The Boy in the Boat

A Memoir

Brian O'Raleigh

—

Brian O'Raleigh

The Boy in the Boat

Originally Distributed by Pan McMillan

I dedicate this book
To my mother and father
To thank them for my life
The invitation to the dance

Being born, coming into this particular body
These particular parents and in such a place
And what we call external circumstances
Form a unity and are as it were
Spun together

Plotinus AD 205–270

Prologue

West Coast of England

My mother and father were Irish and, as far back as I can ever remember, they did not get along. He was an aggressive man, powerfully built and prone to sudden rages, dangerous and unpredictable even when he was sober. One of my earliest memories is of sitting up in bed with my mother, knowing that we had to be quiet but not knowing why; he'd been out drinking all day and now he was demanding that she get up and serve him his dinner.

"Open up!" He was banging his fist on the bedroom door, shouting at the top of his voice. "Open up!" The pounding grew louder, and I could see the door shuddering as he flung his shoulder against it. "Open up! Open the door!" He was screaming now. "Get up! Get me my dinner! Open the door!" There was a crash and then a splintering sound as one of the top panels began to give way.

We sat there in the bed, staring at the door. My mother had one arm around me and the other around my brother. There was another heavy blow to the door and the panels began to cave inwards. I could see his crazed eyes glaring at us through the shattered wood. He disappeared for a second but then came crashing back again, his head coming right through one of the broken panels. The rest of the door was beginning to give way.

My mother's head was bowed, her eyes shut, and she was clutching me so tightly around my neck that it was hurting. One last blow and he came smashing through the opening, bits and pieces of wood flying about in front of him as he fell forwards onto the floor. In a second, he was up and onto the bed, slapping and punching at her.

She was knocked over sideways and fell down on top of me, her arm crushing against my nose.

I couldn't breathe, suffocating under their weight. She was screaming and I was too, but I don't know if any sound was coming out.

I don't know what happened after that, I don't remember, but I know the next day, she wasn't well and she had to go away for a week and we weren't allowed to see her until she got better.

When she returned, things were good again for a while. My father didn't go out drinking at all and even when one of the guests at our hotel offered to buy him a drink, he wouldn't have one.

The Alexandra Private Hotel was our home. I was brought up there from earliest childhood and knew of no other place. It stood on the corner of Alexandra Road, South Shore, Blackpool. From the front rooms, you could see the Irish Sea and, at low tide, glimpses of the long, sandy beach. It was a well-kept, three-story building with a steeply gabled roof and bay windows that jutted out over a concrete-covered yard, surrounded on three sides by a low brick wall.

During the holiday period, the hotel was always busy, full of happy, noisy strangers, talking and laughing together. On those summer evenings, I would sit by the lounge room window and watch the nightly procession of seagulls gliding past the end of the road, floating on the breeze towards the sand dunes at the far end of town.

It was as if we led two lives; in winter Blackpool lay deserted, a ghost town awaiting the turn of the seasons. I awoke each morning to an eerie silence, the hotel as quiet as the grave, the corridors silent and empty, the bedrooms tidy, sterile and pristine, as if in some deserted hospital.

Sometimes, when I was very young, I would wonder if the visitors had discovered some dreadful secret and had fled the town forever, never to return.

—

Chapter 1

The Boy in the Boat

I found the boats late one afternoon. They were drawn up on the tarmac by the sea wall, close to the end of Waterloo Road. I guess they'd always been there; the fishermen brought them up out of the water after every trip, but it was the first time I'd ever noticed them.

I was seven or eight at the time, a frightened boy with a wooden sword, wandering along a seaweed-strewn beach, deserted except for a few cold, unhappy-looking seagulls leaning forward on spindly legs, squinting into the wind.

I was frightened of going home, afraid of what I might find there, feeling sad and looking for refuge. I wanted to get as far away from the hotel as possible. My father had been out drinking again and my parents had been arguing and shouting at each other when I'd picked up my sword and slipped out the back door. From long experience, I knew that it had to end in violence. My mother's pride would not allow her to surrender to my father's verbal abuse and threats. He could only cower her by physical violence and frequently, not even then. I used to silently beg her not to respond, to stay quiet but she just couldn't seem to do that. Too much courage, I guess, and too much contempt for him.

I'd tried many times in the past to save her during these attacks, flailing at him uselessly with my fists or trying to hold onto his arms and screaming for him to stop, but that only served to enrage him further. He'd slap me aside as carelessly as you would a cat and, over the years, as I'd grown to fear him more, I'd had less and less courage to face him.

One dreadful day, he had come at me like a madman, arms outstretched, his eyes enraged. I was so terrified of him by then that, in my panic, I wet myself. The sense of shame I felt was overwhelming, made all the worse because my mother was there when it happened. I was seven years old and a coward now along with everything else.

After that, I began to disappear before the violence started, slipping out the back door of the hotel at the first signs of trouble. To see my mother's bruised face at the breakfast table and to know that I'd done nothing to stop her humiliation was to scar my mind for life.

The sickening hypocrisy of the following days was almost worse. Watching my father posing for the hotel guests, smiling broadly, his arm around my mother as he explained how 'Chrissie had fallen down the stairs' or 'had walked into a door', confused and revolted me.

He was always the actor, the gracious host of the Alexandra Private Hotel, the loving husband and father. He spoke of decency and honor and of how one should behave in life. He helped my mother and opened doors for the waitresses in a gentlemanly manner. He would tell the hotel guests earnestly: "If there's any way we can improve your stay with us, please don't hesitate to ask." The guests would be enchanted when, after a few drinks, he'd close his eyes and sing to my mother in his Irish brogue:

> *I'll take you home again Kathleen*
> *Across the ocean wild and wide*
> *To where your heart has ever been*
> *Since first you were my blushing bride.*

Teary women would bend and whisper in my ear what a "fine father" he was, but behind the scenes, he was a different man altogether. On the occasions when he went too far, my mother would have to go away for a 'holiday' and then I'd watch him drinking and laughing with the hotel guests, flirting with the waitresses and fondling them whenever he could.

Knowing that my mother was languishing in some distant town, recovering from his violent excesses, my heart, mind and soul turned against him forever and I swore to God that I'd kill him one day and set my family free from his terrible rages.

*   *   *

He was still shouting at Mum as I closed the back door quietly behind me. By that time, I had learned how to move into a different world at will. Crossing the promenade, I was on the beach. It was a winter afternoon, grey skies and a cold wind hurrying dark clouds across a bleak ocean.

I walked out to meet the sea. The tide was low, the sands corrugated by the ebbing waters. I continued along the high-water mark, searching through the bits and pieces washed up by the ocean. It was then that I saw the boats.

There were three of them in a row, almost identical, about twenty feet long, wooden clinker construction, the planking curving graciously from stem to stern. A short, sturdy mast protruded from each of the canvas covers protecting them from the threatening rains.

I approached cautiously. There seemed to be a life about them somehow, a presence. I was drawn to the boat in the middle and walked around her, admiring her black hull. On her bow, scripted in faded gold paint on a dark red background, were the words *Kathleen R.*

I traced the groove of each letter with my finger. The letters were carved deep into the wood and then painted over. I looked around from where the boats lay nestled together. The promenade was deserted, not a soul in sight; winter held sway.

The canvas cover was held down by a light rope threaded through holes and then lashed to sturdy brass hoops on the boat's gunwale. My heart beat quickly as I undid enough canvas to peer inside. Saltwater and tar, fish and foreign lands, the smell enveloped me like a dream. I hurriedly pulled more rope away, tossed in my sword and wriggled under the cover. I was inside the boat.

I pushed my head and shoulders back out through the hole in the canvas to make sure no-one had seen me. The coast was clear, nobody in sight. I waved my sword and screamed out into the wind and sea: "I'm the captain! I'm in charge! I'll kill anybody that comes near my boat!"

I slashed about wildly with the blade. *That* should terrify them all! After a final victorious look around, I retreated back into the boat, tidying up the canvas so as not to give away my presence, then sat down on a pile of fishing nets and took stock of my surroundings.

The nets were still damp and, here and there, caught in the folds were small, dead fish, remnants of the night's trawling.

I lay there for a while, worrying. Evening was drawing near, the skies darkening, wondering what had happened at home in my absence. Was she alright? Had he hurt her? Oh God, why does he have to live with us? Why can't he stay in Manchester all the time?

As I lay there, I stared at the dead fish caught in the nets, too small for the fishermen to bother about, staring eyes, open mouths, singing for a help that would never come.

Suddenly, there was a glitter, a movement at the bottom of the net. I peered closer. There it was again! In the net's lower folds, half submerged in seawater at the very bottom of the boat, a small silver fish was moving. I pulled away the strands of rope and there he was, sharing his tiny pond with a few seashells and some rusting keel bolts, with barely enough water to stay alive.

I looked around. At the forward end of the boat, an old galvanized bucket poked out from beneath a sail. I grabbed it, climbed out through the canvas cover, and ran as fast as possible down to the sea. Minutes later, I was back, the bucket half full of fresh seawater.

The tiny fish stared back impassively from his watery dungeon. With the greatest care, I scooped him up, palms full of water, and slipped him into the bucket. He didn't look too bad and I knew he'd be fine once he was back in the ocean.

I climbed out of the boat and carried my precious cargo down to the sea. I warned him to stay away from fishing boats and then released him back into the ocean. With a grateful glance and a flick of his silver tail, he was gone.

I stood there for a while watching, wondering whether he'd be alright out there alone with all his friend's dead and gone. I waved after him and imagined he was thinking of me with affection as he swam away from the shore towards safety, the sole survivor of a terrible adventure.

*   *   *

It was getting dark. I went back to the boat, removed all traces of my visit, and retied the canvas cover. Then, going to her bow, I touched the golden words, *Kathleen R,* once again and bade her farewell before reluctantly turning towards home. I paused at the corner for one last look. The three fishing boats remained huddled together in the failing light. My world had changed. I'd found a refuge and a sanctuary, a place to hide from the dark family secrets of the Alexandra Private Hotel.

Chapter 2

The Hotel

Throughout the year, my father worked in Manchester. He only came home on the weekends and the hotel was always much more peaceful in his absence.

In the summer, with the town packed with tourists, Blackpool was a different world. My mother didn't worry so much about the money then and she was busy all the time. There were always three or four Irish girls working with her, everyone had a job to do and you answered to her if it wasn't done.

During the quiet times, the hotel was more like a home. We were allowed to choose our own bedrooms anywhere in the hotel and they would be ours until the beginning of the following season.

I spent the long winter months in Number Three because it had a view of the ocean. Number Four had a better view, but it was the best room we had, so it was kept vacant in case a travelling salesman might happen along for a night or two.

During the wintertime, mum was always short of money and the mail was of great importance to us. Guests had to confirm their bookings for the next season with a deposit of two pounds and each day, we watched and waited for those letters to arrive.

On the mornings when we weren't at school, I'd sit at the breakfast table with my brothers, Bernard and Peter, listening for the postman. It was like a game. When we heard the clatter of the letterbox, we'd stampede down the hallway to see who'd get to bring the letters back to mum.

My mother would sit there at the table, staring at the little pile of envelopes while we watched her, assessing them carefully like a fortune-teller studying the cards. Then, after choosing one from the pile, she'd examine the postmark and feel the thickness of the envelope.

"Manchester," she'd declare, looking very serious, "umm, this could be a good one!" We'd wait expectantly; she was almost never wrong. She'd slit open the envelope, pull out the letter and then hold up the two-pound notes with a flourish. "Ah, thank God for the Manchurians!" She'd be smiling around at us all, "they're grand people." Then she'd pick up the next one. "Birmingham … umm, feels a bit slim, does Brumich!" She'd open it up, frowning as she read the enclosed letter, so I knew there was no two pounds there. It was just an inquiry or a booking without a deposit. "Miserable people those Brumichers," she'd say, still smiling. Then on to the next one, peering at the postmark. "Now, where are you from, mister?"

Each morning was like a lottery; on a good day, we might have six or eight deposits, other times, we could go for a week or more without anything at all.

*   *   *

Bernard was the oldest boy, then me and then Peter. Mary was older than all of us, but she was away at boarding school most of the time. We only saw her on holidays or when we visited her on some special occasion. I missed her and worried about her a lot. The convent was only a few miles away and we never knew why she was sent there, year after year.

I would sit in her room at the hotel sometimes when she was away, thinking about the convent and wondering why she was sent there, and what about those nuns in the long black robes? Were they kind to her? Would she ever be allowed to come home?

It was always exciting when we went to the convent to visit, the car turning into the long-graveled driveway, crunching along through the avenue of trees, gliding past the nuns as they moved silently down the pathways, smothered in black, heads bowed and covered, holy and sinister, speechless and serene.

Bernard always seemed much older than me although there were only two years between us. He was a big lad and, from the earliest memories I have, everyone respected him. He seemed to know what was going on all the time and the house always felt safer when he was around.

Sometimes when Mum and Dad were arguing, Bernard would try to stop them but that only made things worse. After it was over, Mum would call us in and plead with Bernard never to interfere again. He'd stand there, stony-faced as she talked, and he'd always say the same thing. "He's not allowed to hurt you mum. I'm not going to let him hurt you." Bernard was the bravest of us all.

Peter was the youngest, a shy, sensitive boy who spent much of his time reading. He avoided the troubles in the house by not being there when things happened, slipping away quietly to his room at the first signs of a row, disappearing into his books for hours on end

When I was five, I was sent to St Cuthbert's. I don't know where my fear of school came from, but I dreaded the place long before I ever went there and when the day came, I was determined not to go. It was wintertime, bleak and freezing cold and I was convinced that my mother was going to give me away when we got there.

She dragged me up the road by my arm and, by the time we arrived, she was in a terrible mood. As we approached the classroom, I was terrified. The door was made up of small panes of glass and through them, I could see rows and rows of desks filled with strange-looking children. At the front of the room, a blackboard covered in chalk marks stood next to a large open fire. A tall, thin woman came towards the door, her hand outstretched, staring at me through the glass panes. I panicked and made one last desperate effort to escape but the door opened, and I was pushed into the room, the whole class turning around to stare at me.

"You can leave him with us now, Mrs. O'Raleigh." The thin woman's hand had closed like a talon around my arm. "He'll be fine once you're gone."

I clung to my mother.

"You'll be alright, son." Mum was prizing my fingers off her wrist. "Mrs. Russell will look after you."

"It's best if you go now, Mrs. O'Raleigh." The teacher was pulling me further into the room. "He'll settle down just as soon as you leave."

I watched in despair as my mother walked away, convinced I would never see her again.

Mrs. Russell took me to the front of the room and sat me down on the hearth, close to the fire, facing the class.

As I sat there feeling absolutely worthless, I became aware of the heat from the fire on my back and I knew immediately what I had to do. I was wearing a thick jacket over a heavy wool jumper. Very slowly, I eased myself backward towards the flames. Now I could feel the heat even more. I moved again, still closer. The heat was intense, but I had to get out of that room. The flames were scorching my jacket; the pain was unbearable.

Suddenly a girl jumped up. "Miss … Miss!" She was pointing at me. "He's on fire, Miss!"

Mrs. Russell let out a shriek as she grabbed me, beating her hand on my back, tugging frantically at my jacket. I screamed as the charred material pressed against my skin.

"Stand still! Stand still! I'm trying to help you!" I was struggling to get away from her, trying to get from the pain, but she got the coat off and threw it on the floor. "Oh my God, how could that have happened? Didn't you feel the heat? Are you alright?"

Moments later, we were in the headmistress's office.

"I have no idea how he managed to burn himself, Miss Nicholson! No idea at all!"

Fifteen minutes later, my mother appeared at the office door. She was furious and she shouted at me all the way home.

"How did I end up with a child like you? God, you're a problem! You set yourself on fire, for Christ's sake! You did that intentionally. You might have fooled that poor woman, but you can't fool me." When we arrived at the hotel, she slapped me across the back of the head and pushed me in through the front door. "Get up to your bedroom now! Go on, up to bed and stay there! I don't want to see your face again today! Do you hear me? Go on, get out of my sight!"

She came up to my room later and examined my back. "That was a terrible thing to do, son, you could have burnt yourself alive for God's sake! Don't turn out like your father, whatever else you do. We don't need any more mad people in this house."

When she'd left, I curled up in the bed, thankfully. On any other day, her words would have cut into me but today, they had no effect at all. I was home, safe and sound, with my mother.

The following day, she took me back up to the school again. She'd talked to me for hours the night before and I'd somehow resigned myself to the fact that there was no way out of it.

We arrived just as the bell was ringing and I went straight into the classroom with all the other children. I still felt bad about being there, but the events of the previous day seemed to have broken the ice somehow.

When the bell rang at ten-thirty for the morning break, everyone poured out into the playground. I was one of the last out and as I stepped through the doorway, a group of kids was standing there, waiting for me. I tried to avoid them, but they followed me across the yard and I ended up with my back against a wall with them standing around me, chanting: "Cry baby! Cry baby!"

Their leader was an overweight boy with angry eyes and short, cropped hair and, as the rest of them crowded around, he jabbed a finger in my chest. For a moment I felt close to tears again but then something inside me snapped and I lashed out and punched him in the face as hard as I could. As he fell to the ground, I threw myself on him and began pummelling him furiously, the rest of the crowd scattering in panic, shocked at his sudden demise.

A moment or two later, a teacher was dragging me off my sobbing opponent and I was hauled off to the headmistress's office in disgrace and given a severe telling off. It was my first taste of school and from that day on, I was involved in all sorts of petty troubles.

I hated St Cuthbert's; things were bad enough at home with my father ranting and raving all the time without being ordered around at school all day too. At the end of that first school year, on the bottom of my very first school report, Mrs. Russell scrawled the words: *Brian is very fond of fighting.*

*   *   *

I met Des Reagan on my second day at St Cuthbert's. He came across to my desk and told me that the fat kid that I'd fought with had been bullying him too. Des was smaller than me, slim and wiry with pale blue eyes and blond hair that looked almost white in the sunlight. He lived with his mother a few streets away and after school, we'd go down to the beach and wander along the sands together, searching for treasure amongst the rubbish that littered the high water mark, or chasing seagulls, running along the sands after them, screaming and laughing.

Des became my best friend and I told him, if anybody ever bullied him again, I would stick up for him, but I never took him to the *Kathleen R*, she was my greatest secret and I knew that I could never share her with anybody.

Some evenings, I'd slip down to the beach by myself and walk along the sands to the black granite slopes at the end of Waterloo Road. Then, after making sure that nobody was watching, I'd climb up into the *Kathleen R*. There was always a sense of peace about the fishing boat. She was sturdy and reliable and welcoming, the heavy timber keel and solid planking of her hull, surrounding and protecting me as I lay on the nets dreaming.

Besides the *Kathleen R*, the church was my other sanctuary. From my youngest days, the sights, sounds and smells of the Catholic faith had captured my imagination entirely. My favorite service was the Benediction and I'd sit there in awe, watching as the priest moved about the altar, trying to remember when to stand up and when to kneel down. I always sat close to the front so that I could see everything.

I'd wait for the priest to light the incense; it was the most special moment. He'd move about the altar in his brilliantly-coloured robes as the organ played in the background and then he'd kneel down with the altar boys and prepare the incense in the little silver pot and then, after what seemed like an age, there'd be a puff of smoke and he'd start chanting the prayers and swinging the incense backwards and forwards. The thick white smoke would come billowing out immediately, rising up towards the rafters like the Holy Ghost they were always talking about, as the choir broke into a hymn and we all joined in …

> *Faaaethof Our Faaaatherss Hooollyname*
> *Weeee wiiil betrueuue tethee till death!*
> *Faaaethof Our Faaaatherss Hooollyname,*
> *Innnspiiite of dungeonfirensword!*
> *Innnspiiite of dungeonfirensword!*

Oh, God! All I ever wanted was if they would give me a sword! I'd prove how much I loved Jesus then! I'd fight anyone for him and I knew I'd face death fearlessly in his name. I almost felt like crying sometimes with the frustration of it all. They wanted to treat me like a child but, if they only knew how brave I could be for Jesus, they'd know different then. And if any one of them didn't believe in God's love or that the Holy Roman Catholic Church was the one true faith, they deserved to get killed anyway.

Joey Brennan had told me once that he was a Protestant but my mother said he couldn't be with a name like that. But he was a friend of mine and he never talked about religious stuff or anything like that, so it didn't seem so bad. Mum used to say that he was probably a heathen, but I think she was only joking.

The priest kept on swinging away with the incense, backwards and forwards, and I could hear it slapping against the silver chain with every swing, until finally, after the longest wait, the smell would arrive. A rich, powerful aroma of frankincense, so strong you could taste it, wafting down the aisles, drifting through the congregation, filling your senses with hope like a blessing from above.

I loved the Benediction. The mass was good but the Benediction was better with all the smoke and the songs about dungeons and swords and martyrs, it was more like an adventure.

* * *

Father Boyle was our local priest and every year he'd come to visit us just before Christmas. I knew my mother was going to give him some money for the poor people because I'd been there when she'd put it in the envelope. I'd asked her could I give it to him but she wouldn't let me. "Give him as much as you want of your own money son, but don't be giving away any of mine!"

"How does he give it to the poor, mum? Does he go around and give it to them himself or does he post it to them?"

"That's a good question and one that no living creature could answer." She was giggling. "Oh, God bless you, you're like an empty dustbin, are you not? Sure you'd take anything in! Oh no, it's not as simple as that! Oh no, you see, Old Red Socks has to get his share first before anyone else. Then there's all the bishops to feed and their servants. And then there's the priests and there's hundreds of them, and then finally, you have the sheep, God bless them, standing in line waiting, starving to death."

She was laughing but I didn't like it when she made fun of holy things and I never asked her who Old Red Socks was because it didn't feel good.

Father Boyle was Irish, too and when he arrived, he and my mother sat in the front room talking about Ireland and the weather and how the hotel was doing. I was excited to see him: he said the main mass at St Cuthbert's every Sunday morning, everyone knew he was very important.

I waited there patiently until my mother asked me to make the tea, then I ran out to the kitchen to boil the water and slice the cake the way she'd told me, before taking it back in very slowly on the tray so as not to spill anything and leaving it down next to her on the table.

Father Boyle was sitting in one of the leather armchairs near the front window, talking away as my mother poured the tea. I sat next to them quietly, hoping that I would be allowed to stay. Everything seemed good at first and they both sat there, smiling, and laughing, but then, after a while, things began to change.

"And so, what brings you here today, Father?" my mother asked, "You're not looking for another donation for that steeple of yours, are you?"

Father Boyle was smiling. "Well now, Mrs. O'Raleigh, I wanted to call in and see you anyway but, as it happens, we are raising money for Christmas. It's for the poor, you know, for their annual dinner."

"Do they only get dinner at Christmas time? Sure the poor souls must be famished!"

He was sitting back comfortably in the leather chair, smiling and sipping at his tea, a big slab of fruit cake on the plate next to him.

"Oh no, it's a year-round thing! But of course, we do like to make sure they have a good meal on Our Lord's birthday."

"Ah, you're a grand lad, we should all be proud of you. It's always nice to have a good meal on someone's birthday. I just wonder where you are the rest of the year sometimes. The last time I saw you, you were asking for money for that steeple of yours. It would be nice if you dropped in once just to say hello, without having to come here begging all the time."

Father Boyle's smile had changed a little.

"Ah, sure you have a great sense of humor, there's no doubt about that."

"Well, you need a good sense of humor nowadays with people coming around begging for money all the time."

I was beginning to feel embarrassed and hoped she would stop.

"Ah, now Mrs. O'Raleigh, we all have to do our bit to help the poor, especially at this time of the year."

"If it's the poor you're looking for, then go no further. Sure we're as poor as church mice here ourselves. I'm not at all sure whether you should be picking up money at this house or delivering it! And to be honest, I don't feel too inclined to put any more of my hard-earned cash into that wretched steeple of yours."

"But it's not for a steeple, we don't have a steeple on our church. Like I said, we're collecting money for the poor of the parish."

But it was as if she didn't hear him and she kept going on about the steeple, even though he told her, over and over, that the money was for the poor. Finally, he was red with embarrassment.

"Ah, and now you're blushing! Sure isn't that always a sign of a guilty conscience? There's probably nothing wrong with the steeple at all!"

I was feeling sorry for him now and praying that she would just stop and give him the money but she kept on saying things to him about the steeple until eventually he got up and told her he had to go even though he hadn't finished his Christmas cake. But then, finally, just as he was about to leave, she pulled out the envelope with the money in it.

"There you are now, don't you forget that, don't you forget what you came here for." She handed him the envelope. "There you are now, that's my contribution for the new steeple and make damn sure it's on there by this time next year or there'll be no more money from this house."

"But I've told you, it's not for any steeple, it's for the poor …"
She cut him off, shaking her head.

"Ah sure you'd tell us anything Father, and you a priest; sure I don't know what to believe now!"

He went off out the front door then, clutching the envelope in his hand, and she stood there looking after him through the small square panes of glass as he peddled his bike away off up the road.

"Well, I hope for his sake that's the hardest two pounds he'll ever have to beg for, the bloody parasite!" She was laughing. "They're all the same. Every one of them! We all know who the poor are! You'll never see one of them buggers going hungry to give a starving man his dinner! You can bet your bottom dollar on that!"

I was worried now in case Father Boyle was angry with us, but she thought it was a great joke and she went off up the hallway, laughing like mad.

*   *   *

The following Sunday, I was up at 7 am; St Cuthbert's was always crowded for the morning mass and if you were late, it was difficult to get in there at all. I got a seat about halfway up the aisle to get into the Holy Communion queue early. The church was full, and it had that smell of old incense and candles and holy water.

When things were bad at home, I used to pray every night that my father would stop drinking, but on those Sunday mornings, it felt so much more powerful to be at the mass and to speak to God directly, as it were.

When the time came, I walked forward to the altar and knelt there waiting for Father Boyle to pass along the row of worshippers. There was a flurry of movement to one side and then the murmured prayers. I didn't look, staring straight ahead fixedly, afraid of spoiling something, and then the green, red and golden robes swung into view and the hand came towards me, offering me the Holy Communion, the body and blood of Christ. I looked up, trying to catch his eye, wondering if he remembered who I was.

"*Corpus Domini nostri Jesu Christi custodiat animam tuam in vitam aeternan, Amen,*" he intoned.

It felt good when he said that to me. I didn't really know what it meant but I wished he would just look at me so I knew everything was alright about the money for the poor people and everything.

He chanted the blessing, making the sign of the cross before me in the air and then the wafer was on my tongue and he was gone on to the next person.

I stayed there for a few moments, staring up in awe at the majestic golden tabernacle standing star-like above me on the altar, and then, with the pure clean taste of the Holy Communion clinging to the roof of my mouth, the smell of the scented candles all around me, and the organ playing softly in the background, I prayed with all my heart that Jesus would help change my father.

I felt guilty though because I knew I was partly to blame. I was always breaking some commandment or other and I knew if I did that, God couldn't help me at all. I knelt there, asking for forgiveness, begging for Jesus to help us, promising to be good from then on. I swore that I would do anything in the world for him if he would only help my mother.

By the time the mass was over, I was convinced that he'd heard me. If I was good, and I would be, then the trouble between my parents would stop.

I walked out into the sunlight afterwards, filled with a great sense of hope, feeling at peace with God and the world and every living creature in it. I had been forgiven and blessed. It was the start of a new week. It was a new beginning. And then we all ran home together, Bernard, Peter and me, bursting into the house, shouting and laughing. I rushed through into the kitchen, expecting miracles to have happened already.

My mother was in there, cooking breakfast. Bacon and eggs, black pudding and white pudding, sausages and toast and marmalade and, seeing her standing there smiling, I was sure that from now on, everything was going to be alright.

We carried our plates through into the dining room. My father was already in there, reading the Sunday papers and I watched him across the table, knowing that Jesus was working in him and searching for signs of change. But he was the same as he always was after a night at the Red Lion Hotel. He didn't look up or speak, so we just sat there quietly, eating our breakfast.

Chapter 3

The Stewarts of Galway

When I was young, I used to catch them sometimes, laughing together and looking into each other's eyes. It didn't happen much, usually after he'd had a few drinks, but it made me think that he must have loved her.

My mother was a tall, slim, proud woman, fiercely independent and used to having her own way. One of thirteen children, she came from the West Coast of Ireland. Her father, Jack Stewart, had been a big-boned, hard-working, Galway man, firm in his faith and respected by all. A master tradesman, he had built up a major construction company from nothing.

The Stewart brothers contracted to the Catholic Church, building schools, monasteries, and churches all over Ireland. Her mother was a simple, homely woman whose family had sprung from Inis Mór, one of the three wild, windswept Aran Islands that lay sprawled across the mouth of Galway Bay.

When we were young, we'd sit there listening entranced as Mum told us stories of all her sisters and brothers.

"Jimmy was the best of us all," she'd say, and we knew then that she'd end up in tears, "He was a saint, God rest his soul." She'd tell us how he died of the TB and no-one could help him. She'd heard the banshee wailing outside her bedroom window late one night and within a week of that, Jimmy was gone. And she'd talk of her father, Jack. "Everyone respected your grandfather," she'd say proudly. "Everyone who knew him respected him. He was a hard man, but he was a fair man, he was always fair."

Then she'd go all dreamy and tell us how she'd been her father's favorite. "He thought the sun shone out of me." She'd be smiling. "He called me Christine, never Chrissie, like the rest of them. He could see no wrong in me, God bless him." Then she'd laugh, but I knew she was sad. "I broke his heart, the poor man, God forgive me, I broke his heart."

She'd been sent to school with the nuns and when she left at eighteen, she'd gone to work in her father's office in Salthill. It was there that she met with Sean McDermott.

"Ah, now there was a lad for you," she'd say, her eyes twinkling, "he looked like a movie star. All the girls were mad for him but he only had eyes for me." She laughed as she remembered. "But oh boy, did he love the drink! Sure he was worse than your Da." And she'd tell us how he got so drunk one night that he couldn't even ride his pushbike home and he ended up sleeping in a stable all night with three horses.

When Jack Stewart heard that his daughter was out walking with one of his workmen, that was the end of Sean McDermott, and a few weeks later, Mum was packed off to America to make quite sure the friendship was at an end.

They sent her to Chicago to stay with our great uncle Frank. "Frank the Yank," she called him, and she told us stories about how Al Capone and all the other gangsters were running around Chicago at the same time, having gun battles in the streets.

She stayed in America for two and a half years. Time enough for her to get over Sean McDermott. But then, when she returned to Galway, there was another man waiting for her.

Walter O'Raleigh was a carpenter working for the Stewart Brothers, and even before she met him, she'd heard of his reputation. He was from Garryowen, an impoverished district of Limerick, and he'd already made a name for himself as a drinker, a fighter and a lady's man.

"He was the boldest man I ever laid eyes on," she'd say, "and he had a smile on him that would bend your heart. He'd wink at me through the office window and he didn't give a tinker's curse who saw him." She'd be laughing. "Sure he was as bold as brass was your Da."

They met secretly after church on Sunday mornings and went walking in the fields around Galway. He took her everywhere, boating on the river, horse-riding in the hills outside the town and sometimes on the ferry to Inis Mór and within weeks, she'd fallen in love.

"He came from a slum," she'd say, laughing, "but he dressed like a peacock. Fancy clothes that were all the rage in America, but he was the only man in Galway game to wear them. Sure he had no shame at all."

Walter O'Raleigh courted her secretly for months and by the time Jack Stewart found out, it was way too late. He fired Dad immediately and told Mum to get ready for another trip to America, but they turned up together at his office the following morning and told him they were getting married.

"I told him to his face," Mum would say, "I love him, Da, and I won't be letting him go. We're to marry here in Galway with your blessing or in England without, but we are to marry." There was a huge row. Some of Mum's brothers came rushing into the office when they heard the shouting and it nearly ended up in a fist fight.

Mum and Dad left the office with her father still shouting threats after them, but two weeks later, as they were preparing to leave for England, old Jack relented. They were married in the cathedral in Galway City and her father gave her away.

A year or so later, both of Mum's parents died within months of each other. Neither of them left a will and soon the whole family was arguing and fighting over the inheritance.

There was something else that happened about that time that Mum would never talk about. It had to do with Dad and the loss of a baby. We never knew what it was, but we knew it was something terrible.

My sister Mary was born in Galway, but after that, the trouble with the Stewarts became even worse. Whatever had happened had turned the whole family against our Dad and finally, the brothers gave mum an ultimatum: she had to leave Dad, or she had to leave Galway.

That was the end of Ireland for them. They sold what they had, packed up, and moved to England. She never spoke to any of her family again except for Aunty May who'd moved to England the previous year.

Mum's birthday was the twenty-fifth of December, and every year just before Christmas, the cards would begin arriving from Ireland: big ones, small ones and sometimes a parcel or two. She never opened any of them. It was like a ritual each year. She'd look at the letters, examine the postmarks and then study the handwriting.

"That's Kathleen's writing, no doubt about that." She'd toss it onto the fire, unopened, before going on to the next one. "That's Jack's hand," she'd say, "my oldest brother. He still writes like a drunken spider."

The parcels got the same treatment. After working out whose handwriting was on them, she'd shake the item suspiciously and then take a guess. "Books, I think, or some old rubbish like that."

"Open it up, Mum, *please*," we'd beg her. We thought there might be something inside for us.

But no, she was unrelenting. "They didn't want me then, they can do without me now," she'd say as she tossed it onto the fire. Her face would be set like stone and we'd sit there watching her, wondering what it was all about.

* * *

Mum would always talk about Ireland at Christmas time, looking up at the kitchen clock as she prepared the breakfast on Christmas morning.

"They'll all be heading up the road now, the whole tribe of them, dressed up like stuffed ducks, God help them. Off to get the blessing from His Majesty, the Archbishop," she'd laugh like mad. "Jack will be in the lead, of course. He's a good lad, is Jack. If prayers ever got anyone to heaven, then you'll be sure to meet your Uncle Jack up there when you arrive."

She'd be giggling away as she fussed around the kitchen, checking on each plate before the waitresses were allowed to take it into the dining room. "Sure Jaysus, if the Stewarts missed mass there one day, the bloody church would collapse!"

I'd try to smile, but I was worried sick about her soul. I knew that if you missed mass, it was a mortal sin and if anything happened to you, or you got run over by a bus or something, you'd go straight to hell. There were no excuses.

She'd told me one day when I was crying about her going to hell that it wasn't true, but I'd asked a Christian Brother and he told me it *was* true.

"If somebody has to work on Sundays and they can't get to the mass, is it still a mortal sin, sir?"

"Of course, it's a mortal sin. What else would it be?" The Brother was glaring down at me. "Have you not been listening at all? It's a mortal sin right enough and if you die in that state, your soul will be damned for all eternity!"

I was sickened by what he said. My mum and dad almost never went to church. There was always some excuse about having to work or something like that, but I was terrified for her. I never worried too much about Dad, I knew he could take care of himself, but I couldn't bear to think of my mother being in hell.

"If somebody you loved went to hell, sir, and you were in heaven, how could you be happy in heaven, knowing that they were in hell?"

"Who is this somebody you're talking about, O'Raleigh? Is it yourself?"

"No sir, I was just wondering, that's all, sir."

"Look now, if this mysterious person has missed mass intentionally and they go to hell and you're up there in heaven looking down on them, then you'll understand just how evil they've been. It won't be just the mass, they'll have been up to other things too, and you'll understand then that they have no right whatsoever to be allowed into heaven! Is that clear now?"

It troubled me deeply listening to all this but I knew without a doubt that, if my mother was sent to hell, then I would go there too. There was no way in the world that I would leave her there alone.

*   *   *

"They'll be drenched in holy water by now." She was serving out eggs onto big white plates, still laughing about the Stewarts. "It'll do them the world of good, I'm sure. It's a wonder they don't bottle it and sell it on street corners."

I hated this type of talk; it was exactly what I was worried about.

"Are you coming to mass today, mum?" I said, "It's Christmas day, mum, it's Jesus' birthday."

"Well now son, I'd be the first one up there if I could, as you know. But if you just have a look around, you'll notice that, on the other side of that door, there's forty or fifty people waiting in line, starving to death. And if I don't cook breakfast for them shortly, there'll be a riot for sure and we'll all be killed."

"But mum," I protested, "we could all help. We could all cook breakfast. Mary can cook and Bernard and I can help her. You should go to church, Mum, it's a mortal sin if you don't."

She'd be laughing away as she whisked around the kitchen, issuing orders to waitresses. "Over here, Bridey. Come on now. Get some sausages on those plates and make sure they're hot." She turned back to me. "Oh, God love you, you have no connection with reality at all, do you? I'll tell you now, son, if Jesus was all that keen on having me up there at the mass, you could bet your boots he'd have sent me a decent cook before now. So don't you go worrying your head about my immortal soul, Jesus and me have an understanding. As soon as he sends me a decent cook, I'll be up the road in a flash, celebrating his birthday, God bless him."

"But mum …"

But she'd had enough. "That's it now, on your way, you can say a prayer for your mother, if you like, it's her birthday too, you know. But let's hear no more of your nonsense, I'm too busy. On your way now or I'll put my boot up your backside." She was laughing but I knew not to go any further.

Later on, when things had quieted down, she took me aside. "Don't you go worrying your head about me son. I have my own beliefs. God knows what's going on here, son. We do the best we can. Sure that's all any of us can do."

In the evening when her work was finished for the day, she'd settle back into the big armchair in the living room to have her first Guinness. She'd pour it out carefully and then hold up the glass to the light. "God bless Arthur Guinness," she'd say loudly, "God bless his cotton socks. Sure, the man was a saint!" and then she'd take a drink. "Oh boy, that's grand! That man has done more for world peace than the Pope!" Then she'd take another drink and settle back in the chair. "Now then," she'd say sternly, looking around at us all. "What have you young rascals been up to today, eh?" But she wasn't serious. "Causing mischief somewhere, I'll bet!"

—

Mum always drank six or seven big bottles of Guinness each night. Her medicine, she called it, but she never touched a drop during the day. Around eight o'clock, she'd stand up and the evening ritual would begin.

"Right," she'd declare, 'time for more supplies!" I knew what to do. I'd go out to the back kitchen where the empty bottles were kept and put them all in the bitter-sweet smelling bag that was used only for the off-licence. Then we'd pull on our coats and scarves if it was wintertime and head off along Bolton Street to Mr. Hargrave's bottle shop. I loved strolling along the quiet streets with my mother at night, her arm through mine. It was the only time we ever really talked alone together.

"You see that bright ring around the moon," she'd say some nights, looking up into the winter sky, "that's a sure sign of snow. Mark my words now, we'll have snow before the week's out." She'd always make sure I walked on the outside of her, the side closest to the road. "A gentleman always walks on the outside of the lady," she'd say, "it comes from the old days when horses would throw mud up from the road. It's the mark of a gentleman, never forget that. If it's not bred into you early then you'll never be easy with it, and without manners, son, you'll be no good to man nor beast."

—

Chapter 4

The Armchair

I was always afraid of him. His presence hung over the hotel like a shadow each weekend, flickering around us all, hovering over every room even when he wasn't drunk, so it was a relief to wake up on Monday mornings and know that he was gone. On those days, I'd creep downstairs to peer hopefully out of the kitchen window. If the car was gone from the back yard, then so was he and we could all breathe freely again.

He'd lived away from home for as long as I could remember. My mother ran the hotel whilst he worked in Manchester as a carpenter, coming home on Friday evenings and leaving again early Monday morning. Mum and dad always slept in separate rooms. We never knew why; it was the way it was.

Occasionally when I was very young, they'd go out together to a fancy-dress ball or the local club, but over the years that had gradually changed until finally, they just lived their own separate lives. Separate that is, except for the trouble that lay between them.

Sometimes there'd be a stilted truce, a few smiles and maybe some laughter. Fragile awakenings of hope, always to be carelessly crushed by some trivial happening and then he'd be at it again. Shouting and swearing, bellowing threats and abuse. Us children scattering away from him like startled seagulls, disappearing into different rooms so as not to be involved.

He was a thickset, powerfully built man, with a broad strong Irish face and eyes that would put the fear of God in you when he turned on you in anger. I had good reason to be frightened of him. I knew the sort of power he had. I'd been there the evening he'd attacked the three strangers. They weren't staying at our place, but they'd wandered into the forecourt of the hotel. They were tourists, tipsy from the drink but harmless enough. He'd claimed afterwards that they were stealing the deckchairs. Whatever the reason, they'd made the mistake of wandering onto his territory.

He stood at the front window, half concealed by the curtains, watching them, quiet and motionless like a lion stalking its prey. When one of the men picked up a deckchair, he sprang into action. He went rushing out of the main entrance and then, still running, he punched the man a vicious blow to the side of the head. The man went limp instantly, crashing to the ground, unconscious.

The other two fared no better. Before they could collect themselves, he'd overwhelmed the second man, punching at him savagely until he collapsed down onto the pavement. The third man held his hands up in a futile attempt to placate my father, but he received the same treatment. Within a few minutes, they were all on the ground, one unconscious, the other two dazed and bleeding. It was terrifying watching him, it was as if nothing could stop him, he seemed indestructible.

My mother must have been afraid of him - we all were - but I never once saw her show it. That was the problem. When the rows started, she just wouldn't give in. I felt sure, if she'd only not answer him back, he might stop, but no, that was never the way it was. She had a fierce Irish pride and a caustic tongue, and she would never allow herself to be intimidated by him.

Nighttime's were the worst, lying there in bed, listening to him raging at her after he came home from the pub. I would lie there, desperately trying to block out the muffled curses and crashing sounds, dreading that he was going to hurt her again. The shock of the screams piercing through my bedroom door would leave me weeping and unable to sleep for hours.

The following day, the tension at the dining table was unbearable. There was an overwhelming sense of suppression that stifled all conversation. The frigid silences stretched on and on until I could hardly eat at all. But that was a danger, for it would draw his attention to you. Nobody dared to look at him when he was like that. We'd sit there, mute and terrified, never knowing if he was going to explode again. I'd hold my breath and stare down at my plate, too frightened to move, praying that somebody would say something, anything, to break the terrible silence.

It was like an evil presence hanging over the table. To remain silent was almost unbearable but to dare to speak risked drawing his full attention to you. I would look up eventually and glance out the window, trying to guess from the corner of my eye whether he was still angry or if it was over.

"What are you looking at?"

I'd glance towards him, making sure not to meet his eye.

"Nothing. I was just looking out the window."

"Look at me."

It was hard to look at him, his rage showed clearly in his face, flickering like dark shadows behind his troubled eyes.

There was a feeling of madness about him even when he wasn't drunk. His moods were like quicksilver and I'd learnt over the years that the broad flashing smiles and laughter hid something entirely different. He could change in a moment from a happy, laughing man into a dangerous, raging lunatic capable of attacking anybody.

I was eight years old when he knocked me unconscious for the first time. It was just before summer and there were only a few guests at the hotel. My father's brother, Vincent, was over from Ireland, staying with us for his honeymoon, and we were all excited to meet him and his new wife

Uncle Vincent and Irene had their meals in the dining room like the other guests but every evening after dinner, they'd come into our living room and talk for hours with my parents.

We'd never met his brother before, so it was exciting sitting there on the floor as they drank their Guinness, listening to the stories Vincent and Dad told about when they were young lads in Limerick. One night, my father was telling a story about stealing candles from the church in Garryowen when Vincent interrupted him, shaking his head.

"Ah, sure now Walter, you haven't changed a bit. Why don't you tell them the truth, for God's sake?"

"The truth!" My father was laughing. "Will you listen to him? Sure what would you know about the truth? You were only a baby, for Christ's sake! Be careful of him now, Irene. You have no idea at all of who you've tied yourself up with!"

Vincent looked across at my mother.

"Could you believe that now, the pot calling the kettle black! Listen now and I'll tell you the truth about who stole the candles."

And he took over and finished the story and they both set off laughing about what they'd done to the priest. We all joined in, laughing like mad, although I didn't really understand what was funny about it.

They sat there every night, talking and joking, and dad would have his arm around mum, and everything seemed so good, I wanted Vincent to stay with us forever.

Every now and then, someone would bring out a packet of Players and pass them around and Vincent would get up and produce his silver lighter. It was like magic, a quick flick of his thumb and everyone was puffing away happily. I was fascinated. I wanted to light the cigarettes myself but I knew I wouldn't be allowed to so I just sat there and watched.

Uncle Vincent looked like my father, but he was younger and he was always smiling and hugging his new wife, Irene. The two of them talked a lot about going to Canada to start a new life but I hoped they might change their minds and stay with us at the hotel and I spent as much time with them as I could.

My mother had warned me that I should always ask Vincent first, did they want to be by themselves. Sometimes he said they did but sometimes he would bring me with them on the walks along the beach.

I showed them all my secret places and things they would never have seen if I wasn't there, so I was really disappointed when my father called me into the living room one day and warned me to stay away from them.

"They're honeymooners, they want to be left alone. Stay away from them from now, do you hear me?"

"But Vincent wants me to take him to Stanley Park tomorrow! He asked me to, honest. I always ask them do they want to be left alone; mum told me to!"

He caught hold of my shoulder, his face close to mine.

"Stay away from them, I'm telling you now! You're pestering them. If you go near them again, you're in trouble, understand?"

I knew not to go any further. "Yes, Dad." I was flattened and I went into the kitchen and told my mother what had happened.

"Leave it be, son, don't upset him. Leave them alone for a few days. I'll talk to him about it but leave it alone for now."

After that, I stayed away from them and I only saw Vincent when they came in after dinner at nights. But then, one morning as I was helping mum clean up the lounge room, I spotted my uncle's cigarette lighter lying next to the ashtray and I slipped it in my pocket before she saw it.

I decided that if I could learn how to use it quickly, I would wait until the cigarettes were passed around that evening and then I'd jump up and light them all. That would surprise them!

As soon as I'd finished all my jobs, I went to the sitting room. There was a cupboard in there behind the armchair, down on floor level. It had been one of my hideaways for years. Sometimes when my parents were shouting at each other, I'd open it up and crawl inside. It had a wooden shelf in the middle, and I'd slip in under that into the bottom part where it was quiet and dark then pull the door closed behind me. The floor inside was lower than the living room floor and you had to be careful not to scrape your shins as you crawled in over the edge.

I slipped in behind the armchair and examined the lighter. It was a silver color, shiny and smooth. I studied it for a while and then flicked it the way I'd seen Vincent do. There was a flash of a spark but nothing else. I tried again, still nothing. I was disappointed; it looked really easy when he did it. I kept on trying, flicking and flicking at the lighter until my thumb was sore. I sat there feeling dejected, wondering whether I should give it back to him or just leave it in the lounge next to the ashtray.

I flicked it again without much hope and it sprang into life instantly, a slim flame rising up from the little wick. I was thrilled. I watched it for a moment then I snapped it shut and tried again. It took three flicks this time but then it lit again. I'd done it. I'd learnt how to work the lighter by myself. Now all I had to do was wait for them to pull out their cigarettes then I would step forward and light them up!

As I sat there dreaming, I noticed some tiny little threads sticking out from underneath the armchair. Little wispy threads hanging from the rough Hessian cloth that made up the bottom of the chair. I flicked the lighter and brought the flame to the tip of one of the strands. With a puff of smoke and a sudden tiny flame, it was gone, consumed immediately. I was fascinated and tried again. As soon as the flame touched the end of the next thread, it disappeared instantly, right up to the cloth itself, the tiny strand burning away so quickly that I could hardly keep track of it.

I did it again and again. Soon, I'd burnt off all the threads from the back of the armchair, so I bent over, laying my face flat against the carpet and peered underneath the chair.

The pale brown Hessian cloth covering the underside of the armchair was attached by drawing pins around the edges and sagged down heavily in the middle. Dozens of hairy little strands stuck out underneath like bits of straw from a haystack.

I flicked the lighter again and pushed it in under the chair. Just as I was about to choose a thread, the flame suddenly increased in size and to my horror, I realized the chair itself had caught fire.

I pulled the lighter out quickly and looked around, desperately searching for something to put out the flames with. In my confusion, I grabbed the poker from the fireplace but as I got back in the corner, a yellow flame licked out from underneath the bottom of the chair! I panicked and started bashing at the flames with the poker and as I did, there was a scream.

"Fire! Fire! There's a fire in the living room!"

One of the waitresses was standing in the doorway, screaming. I was terrified, my father was in the kitchen and I knew he'd go crazy. As I jumped out from the corner, smoke was coming from underneath the chair. The waitress was standing in the doorway with one hand over her mouth.

"Get out!" She'd realized the danger. "Get out quick!"

I went to run out of the room but before I could get past her, my father was there, pushing the terrified girl to one side.

"What the fuck's going on in here?" he demanded.

I tried to slip past him, but he spread his arms out either side, crouching over slightly.

"Dad, I'm sorry, dad," I pleaded with him, "I didn't mean to do anything."

I knew there was no hope. I was frozen, paralyzed with fear. I saw his shoulder and head move slightly and then a sharp stabbing pain, followed instantly by a loud snapping sound, went piercing up into my head. An explosion ripped through my brain and then there was a disjointed sense of drifting and a split second of thinking that it wasn't too bad as I fell away into blackness.

I don't know how long I was unconscious but when I came to, it was dark all around and I lay for a long moment, wondering where I was, separating the things of dreams from what might have happened. My jaw was aching, a throbbing pain was beating in my head. Then it came to me, I had set fire to the armchair. Panic gripped me again as I remembered him crouched there, ready to attack.

I looked around. I was downstairs in my mother's bedroom, lying on a stretcher. I could hear muffled voices up above, but I couldn't tell who it was. I was straining to hear what they were saying when I heard the laughter. First one person, then another and then a woman joined in, laughing loudly.

I felt a sense of shock. I didn't know who it was laughing but I lay there without moving in absolute despair. The chair didn't matter anymore. I didn't blame my father for hitting me because I deserved it. But when I heard that laughter, it was as if something inside me had shriveled up and I wasn't sure who I was anymore.

After a while, I drifted off to sleep, numb and not caring much about what would happen now. When I awoke, my mother was sitting by the stretcher stroking my hair. My jaw was still aching.

"He's gone out now, son. That's it now. You'll be fine now. Don't worry, my boy, you'll be fine now."

I didn't say anything. She didn't seem to need me to talk. I stared over at a photograph by her bedside. My mother and father smiled back from behind a glass pane. The house was very quiet, and I wanted to ask her who had been laughing.

Chapter 5

The Dentist

When I turned nine, my mother decided to enroll me at St Joseph's College. By that time, I had been involved in all sorts of petty troubles at St Cuthbert's and the headmistress was happy to see the back of me.

We arrived for the interview at St Joseph's on a cold, wet, winter's morning, made worse for me by a toothache that had been nagging at me for more than a week. We sat on a long, hard bench outside the headmaster's office, Mum brushing at imaginary specks on my coat, smoothing my hair with her hand.

"Now, don't slouch while you're in there, son, and don't forget to call him Sir. Do you hear me now? Be polite, this is your big chance. Put everything else behind you. You have a fresh start here now if you play your cards right."

"I've got a toothache," I told her, "my tooth's killing me."

"Now don't start any of your nonsense, I'm warning you! For God's sake behave yourself in there."

"I'm serious, my tooth's killing me."

"Mrs. O'Raleigh?" A tall, thin, bespectacled man was peering at us through the half open door. "Would you come in please?"

The room was large and dim, a heavy wooden desk with carved legs and a leather-covered top standing directly across from the door.

The headmaster pulled up a chair. "Take a seat, Mrs. O'Raleigh, and you, Brian." He gestured. "Over there, if you would. That's right, just there now, where we can see you."

As he settled into his chair, he looked across at my mother.

"You have another boy here too?"

"Yes, Bernard's been here for a year now and he's doing well. We're all very proud of him."

The headmaster was leafing through some papers on his desk.

"There were a few problems with Brian at St Cuthbert's?"

"Yes Brother, but nothing serious."

"Miss Nicholson tells me that the police were investigating some broken windows at the school. Was Brian involved in that?"

"No, definitely not, Brian had nothing to do with the broken windows. The police are quite satisfied about that."

I'd broken them all, hurling rocks through the windows one night after getting a caning from one of the teachers.

"But he was in trouble there recently, according to this report."

"He was involved in a scuffle with one of the other lads, just high spirits really. You know how boys are."

"Yes, we know how boys are." His eyes flickered across to me, sizing me up. "So," he said, "what have you got to say for yourself, Brian? If we do accept you here, are you willing to put in the effort?"

I could feel my heart dying, the place felt stifling: dark green walls and doors, pictures of the Bleeding Heart of Jesus and statues of the Holy Virgin Mary, black-frocked, unsmiling men, the stale smell of dusty floorboards and old chalk.

"Yes sir, I am."

I listened to my own voice betraying me.

"And what are your hobbies? Do you play rugby or cricket?"

"Yes sir," I lied again, "I play rugby and cricket." Mum had told me to say that the night before.

"Good," he nodded, "you're a big lad. If you work hard and put all that other nonsense behind you, there's no reason you can't make a success of yourself here."

"Oh, thank you, Brother Sheehan." The relief was clear in my mother's voice. "He's a good lad. He'll do well here, you'll see."

As we left the building, she was still chattering on. "There you are now, you're lucky to be getting a second chance. He seems like a reasonable sort of man. You'll have to work hard, mind. You'll have to give it your best."

As we walked off down the driveway, I looked back. The school was perched high up on the top of a rise, fortress-like and foreboding, and I knew in my heart there was no possible way that I could avoid going there.

*   *   *

The toothache became worse each day. I tried pushing and tugging at it, thinking I might be able to pull it out myself, but it was hopeless, it wouldn't budge.

I had a terrible fear of dentists. My mother had taken me to a clinic when I was six to have one of my teeth removed and it had been a bad experience. We'd waited in a big room for almost an hour with rows of chairs and people sitting there, not speaking and I was feeling frightened by the time they called my name.

As I walked into the surgery, the thick, sickly-sweet smell of anesthetic hit me in the face like a sticky fog. A thin, unhappy-looking man in a long white coat was standing there waiting for us. He didn't introduce himself. He just took the papers his assistant handed to him and began talking to my mother as if I wasn't there.

"How old is he?" He was squinting down at the notes through thick, black-rimmed glasses. Then, without waiting for a reply: "He's six. All right, does he want gas or the needle?"

My mother had talked to me about this the night before. "He wants the gas, doctor. Isn't that right, son?"

"Yes, I think so."

I wasn't sure about this place anymore. It didn't feel good. There was a small grey-haired woman with a stooped back and blue uniform standing just behind the dentist, nodding in agreement as he talked, hovering around nervously like a frightened servant. He swung the chair around.

"Jump up there. That's right. Now, sit back." After he'd got me adjusted in the chair, he began his inspection. "Open your mouth lad. Come on now, you can do better than that. That's it, open wide. There's nothing to be afraid of. Come on now, open wide. That's better. Keep it open."

He was poking around in my mouth, grunting orders at his assistant, then he moved away, and I could hear him talking quietly to my mother. I had my mouth open so wide my jaw was beginning to hurt and I knew I couldn't hold it there much longer. I could see a reflection of them both in the shiny steel casing of the light and I wondered what they were whispering about.

He came back and stood in front of me.

"You can close your mouth," he said. "We wouldn't want you catching any flies, now would we?" His face was set in a fixed smile, but I couldn't see his eyes properly through the thick lenses of his glasses. "That tooth's going to have to come out, lad. It'll only take a minute or two and you won't feel a thing." I was still wondering what they'd been whispering about. Why would they want to hide something from me? "If you'd like to wait outside now, Mrs. O'Raleigh, we'll look after him for you."

The nurse moved closer as the door closed. She had a rubber mask in her hand with a long black pipe attached. I wanted to talk to my mother. The tooth didn't seem as painful now and I thought maybe it was all a mistake.

"It's not too bad now," I said to the dentist, "I think the pain's gone."

"They all say that," he said, "last-minute nerves, that's all. Settle back lad, we'll have it out in no time."

The nurse pulled my head forward without speaking and placed the mask over my nose and mouth, snapping the elastic band tight behind my head. The dentist said something to her, and she began fiddling with the knobs on the steel bottles by the chair. I heard a hissing noise and then I smelt the gas and pulled the mask off.

"It smells rotten," I blurted out.

"Don't worry about that, you'll be fine." He was getting impatient. "Come on now, there's other people waiting."

He jerked the mask over my face again. The smell was terrible, a mixture of rubber and gas that almost turned my stomach. He was holding the mask on now, one hand behind my head, the other pressing the smelly rubber against my face. I tried to push it away, I needed air, but he was holding it on firmly.

Suddenly I knew I was about to be sick. I tried to speak but I couldn't. I tried to push the mask off again but I'd lost control of my arms and I wondered vaguely, if I vomited, would I have to eat it to be able to breathe because the dentist wasn't listening to me.

The last thing I remember as I slipped into unconsciousness was his two big bloodshot eyes staring at me from behind bottle-thick lenses, like crazed goldfish trapped in a tiny bowl.

When I woke up, I felt terrible. My jaw was aching and there was a stench of vomit everywhere.

"He's coming to. He'll be fine now, Mrs. O'Raleigh, don't worry."

"He's very pale," voices were spinning all around me.

"Don't worry, he'll be fine now."

Someone was wiping at my chin and I could feel wet, slimy stuff down the front of my neck.

"Can you hear me? Look at me, Brian, look at me."

It was my mother's voice, but I was adrift, going in and out of consciousness, then her face came into focus in front of me.

"You're going to be alright. You've been sick but don't worry, you'll be alright."

A man's voice broke in. "Sit him up, that's right, hold him up. That's right, he'll be fine now."

The dentist was standing there, looking irritated. His assistant was on her knees cleaning the floor. As they half-carried me back out to the waiting room, I vomited again in the hallway.

*   *   *

It had been a frightening experience and I'd sworn that I'd never go near a dentist again, so now, three years later, when the toothache had started, I'd tried to ignore it, hoping it would go away.

The throbbing increased, day by day, and finally, in desperation, I decided to pull it out myself. I prodded and wiggled and pulled at it but it only made the pain worse. It was one of the big ones at the back and it just wouldn't budge.

By the second week, the pain had become so bad that I had to give in. My mother made an appointment with a private dentist. She knew I was frightened.

"Now this man's very good, Brian, he's one of the best there is. So don't worry, son, it won't be anything like the last time."

I was worried sick but there was no choice, I couldn't stand the pain any longer. When we arrived, we were ushered into the dentist's surgery immediately. I looked around, there was the same leather chair lying back waiting for me and the same rack of instruments on the wall.

As my mother told him of the previous experience, he sat there nodding and looking across at me. He was a short, fat man with an almost completely bald head and small steel-rimmed glasses perched high on a red flecked nose. He was smiling.

"There's nothing to worry about Brian. That was years ago, things have changed. You're a big lad now. What are you? You're going on for ten now. We have a new gas that doesn't smell at all. You're not going to feel a thing."

I didn't like the look of him. He was wearing the same white coat that the other dentist had worn and the smell in the room brought back vivid memories of the previous visit. He put a hand on my shoulder.

"Your mother explained what happened but this new gas is completely odorless, you won't smell a thing. Here ..." He was holding out a red rubber mask. "... have a try."

I sniffed at it cautiously but pulled back immediately.

"No!" I told him, "It smells exactly the same!"

He shrugged and put the mask away.

The needle was the only alternative. I looked around the room as he got it ready, trying to gain courage, but I'd lost all confidence by then and I just wished to God I could get away from the place.

"Here we are." He was back, holding a syringe with a long thin needle protruding from one end. It looked huge. "You won't feel a thing..." He was smiling. "just a little prick, that's all." I didn't believe him. "Open up wide ... that's it ... a little wider ... wider." He'd maneuvered himself into position by my side, one arm raised, the needle poised above my face.

"Come on ... you can do a lot better than that ... that's it ... that's it ... just a little prick now ... you won't feel a thing ... that's it ..." He was leaning over me, peering into my mouth, and I could see little white flakes of dandruff scattered through the thin grey hair on the side of his head.

"There we are …" I was gripping on tight to the arms of the chair as the needle began piercing into my upper jaw. It was incredibly painful, but I was determined not to give in. "That's it … there we are now, that wasn't too bad now, was it?" Thank Christ, it was done! But then, he changed position. "That didn't hurt now, did it? OK, open wide again, just another couple, you won't feel a thing." Another couple? Oh, God, I thought it was finished! I was gripping the chair with one hand and clutching onto his arm with the other. He was peering into my mouth again. The needle began to go in for a second time, on the inside of my jaw. "There we are now," he whispered, his stale, warm, breath across my face.

I don't know what happened then, he must have hit a nerve or something, but an excruciating pain shot through my entire body like an electric shock and I raised both my legs instinctively and kicked out as hard as I could. The dentist went staggering across the room backwards before hitting a desk and crashing over onto the floor.

I jumped out of the chair and ran out of the surgery, bolting past my startled mother in the waiting room, then off out the front door and away up the street as fast as I could.

I sat in the bus shelter on the main road holding my jaw, the toothache fading as the anesthetic took hold. My mother came along ten minutes later and stood there, silently staring at me. I stared back.

"I'm not going in there again, he's a liar! He's worse than the last one."

There was a complete silence all the way home. When we got back to the hotel, she took me to the living room.

"Brian, that tooth's rotten, it has to come out. I can't force you to go to the dentist, but you'll have to, sooner or later. It'll drive you mad, son. When you're ready, let me know."

I sat with the pain for the rest of the week, determined not to give in. Some days were worse than others.

That Saturday morning, my father told us he needed a hand with some building materials and shortly after 9 am, my brothers and I jumped in the car and dad drove off towards the centre of town. Bernard and Peter were talking and laughing but I just sat there in silence, engrossed in the pain from my toothache.

I'd never been close to either of my brothers although I always looked up to Bernard. We never went anywhere together but if I ever got into trouble, he was always there to help me. Peter was the closest one to mum. You could tell he was her favorite by the way she talked to him. That didn't bother me, but I always felt apart from them, as if I'd been born into the wrong family.

I didn't pay much attention to where we were going but a little while later, we pulled up in a back lane behind some large brick houses. My father jerked open the door.

"Brian, you come with me. You two, stay there."

Bernard and Peter were pulling faces at me as I walked around the front of the car and followed Dad across the lane. He opened one of the back gates and stood aside to let me in, then he came in behind me, closing the gate after him. I felt his hand on my shoulder as he knocked on the back door of the house.

As the door opened, his grip tightened. A small round figure in a white coat stood there, smiling. I turned to run but my father grabbed me, picked me up bodily and carried me struggling into the dentist's surgery, threw me into the chair and held me there.

Everything was ready. The dentist came at me immediately with the red rubber mask. I struggled desperately but it was hopeless. My father had one knee up on top of me, pressing across my stomach and thighs. One of his hands was grasping my throat whilst the other held both my wrists together. I was wedged into the chair, absolutely helpless. The dentist clamped the mask on my face. When I heard the hissing of the gas, I fought like mad, but my father's hand was like an iron vice.

"I need to use the toilet …!" I was choking out the words.

The dentist ignored me, forcing the mask on tightly as my father held my neck in one of his huge hands. I didn't have a chance. I held my breath for as long as possible but finally, desperate from lack of air, I was forced to take a breath.

"Ah," the dentist murmured, "now we're getting somewhere!"

The anesthetic hit me hard and within seconds, I could feel my strength deserting me. I couldn't fight against my father anymore and I sat there pinned to the chair, just before the darkness came, staring up into his eyes, wondering in a dreamy, far-off kind of way, how he could do this to me so easily.

Chapter 6

Prince

Mrs. Lee was our piano teacher and she lived in an apartment above Notariani's Ice-Cream Parlor at the end of Waterloo Road. The Notarianis were Italian and their ice-cream was fantastic, nobody had ever tasted anything like it.

There was another ice-cream factory in Adrian Street, close to the Alexandra Private Hotel. Their ice-cream was good, too and occasionally Mum would send us off to get some for the guests. We'd take a large pudding bowl and stand by the mixing machine until it was ready.

The man who served us was dressed in white with black rubber boots and we'd watch hopefully as he stuck his long-handled spoon into the big steel bowl as it went around and around above our heads.

"Hmmm ... nearly done. There ye' go now lads, taste that." He'd hold out the spoon. "Ow's that now? Go on, don't be shy."

Then he'd take our bowl and shovel scoops full of the fresh ice-cream into it until it was overflowing, before covering it with the clean white linen napkin my mother had given us.

"Now don't you go pinchin' any afore ye' git 'ome to ye' ma! Thruppence fe' that lot. Go on now, on ye' way."

We'd carry it home carefully like a treasure, knowing there'd be fresh strawberries to go with it after dinner that evening.

Adrian Street ice-cream was good, but it wasn't as good as Notariani's. Notariani's ice-cream was famous all over the world, or so Mr. Notariani told us.

"People coma' here froma' all over the worlt." He'd be digging his big wooden spoon into the pails behind the glass-fronted counter as he talked. "People always aska me, how you make alike dis? I tell them, that'sa my secret, OK? That'sa the family secret, yes? Passa' down from one generation to another, OK? Nobody knows but me, OK? Later my children, but not now, I'ma going to lif' forever!"

Mrs. Lee lived above Notariani's in a unit overlooking the sea. She was a small, round lady, quietly spoken and stooped over with age and we all went to her for piano lessons at one time or another.

Mary took to the piano naturally and when she was home from school, you would hear her of an evening playing away in the lounge room for hours. Bernard was never happy with the lessons and finally he just refused to go anymore. Mum threatened him with no pocket money and peeling potatoes but nothing like that ever seemed to worry Bernard. Once he decided he was finished, he never went again and finally mum just had to accept that.

When my turn came, I knew she didn't have a lot of hope for me and that made me try harder. I went to the lessons each week but, although I practised every night, it never came easily to me. I found it confusing, one week we'd be doing "Buy a broom and sweep the room" with Mrs Lee singing along as we played. "Buy a broom, buy a broom, buy a broom and sweep the room." Plonk, plonk, plonk! Plonk, plonk, plonk! Plonk, plonk, plonk, plonk, plonk, plonk, plonk! And then suddenly, just when I had it right, she'd want to start me off on another tune I'd never heard of. I'd have given the "Buy a broom" tune hours of practice and I'd have it off perfect but then she'd want to move me on to something new and suddenly, I'd be all fingers and thumbs, hitting all the wrong notes and looking stupid again.

And on top of all that, there was Mrs. Lee's dog, Prince. Prince was the oldest dog I'd ever seen. He was of medium height and had at one time been brown, but by the time I was learning the piano, his coat had faded and there were white bits and pieces and bald patches everywhere. He looked like a faded corpse, tired, cloudy, purple-grey eyes staring hopelessly out of a narrow, mean face covered almost entirely in grey-white whiskers.

He was fat and ugly and almost completely blind and he limped on all four legs, listing heavily to the left as he walked. When he had decided to embark on one of his trips, he would stagger across the room towards you, heeled over as if the legs on one side were shorter than those on the other, his cloudy eyes bulging as if he were attempting to peer into the future, a smell of death and decay preceding him like an invisible herald of doom, his tail poking out behind him parallel to the ground. That tail was the only real indication that Prince gave when he was about to pass wind.

When I knocked on Mrs. Lee's door every Wednesday evening at 5.30 pm, there was always a pause for a moment or two that had me hoping that Prince might have died since my last lesson but then I'd hear him, like a dying banshee, soft and confused at first as he struggled to begin his protest.

"Arrrrhooo! … Arrrrrhooo! … Arrrrhooo!"

But then, as he warmed to it, the volume and flow would improve.

"Arrrrhhooooooo!!!Arrrrrrhhoooooooo!!!Arrrrrrhhoooooo!!!"

It was as if he had forgotten how to bark and could only remember the first part. He had problems breathing and, as he staggered up the hallway with Mrs. Lee, I'd hear her reassuring him on the other side of the heavy wooden door.

"Now, now, darling, that's all right, darling. It's only Brian. You know Brian, darling. That's right! That's a good dog! You're a good boy! There, there now baby, that's it now."

She'd open the door then and there he'd be, his mean, grey face squinting up the hallway, angry and confused, until I made a move towards the door and the noise would alert him as to my approximate position.

"Arrrrrrrrrrrrooooohh!!! Arrrrrrrrrrrrooooohh!!" he'd begin again, his already awful features distorting even further.

"Now don't you be unkind to him!" Mrs. Lee would admonish, wagging a finger. "He's only doing his job. Aren't you baby? You're only doing your job, aren't you? Good boy! Good Prince! Good boy! You're looking after your mummy, aren't you? Good boy!"

Mrs. Lee was ancient, too. A small round lady with a kind, vacant smile, she'd lived there alone for years, her only contact with the world outside being the students who arrived at her door each evening.

We'd sit squashed together on the piano stool as she did her best to teach me how to play. The lessons themselves weren't all that bad but from the very beginning, Prince made it clear that he didn't like me at all. Every Wednesday evening, he'd sit in his wicker basket in the corner of the lounge room, glowering across in our general direction as Mrs. Lee and myself hammered away on the piano, growling every so often to remind me that I was still not welcome in his home.

The only time he ever moved from that corner was when he came over to the piano to break wind. It was a ritual with him; there wasn't a Wednesday evening that he did not do it. I was too embarrassed to say anything, and for the first few weeks, I thought perhaps he just smelled that way all the time and that I was just imagining that he was farting. But then I realized that there was a sound involved, too. He would struggle to his feet, eyes enlarged, head wobbling, and begin his voyage across the red carpet, feet swinging falteringly forward, swaying and rolling on his bony, twisted legs, his tail waggling about behind him like a broken rudder. When he arrived in our vicinity, he would stand there for a long moment trying to sense where we were and, if you stayed still for long enough, he would forget what he was about and end up staring fixedly at a leg on the piano or a chair. But once we moved, he would get his bearings immediately and then he would swing his hips around and reverse in under the piano stool. He would pause for a moment, peering up over one arthritic shoulder through those clouded blue-grey eyes, and then he would relax into a long, hissing fart.

Mrs. Lee must have known all about it because, as soon as he reversed in under the stool, she would begin playing the piano, singing loudly as she did.

"Buy a broom! Buy a broom! Buy a broom and sweep the room!"

In those next few moments, I would pray that he hadn't farted, hoping against hope that he was empty. I would tell myself that it wouldn't be too bad even if he had farted. "It's only a smell," I'd tell myself, "that's nothing to worry about!"

But then it would arrive, a nauseatingly rich aroma of death and defilement that defied any description that I was capable of, a warm, fetid, wet stench that arose in an almost visible cloud from beneath the stool, enveloping us both in its wretched embrace, filling our nostrils and our senses with the pure putrefying evil of this dirty little beast. Sometimes, I would try to hold on to my breath until it faded but that only made things worse. For when I was finally forced to inhale, it meant that I took in a much deeper breath than normal. It was a nightmare from which there was no escape, made worse by my conviction that Prince was enjoying every bit of it.

Finally, Mrs. Lee would acknowledge that something had happened, perhaps by way of apology or perhaps to let me know that it had definitely been Prince that had caused the stench.

"Ignore him," she'd say firmly, "He's just showing off."

—

And then we'd go back to the work again, pounding on the keys.

"Buy a broom, buy a broom!" Plonk, plonk, plonk! Plonk, plonk, plonk, as Prince began his shaky journey back home, across the red carpet.

Chapter 7

The Yorkshire terrier

The trouble between my parents ebbed and flowed. Sometimes the rows would go on and on, other times there would be weeks without any serious incidents. It was as if he became normal for a while and then, for some unknown reason, he'd change and turn back into a totally irrational person.

My mother had come to believe over the years that he was deranged, 'moon-mad' as she put it. She believed that his moods and rages were entirely controlled by the planets. Whenever the full moon fell on a weekend, she'd warn us for weeks in advance to be on our best behavior and to give him no excuse to get angry. On those occasions, we'd treat him with the utmost respect, making sure we did everything he told us and avoiding him as much as possible. Once, over breakfast, she'd let out a gasp.

"Oh, God forbid." She was staring up at the calendar. "It's full moon next Friday, that's the very night he's coming home!"

We sat there, staring at her. I was never really sure what the moon madness was, but I knew that, if it frightened her, it had to be deadly serious. I used to wonder whether he changed after we went to bed and the full moon shone, and if she knew that, but just couldn't bring herself to tell us.

I'd seen some of the horror comics that Bernard used to sneak into the house and hide under his bed, so I knew about werewolves and Dracula and things like that. And sometimes, there was a movie on at the Ritz Theatre like *The Isle of the Dead* where people died and

—

then came back again and walked around in the moonlight. But even though I knew that my father was mad, I couldn't bring myself to believe that any of those things were happening to him.

"Now Brian, for God's sake be on your best behavior! Don't do anything stupid this weekend. Don't give him any excuse. And Bernard, make sure the potatoes are done and the yard cleared. And make sure the garage door is open for him when he arrives, you know how angry he gets if it's closed." She looked around at us all. "God help you, you poor creatures, God help us all." It came up every day that week; it was on her mind constantly.

"Brian," she confided in me as I was helping her in the kitchen one evening, "close the door and I'll tell you why I'm so worried." She waited before continuing. "The last time the full moon fell on a Friday was the night he attacked those three men in the front yard. You remember that now. He half killed one of them. For God's sake, don't do anything stupid this weekend, whatever else you do."

I hated to see her like this. She had great courage and I knew it was us she was worrying about.

As the week drew on, I became more and more concerned about the coming Friday. What was this moon madness my father suffered from and why couldn't they do something about it? I'd lie in bed some nights watching the moonlight across my bedroom wall. I'd put my hand into it to see if I could feel it, wondering why it affected him so badly and trying to come up with a solution. But it was hopeless, there was none. We'd just have to wait and hope for the best.

That Thursday evening as we were having dinner, the phone rang. My mother answered in her posh voice, the one we always laughed about behind her back.

"The Alexandra Private Hotel, how can I help you?" But then her tone changed abruptly. "Oh yes Walter, what is it?"

He never called her; we sat there, staring.

"But where would we keep it?" She sounded unsure. "Can't he leave it with somebody in Manchester? There must be ..." I was sitting next to her at the table and I could hear his voice now. "Walter, there's no need to shout. There's no need to get angry now, please. Of course, we can look after it for the weekend. I just thought ..."

She stopped again and I could hear his voice going on and on. We were staring at her, wondering what was wrong. Finally, she spoke again.

"Alright then. That's fine. I'll have Brian fix up the kennel. We'll have it ready for you when you get home. That's grand. Yes, I understand. Good. Yes. Alright then, about seven o'clock, fine." She hung up.

"Well," she declared, looking around at us all, "didn't I tell you he's stone mad. He's bringing a dog home now, a champion pedigree dog no less. A Yorkshire terrier, whatever that is, that's won half the prizes in the world according to him. Well God help us all; sure we're catering for dogs now! Oh sweet Jesus! If this isn't moon madness, then I don't know what is."

"A dog?" I was delighted. "Can we keep him?"

"No, of course you can't, this isn't just any old dog! This dog belongs to his boss at Burtons. It's a show dog; it's worth a small fortune. No, of course you can't keep him. We have to look after him for a few days, that's all. His owner is going away on holiday for the weekend and your father's doing his 'big hearted Arthur' act. Oh, sweet Jesus, the poor man's madder by the minute! Now we're having dogs here as guests, God help us all!"

Peter joined in. "It's OK, Mum, we'll take him on the beach. It'll be good. We'll take him for walks."

"You will not! You won't be taking him anywhere. He's not to leave the house. I've strict instructions. He's to be taken straight to the kennel. Brian, you'll be responsible for that. And he's to be chained up from the moment he arrives till the moment he leaves; no excuses."

"We can't chain it up all weekend, it's not fair! We'll look after him." There was a babble of protest, but she was adamant.

"Look now, what have I been telling you all week? Sure the man's stone mad! There's a full moon on Friday night for God's sake! Have you not been listening? Do exactly what he tells you. No arguments! Use your brains. Stay away from the dog. Chain the brute up and ignore him. Don't give your father any excuse now, for God's sake!" She wasn't going to budge so we had to let it go.

My father had brought home three different dogs for me over the years. He had a liking for dogs that looked like huskies and he would present one to me now and again for my birthday. All of them looked the same. My mother told me later that if he saw one he liked on the way home from Manchester, he'd just grab it and throw it in the back of the car.

My last dog, Jason, had joined the beach dogs only the year before. He'd taken to lapping at the seawater when I took him for walks. It was known that, once a dog drank enough seawater, they'd go a little crazy. I'd tried to stop him drinking the water on many occasions but it was hopeless and over a period of time, he'd spent more and more of his days on the beach, running with the beach dogs that roamed the sands, returning home less often, until finally one day, he didn't come home at all.

I tried for months to get him back. I caught him once and brought him home on a bit of rope. I kept him tied up for a while, but I hadn't the heart to keep him like that, because I knew how he felt. He was unhappy, longing to run free on the beaches, so I untied him. I begged him to stay and he did for a day or so but then, one morning I got up and he was gone again.

I only got close to him once after that. It was months later. I spotted him on the beach near Squires Gate. When I called to him, he left the pack and came across to me.

He was thinner and he looked scruffy, but he was still my dog and I loved him. I talked to him for a while and asked him to come home, but he wouldn't let me touch him. As I talked, he kept looking over his shoulder to where the other dogs were. I made a grab for him then in desperation and caught on to the hair around his neck, but his collar was gone, and I couldn't hold him.

He bounded away out of reach and stood there for a moment, staring back as if some part of him still loved me, but finally he made his decision and trotted away and rejoined the pack.

I only saw him once after that, in the distance, loping along with two other dogs by the ocean edge and then he just disappeared altogether. His kennel was still sitting there in the backyard, the length of rope still attached.

The phone rang again later that day. It was my father giving final instructions. We were to wait inside the front door when he arrived. He would carry the dog from the car to the hotel and then, after the dog was safely inside, he would go out again and drive the car around the back into the garage. I was to tie the dog up immediately and he was to be left there for the entire weekend.

* * *

That evening, we all sat in the lounge room, watching by the window for the car. Sure enough, shortly after seven, dad's Triumph Dolomite, a rakish-looking sports model that had seen better days, slid to a halt directly outside the front gate.

The instructions were absolutely clear. We were not to open the door to the porch. Dad would carry the dog through the main outer door of the hotel. Then, after closing that door behind him, he would open the door leading from the porch into the hallway.

I could see my father's outline through the opaque, pebbled glass as he entered the porch, kicking the door closed behind him with a bang. He was angry, cursing at a small, squirming bundle he was carrying in his arms. The inner door burst open and there they were, my father, angry but triumphant, clutching on tightly to a black and white terrier that was wriggling this way and that, legs thrashing, growling and snapping in a desperate attempt to be free.

"Dirty little bastard pissed in the car," he snarled as he gave the dog a heavy slap across the side of the head. The dog yelped and bit at him and then went crashing to the floor. I made a grab for him, but he was up and running in a split second. He darted through the maze of legs and took off up the hallway like a bullet, tearing past Bernard who'd just appeared around the corner. The last thing we saw as he disappeared into the kitchen was his little white stump of a tail, erect and quivering, like some homing device set firmly on return.

There was a moment's stunned silence, then a stampede, led by my father, thundered after the terrified animal. As we rounded the corner in hot pursuit, I heard dad shout: "Oh Jaysus, the doors are open!"

He was right. The kitchen door swung free. The back door, the same, and the large sliding door of the garage, in preparation for my father's grand entrance, yawned wide and open like an invitation to another world. Of the dog, there was no sign at all. He'd galloped through the whole house unimpeded and disappeared at high speed into the gathering gloom of the street outside.

"Who left the doors open?" Dad was almost screaming.

The only thing that saved Bernard that night was my mother's quick thinking.

"Walter," she leapt in immediately, "quickly! Get in the car! Take Brian with you, he's good with dogs! Quickly now, before you lose him!"

Dad and I ran around to the front of the hotel, piled into the car and took off up the road in pursuit of the little terrier. We drove around for hours, searching the town's streets and alleyways. We called into the local police station and made out a full description of the dog to the bemused Sergeant.

"Jasper, eh? That's a funny name fe' dog! Sounds more like butler's name to me. Any 'ow, what does it look like?"

We dashed back out of the police station and up and down the promenade, questioning people along the way: "Have you seen a black and white spotted terrier anywhere?" We were sent on wild goose chases all over Blackpool.

"There was a little white dog on the corner of Shaw Road, I think..."

We'd tear off to investigate, but to no avail. We scoured the beach, calling: "Jasper! Jasper! Here boy! Here boy! Come on now Jasper, come on now," until well after midnight.

We went back to the hotel several times as ideas struck my father. "He might be asleep in the kennel." or "Maybe he's still in the house somewhere."

We searched every room, my father becoming more desperate by the minute. Finally, long after we were all completely exhausted, my mother talked him into calling off the search for the night. Next morning, it was on again. He woke me at seven, shaking my shoulder: "Come on, up you get, we have to find that dog."

Ten minutes later, bleary-eyed, and resentful, I was in the car with him, cruising along the promenade, chasing shadows again. Occasionally we'd spot a dog in the distance but each time, as we drew near, our hopes would be dashed.

We spent that entire weekend searching for the terrier, scouring Blackpool from morning till evening. We questioned the police and a hundred other people. It was as if he'd slipped out the back door and disappeared off the face of the earth, and to the best of my knowledge, he was never seen again by any living creature.

My mother kept Bernard out of the way for the whole weekend. She told my father he was out searching for Jasper and for some reason, dad never once blamed Bernard for what had happened.

When I came down for breakfast on Monday morning, my father was gone, back to Manchester to face the music.

*   *   *

He phoned through on Monday evening and we all sat there silently listening as mum tried to calm him down.

"Yes, Walter, of course they are. They were out for hours looking everywhere. Yes, yes, we will of course. Yes, we'll do that. Alright, I'll call them right away. No, there's no possibility of that, we've searched the house, high and low. No, it's just not possible. All right then, we'll look. That's right, if anything happens, you'll be the very first to know." Then she hung up the phone and looked around at us all.

"Did any of you see a small dog around here anywhere?" She was looking serious. "A tiny little creature with a row of medals across its chest?" We stared at her for a long moment, puzzled, but then suddenly, she burst out laughing. "I'll tell you what now, I have nothing but admiration for the poor brute! He took one look at this place and bolted! Off back to Yorkshire, no doubt. Fair play to him, sure he has more bloody brains than myself!"

The story of the dog became a family joke, a secret source of humor to be shared with everyone but dad.

Chapter 8

Paint

My father was renovating the hotel that summer and the work had proceeded remorselessly every weekend, mixing concrete, carrying bricks, helping with the painting and then cleaning up after we'd finished each day.

I didn't mind the work, but I was twelve years old and I wanted to do some other things as well. One Sunday dawned quiet and warm and hazy. It was one of those summer mornings that seem heavy with some unspoken promise. I was always captured by days like that. No breeze, just the soft, warm stillness of the early morning calm before the household stirred. It was as if I was the first one awake in the whole world and the day was mine.

I dressed quietly, reluctant to break the spell, then crept up the stairs and went out to the front steps of the hotel. A milkman in a peaked cap and white coat cruised silently past on an electric milk cart, smiling across when he caught sight of me as if there were a secret between us.

I sat there for a while, dreaming, then my dog, Major, came around from the back of the house and stood in front of me, wagging his bushy tail, demanding to be taken for a walk. I had to do some painting that day, I knew that, but the morning was too beautiful to ignore. I grabbed a stick and we were off across the promenade down the old wooden stairs to the beach.

The town was just beginning to stir, a few tourists appearing here and there on the promenade. As Major and I crossed the sands, a couple walking arm in arm smiled as Major sniffed at them. I smiled back. They seemed friendly enough, but I knew there was a difference between them and me. I lived here; the beaches were my home, winter and summer. The visitors only turned up in the season when the sun shone. They arrived from unknown places to talk on and on about the glorious weather or, when it was raining, to complain that they might as well have stayed at home, as if the town only had meaning when the sun shone.

They had no knowledge of the sea or what happened on those beaches when the seasons turned. They'd never witnessed the gales that swept the coast each year, or the Spring tides that roared along those same stretches of promenade, smashing down sections of the seawalls, devastating the structures closest to the ocean, flooding into the low-lying areas and wreaking havoc on the flimsy sideshow stalls that littered the promenade.

When those gales ran in, I would hang on to the railings at the very edge of the promenade, the salt air stinging my nostrils, drenched by the ocean spray whipped up from the white-capped crests as they thundered furiously into the solid black granite, seething and smashing at the seawall as if determined to crash through and ravage the entire town.

Those gales had been known to tip double-decker buses over on their sides as they raged relentlessly through the streets and I would thrill as the winds howled along the coast in winter, screaming through the alleyways at night like demented banshees searching for lost souls. They'd buffet the walls and windows of the hotel so that you thanked God you were safe and dry and warm at home, snuggled down in bed under heavy blankets, made all the more cozy by the elements raging just outside the thin panes of glass.

And most of all, I loved it when the snows came. I looked forward to those glorious winter mornings when I would wake up and know before I'd opened my eyes that the snow had continued falling, as I had prayed, all through the night. I would know at once by the eerie silence the snow always brought, a stillness and a whiteness lying over all, as if the town had been blessed.

Raised up on my elbow on those days, peering out the window, I'd see the soft, pure snow piled up on the windowsill and the fresh white sloping roofs of the houses across the road, transformed overnight into pristine crystal palaces, painted clean and virginal by some silent celestial hand, standing there forgiven, as it were, without a blemish on the crisp white covering.

The silence was always there on those mornings, like a church. I would stare out the window in wonder. Not a footprint or a car track in sight. Occasionally a cat, confused but curious, could be seen picking its way cautiously through the cold white blanket, pausing with each considered step to shake the offending snow from its paws.

On days like that, there was an urgency to dress and run downstairs; the first footprints in the snow had to be mine. I'd wake Peter and Bernard, yelling, "Quick, quick, it snowed all night! Quick, we can make a snowman!"

They'd scramble out of bed, panicking.

"Wait for me! I'll just be a minute, wait!"

We'd tear across the virgin snow to the promenade, hurling snowballs at each other and screaming in ecstasy at this wondrous happening. Then we'd roll a ball of snow over and over until it became big enough to form the base of our statue, working away for hours until we'd built a snowman. Then, when we were finally satisfied, we'd tramp back home for breakfast. Late, freezing cold, hands blue and numb from the snow and the pain, then, as fingers thawed out beneath the warm water.

* * *

Major was off and running, thundering along the ocean's edge, coming back now and again to bark at me, demanding that I at least try to keep up with him. Occasionally, I'd hurl a stick far out into the sea and he would take off with a yelp of delight, plunging into the water and swimming out strongly to retrieve it. We ran up and down the beach for ages, chasing seagulls and sticks until I was brought back to reality by a distant church bell.

Christ, I realized with a shock, it's ten o'clock! My father had told me to be ready for work at 9.30, immediately after church. I felt the old sense of panic as I turned back to the hotel, running as fast as I could, hoping against hope that he'd woken up late but, as soon as I saw my mother, I knew I was in trouble.

"Oh God, why do you do this?" She was frightened. "He's been asking after you. Don't mind now, go out there and start cleaning up, I'll tell him you're working. I'll get your breakfast later."

I went out and began sweeping the front yard. A few minutes later, he was there, standing by the gate, staring at me.

"Have you been to the mass?"

"No, I forgot."

"Where've you been?"

"I was down on the beach."

"You were down there with that dog again, weren't you?"

"Yes."

"You were supposed to be here at 9.30. Didn't I tell you that?"

"Yes, dad."

He was still standing there, motionless, staring at me, when a group of young women came out the front door.

"Good morning, Mr. O'Raleigh," one of them called out.

His manner changed immediately.

"Good morning, girls." Suddenly he was beaming. "So what's on today, then?"

"The Pleasure Beach," she called back, "we're going to spend the day there and then we're going to the Tower Ballroom tonight!"

"Ah Jaysus, you'll break some hearts at the dance tonight, I'll bet." He moved over to where they were and soon, they were chatting away, the whole group laughing and giggling as he flirted with them.

I slipped away to the backyard and began stirring the paint the way he'd showed me but, a few minutes later, he was there again, grim as ever.

"If you take that dog down on the beach one more time when you're supposed to be working, I'll shoot the bastard. Do you understand?" He wasn't angry now, just cold.

"Yes, dad."

"I'm warning you; I'll shoot him if I have to."

"I won't, dad, I promise."

I was frightened. I'd seen him kill animals before and I knew that he meant it. I'd seen him kill a cat one time in the kitchen. The unfortunate creature had wandered into the house, probably attracted by the smell of food. I remembered how my father had come rushing in that day.

"Quick, it's the cat …" He was excited. "… the one that steals the food. I have him trapped in the kitchen! Come on now, help me catch him!"

I thought it was a great adventure at first. We chased the cat backwards and forwards from one kitchen to the other. There were so many places for it to hide, it was impossible to catch. My father had a broom he was using to poke the cat out from under the benches. The terrified animal was hissing and growling as he stabbed at him with the long handle. I was getting worried. It was beginning to feel cruel.

"You're not going to hurt him, are you dad?"

"Not at all." He was grinning. "Sure he won't feel a thing."

Suddenly, the cat burst out again from under a bench and it was on again, around and around the kitchen. A couple of times in desperation, the cat leapt through the small sliding window that led from one kitchen to the other. The third time, my father anticipated the move and the broom came smashing down on the cat in midair. The animal's back was broken immediately, its body twisting up in an unnatural arc from the force of the blow.

I was stunned, unable to grasp what was happening. The cat landed on the table next to the bread-slicing machine, hissing and thrashing around wildly, its front legs clawing frantically at the slippery surface, its back legs flopping about uselessly.

My father grabbed it quickly by the back of the neck. He was smiling. There was a quick twist, then a wrench, and then it was over.

"That's how you kill a rabbit," he said.

I was struck dumb. It was the neighbor's cat; I'd known it for years.

"That'll teach it!" He offered me the body. "There you go now, throw it in the bin."

I pulled back, the dead cat's eyes staring up at me accusingly.

My father was shaking his head. "Ah, you're too soft, son, you're way too soft!"

He'd killed the cat without a second thought, and I knew he'd kill my dog too if he wanted to.

*   *   *

"Make sure you stir that paint properly now the way I showed you, then bring it round the front."

He watched me for a while as I stirred the paint around and around, making sure to scrape the flat stick across the base of the tin every few stirs to get the thick stuff up off the bottom, then he disappeared. I kept stirring. I knew he'd test it as soon as I gave it to him. My mother came out with a bacon sandwich and a glass of milk.

"Sure the slaves in Egypt had it better than this." We both laughed; she had a way of softening things. "He'll be gone back to Manchester tomorrow son, don't get on his bad side."

I stirred the paint for another ten minutes so there was no chance of it being wrong, then I took it around to him. He was halfway up the ladder.

"What took you so long?" Then without waiting for a reply: "Bring it up here."

I climbed the ladder awkwardly, one hand holding the paint tin.

"Come on, pass me up that paint! Jesus Christ, you're slow as a wet week!" I passed it up to him. "Now start sanding those lower windows, make sure all the loose paint's off first."

He'd sing sometimes as he worked and the guests or locals passing by would stop. "You're doing a great job there, Walter," somebody would call up, "and your boy's helping you too, I see."

"Oh yes, he's a grand lad is Brian, he loves helping his da."

Once I'd have felt a surge of pride when he said things like that, but by this time, it had come to mean less than nothing, so I'd just kept working away, scraping and sanding as he painted the woodwork above me.

* * *

Des Reagan turned up just before lunchtime. I heard our secret whistle and there he was, across the road, half-concealed behind a postcard stand outside Dick's shop. I shook my head and he got the message immediately, disappearing into the stream of tourists flowing along the crowded street. Des and I had not been allowed to talk to each other since we'd been caught playing truant together the year before. We'd gone to the Pleasure Beach one day and it probably would have been alright if we hadn't met up with Bobby Jones.

Bobby was completely insane. I don't know if he was actually insane, but he was definitely crazy. We used to go to the Pleasure Beach together sometimes, raiding the slot machines in the fun parlors. Slipping a flat steel hacksaw blade underneath the bottom edge of the small wooden door on the front of the machine and sliding the coins out sideways. Raking, it was called, and we'd sometimes get as much as two or three pounds in an hour. The only trouble was, the attendants got to know you after a while and once that happened, they would watch you like hawks. At some of the places, that didn't matter too much as a lot of them were old guys who couldn't do anything anyhow.

Des was always worried about getting caught. I had been, at first, but then after the thrill of the first few times, I grew to love it. It was like robbing banks on the movies. First, you'd stand across from the arcade and spy on the place, working out who was on duty and how many there were and then you'd wait until the place was crowded and then you'd slip in and start raking. You knew if you got caught, they'd call the police and the least they would do would be to take you home to your parents; you might even end up in court.

But the whole point about it was the excitement. We'd stand there around the machine, hearts pounding, the middle one raking out the coins as quietly as possible, the other two on either side covering him, hiding what he was doing. We'd be right into it sometimes, oblivious to everything and suddenly, you'd hear a shout. "Hey, you buggers!" and the attendant would be running at you full tilt with a mad look on his face. We'd scatter off all in different directions, throwing the money up in the air to confuse them, taking off into the crowd like rabbits from a gun. We'd have planned the whole thing before we ever went in there, sitting in a café, deciding what to do if things went wrong.

But Bobby Jones was a lunatic. He had a reputation that he'd do anything at all, so when we met up with him that day, I knew there'd be trouble. As soon as we arrived at the Pleasure Beach, we went to one of the main arcades. There were dozens of machines lining the walls and we'd been there several times before. We spent fifteen minutes going from one machine to another, pretending to play them as I raked out the money from under the doors and passed it to the others. There were quite a few people around and everything was going well, too well for Bobby, and suddenly without any warning at all, he started shouting. "Thieves! Thieves! We're being robbed! Thieves!" He was hurling money up in the air and screaming like a lunatic at the top of his lungs. Des and I froze for a moment but then, as Bobby ran out of the arcade still screaming, we took off too, rushing past the startled visitors, out into the crowd.

Des ran straight into the arms of two security guards and, when I saw him struggling with them, I turned back to help. But by that time, some of the visitors had joined in too and we both ended up locked in a room until the police arrived. We spent two hours at the police station, denying everything. Neither of us had any money or tools on us and finally, they had to let us go with a warning. Our mothers came up to collect us but, because we were still in our school uniforms, the police had phoned St Joseph's College, so we were in trouble everywhere. After that, Des and I weren't allowed to talk to each other again.

*   *   *

My father was coming down the ladder, complaining with each step. "What's the point in giving me a half-empty tin of paint?" he said, "Get some more red lead in that tin. Come on now, quickly!" He thrust the empty pot at me. "It's on the paint stand at the end of the yard, and make sure you give it a good stir before you tip it in."

I hurried out the back. The stand he kept the paint tins on had six shelves to it, the large tin I needed was perched right on the top shelf, covered in the thick red paint that had dribbled down its sides as we'd poured it into the smaller pots. I reached up. Standing on my toes, I could only just touch it. I ran back out again.

"I can't reach it, it's on the top shelf."

"Jaysus, you're useless! Get the paint for Christ's sake! Go on now, no excuses!"

I hurried back out and looked around. There was a block of wood on the ground. I pulled it across and stood on it. I was closer but I still couldn't get both hands around the tin. I was too frightened to go back again so I jumped up and grabbed at the tin, moving it a little closer to the edge. I knew he'd be out within minutes, looking for the paint. I jumped up again and pulled it out a little more. The bottom of the tin was just showing over the edge of the shelf. I jumped again and it came out some more. It was nearly there. I tried to get a grip on it then but it was still just out of reach. One more should do it. I jumped up again, grasping at the tin but this time I went too far and the tin came tumbling down off the shelf.

I don't know if the lid fell off, or if it had no lid on it, but it came crashing down directly on top of me, covering my head and blinding me immediately. The impact knocked me off the block of wood and I fell sprawling on the floor. The tin freed itself as I landed but I was already completely covered in paint. It was in my eyes, in my mouth, in my ears, I was smothered in it. My mother was screaming.

"Walter! Walter, come quickly! Quickly for Christ's sake!"

My eyes were burning; I couldn't see anything. I was spitting the foul-tasting paint out of my mouth, feeling as if I was about to vomit.

My mother was still screaming. "Walter! Walter, for God's sake come and help him."

I was completely blinded by the paint, but I could hear him shouting as he came through the outer kitchen.

"What's wrong now? What's he done now?" Even through the confusion, when I heard his voice, I felt the fear. "Oh, Jesus Christ almighty, what a fucking eejit!"

I tried to open my eyes but all I could make out was a blurry figure approaching me.

"You fucking eejit!"

The punch landed just above my left eye, knocking me backward into the paint stand. I grabbed at the shelves, trying to hold myself up, but he punched me again in the side of the head and I went down, dragging the stand over with me. I could hear my mother screaming from what seemed like a long way off. It went on and on like a wail.

"Walter, you animal! Help him for God Almighty's sake. Help him! He's blinded, can't you see! Oh! God forgive you, you dirty animal!"

He was snarling. "Get up! Get up, you fucking eejit! Get up! Look what you've done now, there's paint everywhere!" He grabbed on to the front of my shirt, dragging me to my feet. I held on to him tightly with both hands, close to him, so that he couldn't punch me.

"Stand up," he roared, "stand on your own two feet!" He had me by the shoulders, shaking me violently. "Be a man, for Christ's sake! Stand up straight like a man!"

The only thing that registered in my mind in those next terrifying moments was that my mother had stopped screaming. The only thing I'd had to hold on to had been that scream. It was like a thread, a witness, a connection to life itself. I knew she was there somewhere but the only thing that registered through the pain and the blindness was that the screaming had stopped and I felt an absolute despair. I had my hands covering my face but he kept jerking them down.

"Let me look at you! Let me look at you, will you!" He slapped me again, across the face but without much force. "Stop sniveling! Be a man! Open your eyes!"

"I can't," I pleaded with him, "I can't see."

He was rubbing at me with a rough cloth. "Jesus Christ, you're a stupid bastard!" He was rubbing so hard it was burning. "Stand still, will you!" he shouted. "Stand still while I get this off you."

Then finally, finally, I heard her voice.

"Get away from him! Get away from him, you animal! I've called the doctor. I'll call the police too if I have to! Now get away from him, Walter!"

Suddenly, she was there holding me. I could smell her smell and feel her softness as her arms enfolded me.

"Oh God, son, what have you done to yourself!" She was crying, I could feel her shaking.

But suddenly, he was there again.

"Stand back, Chris!" he demanded, "Get away from him, stand back!"

"Oh! Jesus Christ almighty you can't put turps on him, you'll blind him for life!"

"Get out of the way, it'll get the paint off him." He dragged me away from her. "Keep your eyes closed, stupid!"

There was a splash of cool liquid on my face, followed immediately by a searing sensation that tore at my eyes and skin. The pain was intense. I screamed out in terror, stumbling forward blindly before falling over again. There was a crash of a tin on the ground next to me and I could hear them struggling.

"Stop it, you bloody animal, you'll blind him for life!" my mother was crying and screaming. "I've called the doctor already; he'll be here any moment. If you touch that boy once more, I swear to God I'll call the police. I swear to God I will! Miriam! *Miriam*!" She was screaming out for one of the waitresses. *"Miriam, c*all the police! That's an order! Call them now, this instant, do you hear me! *Call the police!"*

"Don't be silly, Chris, there's no need for that, sure Jaysus I'm only trying to help him!"

"Get away from him! Get away from him now or I'll have you arrested; I swear to God I will."

"Calm down now, calm down. He'll be fine now. I was only trying to help him."

Miriam's frightened voice came in. "The doctor's here, Mrs. O'Raleigh. What should I tell him?"

"Put him in the living room, we'll be there in a minute." My mother's voice was low and furious. "If you come near this boy again today, I'll have you arrested, I swear to God I will!"

He went off then, muttering and cursing, but it was over.

She led me into the living room to Dr. Johnson. Both of my eyes were severely affected, but he cleaned them out and covered them over with bandages.

"He'll be fine now, if there's any problem bring him to my surgery in the morning …" He paused. "… is there anything else you need to tell me, about the marks on his face, I mean?"

There was a silence and we all sat there still in the tension.

"Like I said, he fell over, there's no more to it than that."

He didn't say anything for a long moment, and I could hear him collecting his things. Then he spoke again, very quietly.

"If anything else happens, anything at all I mean, you'll give me a ring, won't you? I'm sure we could arrange for some help."

"That's grand, Doctor. I appreciate your help, but we'll be fine now."

I didn't see my father again that weekend and when I came down for breakfast on Monday morning, he'd already left for Manchester.

Chapter 9

Truancy

When Bernard left St Joseph's, my mother enrolled him in a navigation course at the Naval Training School in Fleetwood. He was only fifteen, but she was worried sick about him, and wanted to get him out of Blackpool as soon as possible.

My father's rages were becoming worse and one night, there'd been a terrible scene at the hotel. Bernard and I had run into the kitchen when we'd heard them shouting but dad had knocked Bernard down immediately and then turned on me. In my panic, I'd grabbed a carving knife that was lying on a bench and threatened him with it. My mother screamed but my father just stepped forward quickly and slapped me hard across the side of the head. I was sent flying across the room and ended up half-stunned on the linoleum floor with him standing over me shouting.

"If you ever dare pick up a weapon to me again, I'll break your fucking back." He was jabbing a finger down at me. "As God is my judge, I will!"

It was over then, but as he strode from the kitchen cursing, I swore in my heart that I would kill him one day.

After that night, Mum did everything she could to find Bernard a berth on a ship, and a few months later, he signed onto the *SS Willowbank,* a dirty old tramp steamer outward bound from Liverpool. The night before he was due to leave, we sat in the lounge room, talking. It was a Saturday evening and he was joining the ship the following day.

"I want you to look after mum while I'm away," he said. I was frightened because he was leaving but I didn't know how to tell him that. He was looking out of the window. "Don't do anything stupid with dad. Don't try to fight him or anything like that, OK?" I didn't know what to say, Bernard had been our only hope. "I won't be gone for long," he said.

"How long?" I asked.

There was a pause.

"I didn't want to go; mum wants me to." There was another long pause. "I won't be gone long," he said again.

I ran home the following morning as soon as the mass was over, but Bernard had already left. Ten months later, we received a letter from the company he'd signed on with telling us that he'd jumped ship in Australia. He was sixteen years old and he never returned to Blackpool.

*   *   *

I woke up early Monday morning and stood by the window, staring out to sea. Was Bernard on the ship already? I'd never taken him to the *Kathleen R* and I regretted that now.

I thought about going to school, but the idea revolted me. My sister Mary had been working for eighteen months and now Bernard was gone too. Five straight days of school lay ahead of me and to make things worse, the exams were starting that week. I dreaded the exams more than anything. The previous few years at St Joseph's had been disastrous ones for me. I'd run into problems with the Christian Brothers soon after arriving and from the beginning, I was labeled as a troublemaker. I thought about our form master, Brother O'Rourke, constantly screaming abuse at everyone. I felt disgusted and wondered if I could avoid school that day.

As I stood there looking out the window, my father's voice came floating up the stairs and when I went down, he was sitting at the breakfast table, reading the morning newspaper. He ignored me completely except for a quick glance.

"Chrissie," he called out suddenly, "did you know that Bernard Read died the other day?"

"No," she answered from the kitchen, knowing the routine, "what age was he?"

"Sure, Jaysus, he was only fifty-three! That's still a young man."

"What did he die of?"

"It doesn't say, but they're burying him on Tuesday."

My mother joined us at the breakfast table and there was a long silence as my father ploughed his way through the obituaries. Mum smiled and winked at Peter and me, it was like a secret thing between the three of us.

"Jesus, Mary and Joseph," he exclaimed suddenly, "I don't believe it! John Brady's dead! He died two days ago, and he was exactly the same age as myself!"

"John Brady?" my mother said, trying to sound interested.

"John Brady," he snapped, "from North Shore! You know him well. A tall man with dark hair, he was a big drinker."

"I can't place him." She wasn't the slightest bit interested.

"Sure, Jaysus you've met him a dozen times! He used to drink at the Cliff's Hotel. He only ever drank whisky." He was staring at her now, frustrated.

"I can't place him, Walter."

"John Brady, Chris, for Christ's sake! He was at the fancy dress party last month. He was dressed up as a pirate or something. You knew him well." He put the paper down, exasperated, and I wished to God she would just say, "Oh him. Oh yes, I knew him well," but she never took easily to intimidation.

"I don't know him, Walter. I don't recall ever meeting the man."

I was dreading the worst now; why didn't she just agree with him?

"For Christ's sake, Chris, of course you know him! Why do you go on like that! He was at the Christmas party. He was drunk. He was singing there for a while and then he fell asleep at the table." He was glaring at her now, a time bomb waiting to explode, but she was sick of it, too.

"Walter, I don't know who John Brady is. If I did, I'd say so. But I doubt if I'd want to know him anyhow if he's drunk all the time."

"I didn't say he was drunk all the time," he shouted, "and he's dead anyway, so show the man some bloody respect!" His fist came smashing down on the white linen tablecloth, knives and forks and crockery jumping up in the air. "What's wrong with you?" he bellowed. "Why do you have to cause these scenes? Can't a man have his breakfast in peace in his own house without being insulted?"

I was watching them, terrified. I knew if he went to hurt her, I would have to try to stop him. My younger brother Peter was frozen up solid next to me, staring fixedly down at the tablecloth, but for once, Mum pulled back … for our sake, I knew.

"Oh wait, John Brady, of course! I'm sorry, Walter, of course I know him. He's that big man with the dark hair. I just couldn't place him for a moment." She was lying, I could tell by her voice, but he was still glaring at her, and for a moment, it was touch and go.

"Why do you do that?" he fumed, "You knew all along who I was talking about."

"I'm sorry, Walter, he must have slipped my mind."

He stared at her for a long, tense moment, both fists resting on the table, but she refused to meet his eye and continued pouring cups of tea and fussing over the breakfast things. Finally, he stood up and threw the newspaper down on the table.

"I'm late," he said, glaring around, "and I have a long drive ahead of me. I don't have time for any of this nonsense."

He went to leave the room but then turned back.

"You're going to school today, right?"

The words had an ominous ring.

"Yes, dad."

"Well, on your way then. Go on, get moving."

As soon as he'd said it, I thought: 'That's it, I'm going to wag it!'

My mother gave me my sandwiches and I jumped on my bike and peddled off up the road, my father's suspicious eyes following me all the way. I felt bad about tricking her, but I hated school more each day.

When I got to the top of the road, I turned left as usual but then doubled back and went in the opposite direction. I was headed for the far end of South Shore but first I had to call into the news agency across the road from the Cock and Bull Hotel. At the back of the shop, half-hidden behind a faded curtain, was the lending library. It was dim in there, a pale light filtering in through the dusty windows, the smell of ancient books, old magazines and posters of Hollywood movies creating an aura of mystery and the promise of adventure. The books were all shapes and sizes, some old, some new. There were tales of adventures on the high seas and stories of heroes and the deeds they'd done, all jumbled together, strewn at random across the dusty shelves. Many of them were dog-eared and worn, their jackets frayed with use and before I read the first page, I would always look inside the cover to see if it had been a gift at one time.

To Clare,
Wishing you all the very best
On your 16th Birthday.

Or another, taking up most of the page, in a graceful flowing hand:

To my dear son Robert,
Happy Christmas.
Love Mum.
1936

Where was Clare now, I wondered and what had become of Robert? 1936 … that had been before the war, had he been a soldier, was he still alive, had he read the book and then gone off somewhere on adventures of his own?

One title caught my eye: *The Devil Rides Out*, by Dennis Waitley. I'd read one of his books before, so I pulled it out and leafed through the pages; it looked interesting. Threepence allowed you to take out two fiction and one non-fiction. I would have preferred three fiction but that wasn't allowed. I could have got them for nothing at the public library, but it felt better paying for my own books; it was more mature.

I found an old detective novel that looked good and then went over to the non-fiction shelves. I couldn't see anything there, so I took the books up the front counter.

"No school today?" The man behind the counter opened up the lending book. "You're at St. Joseph's, aren't you?"

I felt a stab of panic as I realized I'd forgotten to take off my school scarf. "Yes, but I'm sick, I can't go to school today, the doctor told my mother to keep me home."

"Oh, that's no good, lad. Nothing bad, I hope?"

"No, it's asthma, they're going to give me some tests."

That sounded good. The doctor had said that the year before when I had bronchitis.

"Well, you look after yourself, lad. We don't want you dying on us now, do we?"

I escaped out the door, clutching my treasures, shoved my scarf in my school satchel and sped off down a side street. Once I was out of South Shore, I'd be safe.

Within minutes, I was on the Promenade. It was off-season and the place was like a ghost town, the hotels and boarding houses standing mute and silent, their front yards empty, their large bay windows staring out hopelessly across the ocean, searching for the first signs of the next invasion.

Soon, I came within sight of the Pleasure Beach. It was fenced off and shuttered down for its winter's hibernation. Directly across the road lay South Pier. Crossing the tramlines, I arrived at the steep flight of stairs that led down to the beach. The seawalls in that area were much higher, built out of smooth shiny black granite chunks that had been cemented in place years before when Blackpool had been one of the major seaside resort towns in England. The stairs were wide, wooden and solid with ornate steel railings on either side, painted as always in the Council colors of cream and green.

The huge sweeping seawall that supported and protected the Open-Air Swimming Baths on the left and the elaborate Victorian architecture of South Pier on the right lent an air of grandeur to that part of town.

Going down those endless stairs to the beach, the broad expanse of the sands stretching out before me, seabirds wheeling and screeching overhead in welcome, was like passing through a doorway to freedom. I was leaving behind the problems of home and school and entering a magical world full of hope and promise. I knew every inch of those beaches, every curve in the seawall that protected the town from the ocean's fury and every stair and tread that led down to the sands. During the summer months when the town was crowded with tourists, we'd crawl underneath their broad wooden treads, shoveling sand into homemade "riddles", roughly-made wooden sieves with wire mesh bottoms, fossicking for coins or other things dropped by the hordes of visitors who sat on the steps, eating fish and chips by day and drinking beer and making love by night.

But today was different. Winter had emptied the beaches and there was not a soul to be seen. Far away toward the horizon, dirty white waves tossed about in the distance, anxiously awaiting the turn of the tide. On the beaches, the piers were the only aberrations, their gaudy, painted superstructures, and dark rusting steel undersides contrasting starkly with the openness and purity of the endless sands.

South Pier was an impressive sight. Built at the turn of the century and beginning to show its age, the pier's main deck was taken up by sideshow stalls, slot-machine parlors and fortune tellers with names like *Gypsy Rose Lee* or *Madame Bovary: Fortune Teller to the Aristocracy*. They came complete with gypsy clothes and crystal balls and for a small fee, they would forecast your future by reading your stars.

Further along, you could play darts or put ping-pong balls in rotating cast-iron clowns' gaping mouths to win prizes. The middle section of the pier broadened out to accommodate 'The Ballroom,' a large dance floor enclosed on all sides by glass doors and windows. Here in summer, beneath the spotlights and the revolving multi-colored mirrored ball suspended from the ceiling, the visitors who swarmed into Blackpool from the mills and factories of the industrial north would drink and sing and dance the night away.

At the far end of the pier, beyond all these diversions, a flight of solid iron stairs led down to the jetty. This was a world stripped of pretense. The surface underneath your feet, cold, hard, steel gratings supported by heavy rust-caked girders, the fittings plain and sturdy, the heavy steel post handrails welded at the joints and capable of supporting a man's full weight, the entire structure had an air of utility and hardship about it.

Usually a chain swung across the entrance to this area to deter the tourists. Only the local fishermen came here, fishing from the jetty in all but the very worst weather when the pier would be officially closed to the public. On those stormy days when the gales battered the coast and the wind and waves sent torrents of white water foaming across the promenade, Des Reagan and I would climb over the locked turnstiles and advance cautiously to the end of the pier. We'd cling onto the railings in the heaviest gusts, screaming with glee and hanging on for grim life as the foaming ocean swept the full length of the jetty.

Nothing could have survived at the end of the jetty during those storms. It was like watching a submarine sloughing its way through the deep. One minute, it would be above water, the next, huge, roaring, breaking crests would sweep along its entire length, pounding waves hissing through the aging girders and spurting up through the trembling gratings.

The fishermen stood on the jetty stoically through winter and summer. I spent hours watching them, two lines of silent men on either side, backs turned to each other, far enough apart from the next man so they would not foul the wide sweeping arc of each other's rods as they hurled their multi-hooked paternosters, lead sinkers and bait far off out into the dark waters. They were a solitary lot, seemingly content to stand there all day without the need to talk or socialize with each other, just the odd comment occasionally, usually about a fish just caught.

"That's a nice one there now."

"Ay, 'tis indeed."

And then back to their own silent worlds, standing mute by the railings, hands clutching their rods, heads bowed against the weather as if in prayer, watching and waiting for the next bite.

Occasionally tourists would find their way down to the lower jetty and the fishermen would tolerate them as long as they kept to themselves, but if tourists, in their ignorance, were silly enough to proffer such trivialities as: "Are you catching anything today?" the question would be met with a cold, blank stare, a stony silence and a turned back.

Underneath South Pier was a different place again. Dark, sinister, shadowy, and dripping wet. The old steel columns that had supported the pier since Victorian days covered in dense scales of heavy rust and coated below with barnacles and shellfish of all varieties. Where the columns disappeared, the sands had fallen in a concave shape around the encrusted steel, creating a circular pool at their base. The sand in the pool was soft and waterlogged and for years, we'd heard stories of how children who had stood too close to the base of these piers had been sucked down to their deaths by the sinking sands around them. We all swore that we didn't believe it but none of us would have dared to put it to the test.

Looking seaward towards the far end of the pier, you were confronted by a mass of aging steel girders that became denser as the pier swelled out in size. Beneath this area, heavy shadows fell on even the brightest day and a shallow lake of seawater, ominous, still, and silent, always remained there.

I'd attempted to cross this area many times over the years, leaping from one dry patch to another, trying to maneuver a way through the dangerous territory. But on each occasion as I progressed further into that shadowy world, the echoing drip, drip, drip of water falling from the rusting girders overhead, the acrid smell of rotting steel submerged in cold salt water, and the eerie echoing noise of my own feet jumping on the rapidly disappearing sand banks would always stop me before I was halfway across.

Once paused, I would be overwhelmed by a sense of dread; all I could see around me was death and decay and with the sands underneath my feet waterlogged and sinking and the long dark strands of seaweed hanging like hag's hair from the corroding cross braces, I would panic and turn to flee. Heading back toward the sunlight, running as fast as I could, weaving in and out of the rusting stumps as if pursued by demons, splashing through the shallows, oblivious to the cold waters, intent only on breaking out from under that dark and menacing place. But today was different. Today, I was grateful just to wander along the beaches alone, away from home and school.

After exploring under the pier for a while, I began to feel hungry and I pulled out my sandwiches. Then I sat there in the cold, brittle, winter sunlight, eating, daydreaming, and relishing my newfound freedom. A few hopeful seagulls turned up to beg for scraps, but I didn't feed them. I knew if I did, they would begin fighting and screeching and then they'd be followed by hundreds of squabbling seabirds that could only draw attention to me.

As soon as lunch was over, I climbed back up the long wooden stairs, crossed the tramlines and headed off along the Promenade. The day was cold, the sky leaden with the threat of snow. The wind had increased overnight and was now blowing strongly, bringing with it the realization that I wouldn't be able to stay outdoors all day. What could I do? I had no money. It would be warm in one of the public libraries but that would be dangerous.

I came across some shelters near the swimming baths and tried huddling in the corner of one of them, but it was useless, the wind was everywhere. I set off again, heading further south. It was then that I spotted a small building near the sunken gardens. It was shaped differently to all the other shelters. The base was circular, divided into four separate sections by wooden partitions that crossed in the middle.

I tried each section in turn, but the wind was howling through them all, so I chose one at random, lay down on my back and pulled my coat tight around me. It was then that I spotted the trapdoor in the ceiling. My heart leaped. I climbed up on the back of the seat and when I pushed at the little door, it swung open easily, falling backwards to reveal a man-sized opening. I took a quick look around the Promenade, the coast was clear. I reached up, grabbed the sides with both hands and hauled myself up into the loft.

It took a moment for my eyes to adjust to the light, but as they did, I began to make out my surroundings. The interior was like the inside of a pyramid and I could stand up straight as long as I stayed close to the centre. The floor was made up of wooden planks laid side by side. I was thrilled, this was incredible, it was a perfect refuge, totally safe and secure. I could live here forever, I thought, looking around. All I needed was food and some blankets and this could be my secret hideaway, winter, and summer.

I was jolted out of my dream world by voices nearby and I held my breath, trying to make out what was being said. The voices began again followed by a woman's laughter. I crept closer to the trapdoor and peered down. There were two women sitting on the bench closest to the road. They were laughing and talking to someone I couldn't see.

"You look daft, Jack, take that silly bloody cap off."

There was more laughter. My satchel was on the seat next to them. *Damn!* That's what they were laughing at. My school cap had been on the satchel.

I moved quietly to one side and knelt. A pair of legs came into view, dancing around in circles. Then they moved closer and I could see him clearly: a heavy, middle-aged man in a dark brown overcoat and glasses was dancing around with his hands on his hips, my school cap perched on top of his head.

"There's a tram comin,' Jack. Come on, ye' daft bugger."

"What should we do wi' bag?"

"Leave it be, it's none of our business."

There was more laughter and my cap was tossed back on the seat. As they walked away, I lowered my head upside down out of the hole to watch them. This was fantastic; they'd had no idea I'd been spying on them. I watched as they boarded the tram and, as it rattled away, I slid out of the manhole and retrieved my cap and bag.

Back up in my hideaway, I took stock. This was serious business. I could hide here forever. I looked around; how could I be discovered? As long as no-one saw me go up or down, my hideaway was invincible. The open trapdoor could be a giveaway, though. I pulled it closed; darkness fell immediately. Jesus, I thought, candles are what I need! We had plenty of them at home. I opened the trapdoor again to let in some light and looked around. There was a lot of dust on the floor but that was OK. I could lay some sheets down like a carpet. We had plenty of old sheets at home that my father used when he was painting.

I opened my satchel. There was nothing left but a small piece of cake. I ate it. I'll need something to drink, too and a cup to drink out of; maybe I should bring a knife and fork, too.

I stayed there for hours, dreaming, and making plans. One day I'd tell Des Reagan about it but not just yet, not until I'd fixed the place up properly. If things got too bad at home, maybe I could move in here. Why not? If nobody else even knew about the place, then it belonged to me.

I opened my book, *The Devil Rides Out.* The light was poor, I had to stay close to the trapdoor to be able to see. As I read, the wind began to moan outside and with the dim light from the trapdoor barely illuminating the words, I was carried away into a fantasy world where I stayed for hours.

Before I left, I hung my head out the hole once again to make sure the coast was clear, then I dropped down quietly, closing the trapdoor behind me. I made sure the shelter looked exactly the way I found it and then I headed off home, arriving the same time as usual. I was a little worried but, when my mother called out a greeting in her usual voice, I relaxed.

That night after dinner, I assembled the things I needed for the morning and the following day, I was up early, eager to be on my way. I'd taken a tin of beans from the cupboard and a can opener, I had enough money for a bottle of Tizer, and I had six candles in my pockets and a full box of matches, too. I'd tied two old painting sheets to the bike the night before and a thin blanket was stuffed in my satchel. I was ready to go.

I shouted goodbye to my mother and then cycled up the road as usual. As soon as I was out of sight, I dived off down a back lane, circled around the block and headed for freedom. The Promenade was deserted but I rode up and down for a while, just to make sure the coast was clear, then I approached the shelter. Soon I was safely back inside again.

This time it was different; this was my den. I organized the sheets close to the trapdoor and then placed several candles together on a ledge and lit them. Even with the door closed, I could now read comfortably. The place looked fantastic, just like a pirate's cave. This was even better than I'd imagined, and this was only the beginning. I pulled out my book, sprawled out on the floor and began to read.

The Devil Rides Out was spooky, but even with the flickering shadows dancing around my head, the wind whistling about the shelter roof and Dennis Waitley's ghosts and demons howling through the pages, I still felt entirely safe and secure in my secret hideaway. Occasionally I'd hear footsteps or voices. Sometimes, they'd pass by and sometimes people would come and sit in the shelter. At first, I'd spy on everyone who came by, but after a while, I'd just take a peep and then go back to my book, only bothering to check on them if they sounded really interesting.

I had my first meal up there that day, my school sandwiches laid out on a sheet and cold baked beans fished from the can with a teaspoon. Sitting up there, quietly eating my lunch while people were down below talking, gave me an incredible sense of adventure. Nobody could ever guess that I was up there. Robin Hood must have felt the same way, normal people completely unaware of his presence or his real identity. He'd emerge from his hideaway only when he wanted to take part in some incredible adventure.

After I finished lunch, I lay down on the sheets. It was getting colder and I realized I was going to need more blankets. That's alright, I thought, that's tonight's secret mission, when the moon is full.

The people downstairs were still there, a middle-aged man with an incredibly old woman. They had been there for a long time and I was wondering what was going on. They would go silent for ages and I would think that maybe they'd left, so I would ease open the door and peep down. The old woman just sat there, staring fixedly ahead, a blanket over her knees, while the man read a newspaper and commented occasionally on some item or other.

"Ere luv, they caught that bloke that stole money from Pleasure Beach. Not before time."

The woman didn't speak, content to just sit there, staring out to sea. I was starting to get worried; I needed a pee. How long were they going to stay there? Then I realized that Robin Hood must have had the same sort of problems sometimes. 'Get a grip on yourself,' I told myself sternly, 'be a man!'

I thought it over and decided I would hibernate until the danger had passed. I pulled the paint sheets across me and lay there quietly, pretending to be a secret agent trapped in an enemy fortress.

As I lay there dreaming, my thoughts drifted back to my brother, Bernard; we'd got a letter from him the week before from Australia. There was a photograph of him inside. He looked different somehow. He was standing near a railroad crossing by the side of a dusty road. All he had on were jeans and a pair of boots. He was cradling a baby kangaroo in his arms and grinning at the camera. Mum was forever talking about us all going to Australia. Dad always laughed, but I was beginning to wonder if we would, one day. I wasn't even sure if I wanted to go and live with Bernard. I liked being by myself.

As I lay there on my back, I wondered what Australia would be like. I'd seen it on the movies once, sunburnt men with wide-brimmed hats. Anything would be better than St Joseph's. I'd caused a lot of trouble for myself there, talking in class, playing truant, fighting and refusing to play sport. I didn't fit in there. I didn't fit in anywhere. As I drifted off to sleep, I found myself wondering how Bernard had caught the baby kangaroo.

When I awoke, there was an absolute silence all around. The candles had burnt out and my cave was almost black. I eased open the trapdoor; the odd couple were gone. I had no idea what time it was, but I knew it was late.

After tidying up, I dropped out of my cave and retrieved my bicycle from its hiding place across the road. As I rode off towards home, I looked back to my shelter. There were other shelters similar to it further along the promenade but this one was special, this one held a secret, and this one was mine.

Chapter 10

A Decision

I'd only intended taking a few days off school but, after finding the hideaway, I decided to stay away for a little longer. Soon, I was wondering if I had to go back at all. Being away was dangerous. My brother, Peter, was at the same school. If they asked him where I was, I'd be in big trouble. The only way to stop them making inquiries would be to write them a sick note.

The thought frightened me. If my father found out, I knew he would give me an awful thrashing. But I hated school, especially now that I'd found a new way of life. I'd seen plenty of sick notes before. My mother had written one the previous winter when I'd been off for three weeks with bronchitis. Christ, I thought, three weeks! Could I do that again? Three weeks, Jesus! The school record for truancy was only a week. The more I thought about it, the more I liked the idea. I could use the paper with *Alexandra Private Hotel* printed on the top; that would look good.

The following evening, I took a dozen sheets of the hotel paper from my mother's cupboard. What about her signature? I went through a pile papers until I found one she'd signed and stuck everything in my satchel. This work should be done in my secret den. I spent most of the next day pouring over the sick note by candlelight, writing and rewriting the letter.

Dear Brother Sheehan,

I am sorry to inform you that Brian is once again sick with bronchitis. Dr. Johnson has recommended that he be kept home for at least three weeks. I hope you are well and thank you for your help in this matter.

Yours truly,
Mrs. Christine O'Raleigh

The signature was the main problem. I tried over and over again but each time, it didn't seem quite good enough. Finally, I ran out of paper, so I just picked the best one, put the note in an envelope and addressed it carefully.

That evening with my heart in my mouth I stood outside the post office in Waterloo Road, holding the letter half in and half out of the post box. If I dropped the letter in, it was done; there could be no turning back. The only other option now was to write another letter explaining my three days off school and return to class the next day.

Suddenly, I was terrified. I pulled the letter back out. This was ridiculous, how could I expect to get away with it? I thought of my father's face the last time he'd beaten me, and even though he was miles away in Manchester, I felt frightened. He'd kill me if he knew what I was doing now.

I put the letter into the slot again, still holding on to a corner. I thought about Robin Hood. What would he have done? Either way, I had to post a letter to the school. I let go of the envelope and heard it falling down to the bottom of the box. It was done. There was no turning back now.

I returned home through the back lanes, climbing over brick walls that separated the narrow streets, creeping silently through people's backyards.

The next morning, I was up early again. I'd hidden a heavy blanket in the rubbish bin outside the back door and I had to retrieve it without being seen.

"What's got into you?" My mother looked up from her breakfast. "You're awfully keen to get to school."

"It's a sports day," I told her.

"Is that what it is." She was smiling.

I draped the blanket over the handlebars and fled up the road. My hideaway was now complete, but I passed the next few days anxiously, waiting and wondering, but by Thursday, I began to relax: if they were going to question the letter, they would have done so by then.

I was starting to feel a bit lonely. It was still good, but it would have been better if Des Reagan was there, too. That night I went around to his place and gave the secret whistle and minutes later, we met up at the end of Bagot Street.

"I thought you were sick ..." he started but I cut him off.

"How would you like to see a hideaway, a real secret hideaway where nobody could ever find you?"

"You're wagging it?"

"Yes, and I might never go back to school. I've got a secret place that nobody knows of. I own it, it's mine."

"Where is it?"

"I can't tell you, it's a secret, but if you come tomorrow after school, I'll show you."

He kept on questioning me, but I wouldn't tell him anymore and before I left, I made him swear our worst secret oath.

"Do you promise never, as long as you live, to tell anyone about what we have talked about just now, and do you swear that, if you tell anyone about my secret hideaway, that you hope your mother will die and rot in hell forever?"

"I do."

"That's no good, you know that! You've got to say it all, all of it. With your hand up, go on!"

He put his hand up, he didn't like doing it, nobody did. Even though you knew you would never break the oath, you didn't like saying things like that and getting your mother involved. That's why it was good; you could believe it, then.

"Do I have to say the part about my mother?"

"Yes, of course you do, otherwise it's no good!"

He took the oath and I gave him the instructions.

"See you tomorrow. Don't be late. Don't bring anybody with you and make sure you're not followed."

I left him there, looking after me and slipped away down a back lane.

* * *

The next day when I hung my head down through the trapdoor just before four o'clock, he was already standing there, outside the hotel across the road.

"Des, over here!" He looked around, bewildered. "Des, are you blind or what, can't you see me?"

When he saw me dropping out of the roof, he looked amazed. "Is that it, is that the hideaway? That's incredible, what's up there?"

"Put your bike over the road behind the pub. Make bloody sure no-one's watching you, then come back here."

By the time he came back, I was already up in the den, peering down, waiting for him. "Don't look up, just sit there for a while looking around and make absolutely sure no-one's watching you."

"It's all clear, can I come up?" He clambered up quickly and stood there, looking around. I'd lit all the candles to impress him. "Whose is it?" He was amazed. "Is it someone's den?"

"It's my den, I come here every day."

"Wow!" He stared around, trying to take it all in. "Does anybody else know about it?"

"No, and nobody ever will. It's a secret den and you can't tell anybody about it, ever, OK?"

"I won't, I promise, on my mother's grave, I won't,"

"You better not, you already made an oath, remember?"

"I won't, I promise. I'll never tell anyone as long as I live."

"If you do, your mother will rot in hell, you know that. I won't let you off."

"I won't, I definitely won't. Never, I promise." He was amazed. "How did you find it? Was it someone else's before?"

"No, nobody knows it exists. This is my own place. Wag it tomorrow, we've got everything we need here."

"If we're caught, we'll be expelled." He was wary, "My mother would kill me."

Des's father was supposed to be an engineer, but he was always away in some other country. Sometimes I wondered if he really had a father but I'd never asked him that because we were friends.

"We'll write you a note," I told him, "that's what I've done."

"If we're both missing from school, somebody will guess." He liked the idea, but he was too scared to make a decision.

*   *   *

On the Wednesday morning of the third week, just as I was settling down to my latest book, I heard our secret whistle. I dropped my head out the hole. Des was standing there, holding on to his bicycle, looking around nervously.

"Don't leave the bike there, take it across the road and hide it in the backyard of the pub."

He was back a few minutes later. He'd brought a whole box of candles and some tins of food for our stores and, after putting things away, we went off and explored the beach before returning to our hideaway to eat. We talked about all sorts of things. We could start a gang now and meet in the shelter every night, if we wanted to; the possibilities were endless.

I returned home later than usual that evening and I could feel something was wrong as soon as I walked in the door. My mother was sitting in the big armchair by the fire.

"Ah," she said, "the wanderer returns, and what did you get up to today?"

"Nothing much," I said cautiously, "just school, that's all."

"And how was school today?"

Peter was watching me, not saying anything.

"It was OK, we did sport."

"And how was sport today?"

There was something wrong. Her voice was different.

"It was OK."

She jumped up suddenly.

"And how was school yesterday and the day before and the day before that?" She was shouting and I knew the game was up. "You haven't been to school for weeks, you little liar." She was furious and, for a moment, I thought she was going to hit me. "Go into the lounge room, wait for me there."

I sat in the lounge room in despair. I couldn't believe it, just when everything seemed perfect, the spell had broken. What now? I thought, my father would be home the following evening. If he knew about this, I was done for. She came into the room, closing the door behind her.

"Where have you been for the past three weeks, tell the truth now, it's the only hope you have."

"I've been wagging it."

"Sure, Jaysus, don't I know that! Didn't the headmaster himself phone me up this morning! You and that Des Reagan brat missing from school for three weeks!"

"It's wasn't his fault, he's only had two days off."

"Don't lie to me!" she shouted, "For God's sake, if your father learns of this, he'll kill you, you stupid boy! Don't you realize that?"

She got up and began pacing around the room.

"Where have you been for three weeks? Where? Where were you each day?"

"I was on the beach, up at Squires Gate." I would never tell her about my hideaway.

"On the beach, in this weather? I don't believe you; you're lying!"

"I was on the beach. If it was too cold, I went to the library. If I had money, I went to the pictures."

She stared at me in silence for a long time.

"I'm taking you up to the school tomorrow morning to see if I can talk the headmaster out of expelling you." She paused again for a long moment. "If your father finds out about this, he will put you in hospital for sure." She stopped, frightened by her own words. "He'll hurt you, son, he must never know about this." She looked away, too upset to go on. "Go on now. Go in and have your meal."

I felt terrible. Not for the shattered dreams but for the fear I saw in her eyes. Her anger had gone as quickly as it had risen. All she knew now was that she'd have to protect me from my father.

The next day we went up to St Joseph's in a taxi. Des Reagan and his mother were leaving just as we arrived. His mother said something to him as they came down the stone steps of the entrance and he ignored me completely.

My mother went into the office first and I sat there listening to the murmur of voices through the heavy door, wondering what she was saying to the headmaster. What would happen? I knew if you were caught wagging for a day, you could get six on each hand. Three weeks was a school record.

The door opened. The expressionless face of Brother Sheehan peered out at me as if he were inspecting some lower form of life.

"Come in ..." He moved to one side and then pointed to a place on the carpet in front of his desk. "... over there."

I stood there self-consciously, not sure of where to put my hands, wondering if I was expelled or not. He sat down in a tall high-backed chair, his palms pressed together, the fingers touching the tip his nose as if in prayer, staring at me as if he had no notion of who I was. Finally, my mother broke the silence.

"Please, Brother Sheehan," she said simply.

He came out of his reverie. "Brian, you have been absent from this school for three weeks. If you tell me any lies in this meeting, I will expel you immediately. Do you understand that?"

"Yes, sir."

He held up a piece of paper by one corner. "Did you write this note?"

"Yes, sir."

"Did you persuade Desmond Reagan to join you in your truancy?"

"Yes, sir."

"Would you say that you were responsible for Desmond Reagan joining you in the act of truancy"?

"Yes, sir."

He paused for a long moment, deep in thought. The old wooden clock on the wall behind him was ticking loudly and I wondered, did he already know the verdict and was he just showing off for my mother.

"Your mother has just told me that your father will give you a thorough thrashing when he gets home." I didn't say anything, and after another moment, he went on. "That is exactly what you deserve." He went silent again, as if not sure of which way to go. "Do you wish to continue your studies at this school?"

"Yes, sir."

He was staring at me blankly, no trace of emotion in his face.

"Wait outside."

I sat outside in the hallway, listening to their voices, wondering why he hadn't asked me where I'd spent the last three weeks. Had Des told him?

My mother came out ten minutes later.

"Don't say a word." She grabbed my arm and almost dragged me out through the doorway. "Never, *ever*, put me in that position again! Do you hear me?" We were heading off down the driveway. She was furious. As soon as we passed through the main gates, she stopped and spun me around. "Listening to that bog Irish idiot going on and on was almost more than I could bear!" She took off again, walking so rapidly, it was hard to keep up with her. "Jaysus, and they're the educated Irish, God forbid! I have no idea why we sent you there in the first place. Sure the man's as thick as a brick! He'd be from somewhere deep in the Bog of Allen, I'm sure!"

I stayed silent; it wasn't often that I saw her this angry. When we got home, she took me into the lounge room and closed the door.

"Your father must never know anything about this. Nobody will ever mention it again, are you clear on that?"

"Yes, mum."

"If he ever found out about this, he would kill you, or he'd put you in the hospital at the very least. Do you understand that"?

Her fear was contagious, and I understood only too well.

"Wait here." She called Peter in and explained the whole thing to him. "You're never to mention this again to anyone. Not even to Mary. Is that understood?"

"Yes, mum," he agreed, impressed by the seriousness of the situation.

My father came home that night. The whole house was on edge, unsure of how we could keep the secret, but the silence held. He never learnt of the truancy.

When we arrived at school on Monday morning, Des Reagan was called into the headmaster's office where he received a severe caning. When he returned to the classroom, he looked destroyed. He was hunched over, holding his hands under his armpits, his eyes red from crying.

As he walked towards his desk, Brother O'Rourke called him back.

"Oh no, Desmond, oh no, it's not as easy as all that."

Des looked terrified.

"Come here now boy, just a little something extra from your form master. Put out your right hand."

Des couldn't at first and I sat there in agony, watching his humiliation. O'Rourke grabbed his hand and gave him three vicious strokes across his open palm. Des broke down immediately, collapsing on the floor sobbing as his knees folded. It was sickening to watch.

"There now, that's better. That's just my own my little contribution. Get up on your feet and off you go now, back to your desk." O'Rourke looked around the classroom smiling, acting stupid. "Now there was something else, wasn't there? What was it now?" His eyes came to rest on me. "Oh yes of course! Brian O'Raleigh! Isn't that terrible! Sure I almost forgot you were down there, Brian. I haven't seen you for so long! Come up here now and let's have a look at you."

I walked up, trying not to look frightened.

O'Rourke was smiling.

"And how's the bronchitis Brian? Are you feeling any better?"

I didn't say anything.

"Well now Brian, the headmaster wants to have a quiet little chat with you, and then after that, you can come back here and we'll get things sorted out between ourselves. Is that alright with you?"

"Yes, sir."

"Good, that's good, and you won't forget to come back and see me now, will you?"

I walked down the corridor slowly. Through the brothers' quarters, past the statue of the Blessed Virgin Mary, then along the dim hallway that led to the headmaster's office. The door was right next to the front entrance. I was frightened, but I was angry, too. I looked at both doors, wondering which one to take. Suddenly, without warning, the headmaster's door jerked open and Brother Brennan came out backwards, nearly knocking me over as he spun around. The headmaster spotted me through the gap and called out.

"Send him in please, Brother."

Oh God, it was on!

"Good luck, son." Brother Brennan was one of the better ones.

I stepped in nervously as the door closed behind me. The headmaster pointed to the carpet in front of his desk. He was a hard-looking man, tall and thin with piercing eyes that seemed to look right into you. He was sitting behind a huge wooden desk in a high-backed chair that looked more like a throne. There was a large blotting pad directly in front of him and, lying across the pad, like a weapon of execution, lay the thick, heavy leather strap that the entire school feared more than any other.

Rumor had it that he'd got it specially made in America to beat the really wild kids with and it was supposed to have strips of metal and whale bone sewn into it to make it hurt more. They said he soaked it in vinegar every night so that it stung for ages. He caught me looking at the strap and a fleeting smile crossed his lips.

"Your father was home on the weekend?"

"Yes, sir."

"And he disciplined you?"

"Yes, sir."

"Good." He was toying with the strap, lifting it up slightly at one end and then letting it fall back down on the blotter. "And what form did the discipline take?"

"He beat me up, sir."

He looked up.

"Explain yourself, O'Raleigh. What does that mean, beat you up?"

I decided to go all the way.

"He beat me up, sir. You know, he punched me in the stomach and then he knocked me out."

He'd stopped playing with the strap now and was staring at me.

"Knocked you out?" I looked down at the floor, trying to look distressed "You mean, knocked you unconscious? Is that what you're saying? So what happened then?"

"I'm not sure, sir. The doctor said I was alright afterwards. My ribs weren't broken or anything like that."

I had his full attention now.

"Your mother called the doctor?"

"Yes, sir. It's happened before, sir."

"I see."

I felt a thrill go through me watching him, he was taking it all in.

"Your father's an Irishman, isn't he?"

"Yes, sir."

He stopped talking for a while and just sat there, staring at me. Then he came to a decision.

"Very well, O'Raleigh, come with me."

He stood up abruptly and swished off out of the room and up the hallway, his black cassock swinging from side to side as he strode ahead of me. When we entered the classroom, O'Rourke was writing on the blackboard.

"Brother O'Rourke," the headmaster gestured, "a moment please."

O'Rourke glanced at me.

"Back to your desk, O'Raleigh."

The two of them huddled together at the front of the room, whispering quietly. O'Rourke turned around once or twice to look at me and then, as soon as the headmaster left, he called me up to his desk.

"So you got a little bit of a thrashing on the weekend, did you?"

He was grinning openly and even though it was a pack of lies, I still hated him for it.

"Yes, sir."

"Well, well now, isn't that a pity!" Then he changed again suddenly. "Get back to your desk now," he snarled, "or I'll do a lot worse."

After that day, nothing was ever said about the truancy and my father never found out. The following week, after making sure that nobody was following me, I returned to my den. A solid brass lock swung from a freshly installed steel bolt. Des Reagan swore that he hadn't told anybody. I never really found out what happened, but it was over.

Chapter 11

The Gypsy

I caught my first glimpse of her on the beach across from Shaw Road. There was a flash of color as she twirled around, dancing and laughing as her younger sister stood there, clapping her hands. They were gypsies, I knew that, looking after a group of donkeys their people hired out to the visitors in the summertime.

Their donkeys were always covered in leather straps decorated with silver and brass bells that hung down beneath their bridles and you could hear them coming from miles away, jingling and jangling as they trotted along the sands.

Now they were tied up together in a bunch, looking sullen and resentful, as if being held against their will. Their dusty, moth-eaten coats and doleful eyes always made me sad and I'd stopped to say hello.

It was an hour or so before sundown and the town was quiet, just a few people strolling along the promenade in the evening sunlight.

As soon as I saw her there dancing, her brightly colored skirt swirling out in a wide arc around her, I was entranced and struck dumb. She must have been fourteen or fifteen, a year or two older than me, and right then and there in that instant, for the very first time in my life, I was captured by the beauty of a woman.

Her long, black, curly hair swung around as she moved, one moment trailing out behind her, the next covering her face. She danced as I had seen women dance in the movies, one hand raised high, snapping her fingers, the other held across her middle in a proud, almost arrogant way. Her skin was darker than anyone I'd ever known, her face strange, exotic, and as foreign to that town as a creature from another planet.

As I stared at her, bewitched, her young sister began to sing. I couldn't understand the words but that didn't matter, I just wanted it to go on.

The gypsy girl wore a white frilly blouse and a long skirt covered in brilliantly colored patterns. She had large golden rings in her ears and silver and gold bracelets on her arms. I stared at her, hypnotized, half afraid and half entranced, not daring to move.

The younger sister saw me standing there and whispered something in her sister's ear. The gypsy girl turned to face me and as our eyes met, she was still smiling.

"Hello," she called out, "what is it you're wanting, a ride on the donkeys? Well it's too late; we're finished for the day." She said something to her sister and they both laughed.

"No," I said awkwardly, "I just like to stroke the donkeys and talk to them."

She burst out laughing, and even though I was embarrassed, I couldn't take my eyes from her face.

"So you talk to the donkeys, do you? They'll take you away if you're not careful."

Her sister joined in.

"You must be mad then, if you talk to donkeys!"

That set the gypsy girl off laughing again but then she softened.

"I talk to them too," she said, "I just don't tell anyone. What's your name?"

"Brian."

"Where're you from?"

"Here, I live here, Alexandra Road," I pointed across the promenade, "over there."

"You live here, you're a local?"

"Yes." I felt awkward.

"Do you want to help us brush the donkeys?"

My heart leapt.

"Yes, I'd like to."

"We'll do one together," she said, "Come on, I'll show you."

She gave me a stiff brush and showed me how to comb down the thick coarse hair on the donkey's back and shoulders as she set about tidying up the plaits and colored bows on his main.

As we worked, she kept teasing me, flashing me smiles that took away my words. She met each look with an open gaze, and I knew, there and then, that I would love this girl all my life.

"You don't say much, do you?" She was smiling again.

"No," I said stupidly, "I don't."

Her young sister joined in.

"Why don't you talk then?"

"Leave him alone," the gypsy girl told her, "He doesn't want to talk, that's all."

"You like him," the younger one shrieked, "you love him!" Then she started screaming hysterically, running around in circles.

The gypsy girl ran after her, pretending to be angry.

"I do not, now shut up, you little pig, shut your mouth!"

She caught her sister and they fell on the sand, struggling and screaming at each other, laughing madly like two crazy people.

I watched them, entranced, longing to join in but unable to and hating myself for it. They tired after a few minutes and got up, brushing themselves off. Then they came back, still laughing and pushing at each other.

"We have to get these done," the gypsy girl told her sister, "Come on now, before da gets back."

She stood close to me as we worked, brushing the donkeys' coats. I longed to say something but I didn't trust myself to speak.

"You're very quiet," she said again, more softly this time.

I didn't answer. I had no idea what to say. We worked on in silence for a while until, unexpectedly, a deep voice called out.

"Do you have them ready, girls?" Two men were striding toward us. "They should have been done hours ago."

The big man was staring at me.

"Who's this?"

"His name's Brian, da, he's a local. He's helping us with the brushing."

Her father looked me over.

"On your way, boy." He jerked his head in the direction of the promenade. "Off you go, you've no business with our people." He stared at me, stony-faced, the two girls standing together next to him. There was nothing I could do.

"Goodbye," I said to the gypsy girl.

She smiled as I walked away. My heart was torn. I paused and turned to look back. They were still standing there, staring after me.

I climbed the stairs to the promenade and looked back again. The men were leading the donkeys off along the beach, one of them riding side-saddle the way they did. As I watched, the girls separated from the group and with a wave to their father, they began walking towards the steps that led off the beach.

My heart leapt, there was a chance! I crossed the road so that the men couldn't see me, then ran along the promenade and waited by the Red Lion Hotel. A few minutes later, as they crossed the tramlines, I ran over to them.

"I told you, he loves you," the younger sister was giggling again, "he's mad about you!"

She went off again into fits of laughter, but I was glad that she'd said it. I wanted the gypsy girl to know how I felt, and I knew I could never have told her.

"My da said to stay away from you. I'm not to talk to you." She was trying to look serious.

"So now you can't talk, and I can," I said, and before I knew it, I'd reached out and touched her arm.

"No!" She looked towards the beach. "They'll see us!"

The first few donkeys were beginning to appear up the slope by Waterloo Road.

"He'll kill me if he catches me talking to you, don't follow us, please." She spun around quickly and walked away, her sister hurrying after her.

My heart couldn't leave it at that. I turned down an alleyway and ran for all I was worth to the top of Shaw Road then hid behind a wall and waited for the girls to appear. As the minutes passed, I became impatient. Finally, I peeped out from behind the wall. The road was empty, they were nowhere in sight, they must have turned off into a side street.

For a moment, I panicked but then I realized that they'd have to cross the Railway Bridge to get to Carmoss Field where the gypsies kept their donkeys. I ran as fast as I could to the bridge and waited there, praying desperately that I would see her again.

Ten minutes later, the donkeys came jangling up the road, hoofs clattering, bells ringing. Her father spotted me standing underneath the lights of the station in the gathering gloom and fixed me with a steady gaze, reading my mind. I waited there until well after dark, but she didn't come; they must have crossed the bridge before I arrived.

The next day, I went down to the beach before breakfast. The donkeys were already there, awaiting the day's work. I walked across cautiously, not knowing if the men were about. When I got closer, I saw two old gypsy women sitting cross-legged in the sand, talking.

"Good morning, young sir," one of them called out, "would you like a ride on the donkeys?"

"No thanks," I told her, "I live here."

They lost interest immediately, returning to their conversation as I continued along the sands to the next group of donkeys, hoping against hope that she'd be there.

Over the next few days, I walked for miles on those beaches, visiting every group of donkeys I came across. I was heartbroken and couldn't get her out of my mind.

I looked for her for the rest of that summer, seeking her face in every crowd, but despite endless hours on the beach and long, lonely evenings by the South Shore Railway Station Bridge, I searched in vain.

* * *

I dreamt about the gypsy girl for months afterwards. She haunted me throughout my waking hours then came to me at night, laughing and dancing in my dreams.

I wandered alone for hours on Carmoss Field, hoping to run into her or her sister, but I never found a trace of either of them. I saw her father once, a few weeks later, up at the far end of town near North Pier, but, as for the girl herself, there was nothing.

I knew that some of the gypsies stayed in Blackpool permanently but most of them left after the summer, moving with the seasonal work all over the country. Finally, in desperation, I told my mother about her.

"Mum, I met a girl a few weeks ago and now I'm not sure how I can contact her."

"What sort of girl?" She was smiling. "Is that what's been wrong with you these past weeks, you're in love?"

"It's not funny, I'm serious about this."

"Ah, God bless you, son, sure it happens to us all." She took me into the living room and closed the door. "Come on now, tell me all about her. Who is she?"

I told her. I told of how we met and how I was sure the gypsy girl liked me. I told her of how I spent half my time looking for her and how I didn't even know her name.

She listened to everything and then she explained to me that the gypsies were different to other people and they were wild and traveled a lot.

"That doesn't make them wrong, son, but it makes them very hard to get to know. They're not like us, they're used to traveling and moving about all the time. Ireland's full of them. The Tinkers, they call them there, but not to their faces, mind. The polite term for them is the Travelers. Never call a Tinker a Tinker to his face, you'll have a fight on your hands for sure."

"Could she be in Ireland, Mum?"

"Sure Jaysus, she could be anywhere, son. Your best hope is if they come back to Blackpool next year for the season. Apart from that, I don't know what to tell you. God only knows where she'd be."

I brooded over the gypsy girl for months, but she was gone, disappeared as if she had never existed, leaving behind a beautiful, painful image that would live in my heart forever.

Chapter 12

Leaving School

Later that same year, my father resigned from his job in Manchester. The doctor had told him that he had high blood pressure and a bad heart, and he was forced into an early retirement at the age of forty-six.

When Mum told me the news, I was worried. It was bad enough him being there on weekends, I couldn't imagine what it would be like having him in the house all of the time.

The first few weeks he was back, I treated him carefully. Keeping out of his way as much as possible and talking to him only when I had to. It soon became obvious that he didn't only drink on weekends and when the rows started up again, I knew I wouldn't be able to live in the hotel much longer.

School was a nightmare for me, too. I'd been involved in a lot of trouble at St Joseph's, mostly of my own creation. I'd been caught out cheating in an exam and Brother O'Rourke had given me a bad thrashing with his strap.

I hated O'Rourke with a passion and when he left the strap behind on the desk one day, I slipped it into my satchel when nobody was looking.

For the next few days, I enjoyed watching O'Rourke making a fool of himself demanding to know who'd stolen it. He threatened the whole classroom with detention and extra homework but nobody knew who'd taken it.

It was fun for a few days so, when it began to die down, I decided to stir things up again. I took the strap home and cut it up into four small pieces and then went in early the following morning and placed them on his desk.

He came swishing in the door as usual, bustling about collecting the homework but when he arrived at his desk, he stopped dead.

When I saw the look on his face, I turned away quickly, not wanting to catch his eye. Then he exploded into one of his mad rages, demanding to know who had done this and threatening all sorts of consequences.

When he finally calmed down and thought for a moment, he asked who had been the first boy in the classroom that morning.

I couldn't deny it, too many people had seen me, so I raised my hand.

"O'Raleigh!" Suddenly he was smiling. "Brian O'Raleigh! The first boy at school today. Now isn't that a nice surprise. You must have turned over a new leaf, have you?" The smile faded. "Come up here, O'Raleigh."

I went up. He couldn't prove anything.

"Did you do this?"

"No, sir."

He raised his eyebrows. "I'll ask you once again and this time, I want you to tell me the truth. Did you do this?"

"No, sir."

"Liar!" he screamed at me so suddenly, I jumped, *"Liar, you're a liar!* Who else but you would do a thing like that? Of course it was you. I should have known."

I'd been in trouble with O'Rourke from the very first day that he'd become our form master. He'd tried to have me expelled the previous year for fighting in the playground, but my mother had managed to talk the headmaster out of it.

He lowered his voice and tried another tack.

"So, you were the first person in here today, is that so?"

"Yes, sir."

"And when you arrived at the classroom, was the strap on my desk?"

"I don't know, sir."

"O'Raleigh," he paused, "look now. It's pretty clear to me that this is your handiwork, but I'm going to give you one last chance. If you own up now, like a man, I will not punish you, do you hear? I just want the matter resolved. Just tell the truth now and we can put all this nonsense behind us." He leaned closer. "Did you cut the strap up?"

"No, sir, definitely not."

He stared at me for a long moment. "You're lying," he said. "I know you are."

"No, sir."

"Go back to your desk." He looked around the room. "The whole class will stay behind tonight and every other night this week, until the culprit confesses, and we all know who the culprit is now, don't we?"

He kept the whole class in after school for the next two nights. On the third morning, when nobody was looking, I slipped a piece of paper onto his desk on the way out for the lunch break. On it I'd written: "Fuck you O'Rourke."

On returning, he spotted the message, and strode across to my desk immediately. Without a word being said, he grabbed my arm and half-dragged me up to the headmaster's office.

I stood in the corridor outside listening to their muffled voices. A moment later, the door opened.

"Get in here," O'Rourke grated.

The headmaster was sitting behind his desk, looking serious.

"Brian," he began, peering at me over the top of his spectacles, "before we go any further, I want to make it clear to you that, whatever you have done, you will be treated much more leniently if you tell me the truth. Do you understand that?"

"Yes, sir."

"Good. Now Brother O'Rourke has explained the situation to me, and I tend to agree with him. You are without a doubt one of the most troublesome students we have ever had here." He paused again, assessing me. "Do you wish to stay on at St Joseph's College?"

"Yes sir, I do." If I'd said anything different, my father would have killed me.

"If that is so, then why do you persist in misbehaving like this?"

"It wasn't me, sir."

"Are you prepared to swear to that?"

"Yes, sir."

He sat there, studying me for a moment before continuing. "And you're prepared to swear on the Holy Bible that you had nothing to do with this filthy little note here?"

"Yes sir."

He jerked his head at O'Rourke.

"Get him out of here. I'll contact his parents."

When I got home that evening, my mother and father were waiting for me. I denied everything and I swore to God that I had nothing to do with the strap or the note.

It was touch and go with my father. He told me he would thrash me to within an inch of my life if he found out that it was true. I was pretty frightened by then, but I must have lied convincingly because finally they accepted my story.

My mother was concerned in case I would be expelled, and she phoned the headmaster the following day and insisted to him that I was innocent. Nothing more happened about the incident with the strap.

The truth was, I couldn't wait to get out of St Joseph's. I was always in trouble there. It was a complete waste of time and I had no interest whatsoever in schooling.

I was nearly fifteen and I'd been working with my father on the weekends for years by then, mixing concrete, carrying bricks and painting the hotel and I knew that I was a lot more grown up than any of my friends.

A few weeks after the strap incident, I awoke late one morning and lay there in my bed, staring at the ceiling and dreading the day ahead. There was some long overdue homework that I still hadn't done and now there was no chance of completing it.

I thought about wagging school again. I could go exploring on the beach or get a book from the library and stow away in the *Kathleen R,* if she was up on the promenade. It was tempting, but I knew if I were caught, it would be the end of me.

I went downstairs. My father was already sitting at the table. He looked up as I walked in, but didn't speak, he just went back to reading the morning newspaper. My mother came in with my breakfast, but I was too preoccupied thinking about my problems to have any appetite. I dragged my way through the meal, my father glancing at me suspiciously from time to time across the silent table.

"What's wrong with you?" he demanded finally, "Why are you so quiet?"

It was pointless trying to explain.

"I'm tired, that's all."

"Get yourself off to school, that'll cure your tiredness."

My mother joined in, anxious to avoid a scene. "Off you go now, there's the lad. You don't want to be late for school."

As I pedaled off, I caught a glimpse of my father at the lounge room window, watching me. He would have stayed there like a statue until I reached the intersection of Lytham Road and Alexandra Road, to see which way I turned, left for school, right for freedom. I turned left, looking back as I did, knowing his eyes were on me and hating him for it.

By the time I got to school, it was well after 9 am. I'd taken my time on the bike, stopping several times, uncertain of my options. It was a few weeks before Christmas and I would turn fifteen in early January. Maybe I could leave school now and get a job somewhere. Anything, I thought, anything at all to get away from there.

I wheeled my bike into the shed and then walked around to the main assembly yard. The playground was enclosed on three sides by the school buildings. They were three stories' high, built in dark-red brick, windows set with mathematical precision along their soulless walls. On the fourth side was a steel fence, the railings topped with pointed spikes and an occasional fleur-de-lis that separated the yard from the playing fields below. The grounds were absolutely deserted, not a uniform in sight.

I walked up the cold stone steps, past the dark-stained wooden staircase that led up to where the boarders lived, those strange creatures from other towns whose parents had sent them away from home for reasons unknown.

My form class was inside the first door on the right. The entrance to the classroom was a large door made up of timber frames and small square panes of pebbled glass. I raised my hand to the handle but then hesitated. Through the opaque panels, I could distinguish O'Rourke's black-cassocked figure pacing about restlessly, booming out nonsense about $X = 2$ *pie squared* or some other indecipherable things in his deep Irish voice.

If I just slipped away and disappeared, I wondered, would anyone in the world even notice that I was gone? Why would they? Everywhere I went, there was trouble … raised voices, angry faces … was it my fault? If I just disappeared, wouldn't it be better for everyone?

What O'Rourke taught in the classroom meant absolutely nothing to me, but I pretended it did because I knew if I told him that, he would go berserk and beat the living Jesus out of me. He was supposed to be an intelligent man but he looked a lot more like a pig to me than an intelligent man, especially when he got angry and his eyes squinted and got small and mean and went red like a pig's eyes. Then, on top of that, he actually grunted as he exploded with anger and came at me with that strap. Well, fuck you, O'Rourke! I turned away from the door. I was not going in there again. I walked outside but stopped suddenly. Where to? I wondered.

I sat down on the bottom step. The stone was stained, worn away over the years by a million pairs of resentful feet. I felt worthless. There was no place for me here and there was no place for me at home. I was trapped.

My satchel lay on the ground in front of me, the dark-brown leather creased and aged. I stared at the words inscribed on the leather in happier days. Brian O'Raleigh, St Joseph's College. I thought about my father. If I missed school one more time, he'd kill me for sure ...

What's it like to get killed? Would it be all that bad? I suspected it wouldn't be too bad once it got started. Just like him belting me was never as bad as I'd thought, just before it started. The waiting was the worst part, not knowing if it was going to start or not. You still felt frightened, but at least you knew it had started and that meant that it would be over soon. Sometimes though, something happened that was different, and even through the confusion and the shock of the blows, I'd feel as if he tricked me somehow. Because he'd done something new this time. Like when he'd hit me around the head a few weeks ago. I'd felt dizzy after the first couple of blows, because you get confused, so I'd covered up my face, and for a second I thought I'd solved problem, but then I got a punch in the back of the head and when I'd tried to cover that up, he'd hit me in the face again and I knew then that I didn't have a chance.

.

Only last time, I'd covered my whole head with my hands and arms, so my elbows were saving my face and my hands were saving the back of my head. But then suddenly, something hit me in the stomach, and I couldn't breathe, and I doubled up and crashed on the floor, gasping and choking for air. I knew he'd betrayed me then. He'd changed everything again. I knew it was my fault, though; I should have let him hit me properly in the face the way he wanted to. So I knew I couldn't really blame him, but I still felt betrayed because he'd never punched me in the stomach before and I knew that he would feel bad about that because he was bigger than I was. Then I felt guilty that I'd made him feel bad and I felt sad too because I knew he must think even less of me now or else he wouldn't have made it worse. And I couldn't even guess at what I'd done that would make him think less of me except that I knew I was wrong somehow. Then my mother had come in screaming.

"Stop! For Jesus Christ sake stop, you'll kill him!"

And I'm on the floor trying not to vomit and trying to breathe, but feeling better already now because Mum has told him what I can't tell him, that I know he's going to kill me one day and I feel really sorry for that and I feel sorry that he hates me so much that he will kill me and I know he must be so disappointed that he has ended up with a son who is so fucking useless that he has to kill him, but a voice was talking to me …

"Aren't you supposed to be in class?"

I looked up. It was the new headmaster. He was six feet tall or more, a long, lean Irishman with steel-rimmed glasses, close-cropped grey hair and a lean, cadaverous face as if he were a prison warden from a boy's home, which is what everyone said he had been when he was in Boston, in America.

"Yes, sir." Could I ask him for help? He was the head man. Maybe I could tell him what was happening at home, or at least I could tell him about Brother O'Rourke and about the strap.

"You're O'Raleigh, aren't you?"

The way he said it destroyed any hope.

"Yes, sir." I looked up into his eyes, searching.

The cold, hard face stared back at me without any sign of emotion.

"I've heard all about you, O'Raleigh. You're a troublemaker. Get into your classroom, now."

I got up and he followed behind me to the class door. I hesitated but he opened the door and prodded me in. O'Rourke was at the front of the room in mid-flight, still raving on about Pythagoras.

"Brother O'Rourke," the new headmaster was looking grim, "I found him outside, sitting on the step."

O'Rourke nodded.

"Thank you, headmaster."

The door closed and a quiet buzz went around the classroom.

I moved toward my desk at the front of the room.

"Oh no, boy, oh no! Come up here now." O'Rourke was grinning like a hyena. "Come on up here now."

I walked back up to the front of the class.

"So, you've decided to join us after all!" He was smiling "What time would you say it was, O'Raleigh?

"I'm not sure."

"You're not sure, *what?*" he demanded, the first signs of anger penetrating the plastic grin.

"I'm not sure, sir."

"That's better now, isn't it? Never forget to show respect. Now let's try again." He was talking to me as if I was retarded. "What time is it now, do you think?"

"It's about 9.30, sir."

"Well done! It's about 9.30, so. Now what time does it say on the clock? Now have a good look."

I glanced at the clock.

"10.30, sir."

"So! It's 9.30, but the clock says it's 10.30. Now I wonder why that would be? Could somebody have moved the clock forward one hour for some reason? Is that at all possible?"

There was a titter from some of the kids in the classroom. Others just sat there watching quietly. I was sick of his play-acting.

"I put it forward last night."

He was caught off guard.

"So, you admit it?"

"Yes, sir."

"And why did you do that?"

"I thought it was unfair to stay back for one and a half hours."

"*Sir,*" he demanded. "Always say *sir* to me, do you understand?"

"Yes, sir."

"Good. So, you thought it was unfair, did you? Well, let's see if you think this is unfair. Put out your right hand." He was speaking quietly now, his most sinister mode. He reached into the side pocket of his cassock and pulled out a long, thick, leather strap. "Now then, we have a nice new strap here for you." He was smiling. "I lost my other one quite recently, as I'm sure you'd remember. Come on now, put out your right hand."

Don't flinch, I told myself. If you think hard enough of something else, you won't feel it.

He brought the strap down viciously. All thoughts of not feeling it were smashed out of my mind.

"Again," he indicated with the strap, "you're getting six."

Oh, Christ! I thought.

It went on and on, each blow harder than the one before. When it was finished, my right hand was a mixture of numbness and intense pain. I held it under my armpit, hugging it to my body, hating myself for showing weakness.

"Well ..." His voice was softer now, almost purring with pleasure. "... that was just a little reminder of what not to do with clocks! Now then," he continued more briskly, "on to more serious business. Where is the homework I set for you last night?"

My heart sank, there was going to be more.

"I didn't do it, sir."

"Oh, I see." He raised his eyebrows. "What a pity!" His piggy little eyes were glinting; he was enjoying his own humor. "Well now, we'd better have another six for that, then."

A murmur went around the class. Twelve strokes were highly unusual.

"Now why don't we try to be fair?" he asked earnestly, "We'll give your left hand a turn." He grabbed my wrist and jerked it up.

The strap came smashing down again. Once, twice, three times. I tried to pull away desperately.

"Stop!" he shouted, "Hold steady! Be a man! Hold your hand steady!"

I gathered my remaining courage and forced myself to hold my hand still. It's nearly over, I told myself. It's nearly done.

Whack! Whack! Whack!

It was finished. My hand was throbbing. The pain intense. The class silent, fixed on the unfolding drama.

"Well then," he nodded, "Now that we have that sorted out, and seeing as you're up here anyhow, you can show us your homework from the night before." He was looking first at me and then at the class. "Come on now," he demanded, "I know you wouldn't be stupid enough not to have done your homework two nights running, so where is it?" He was standing directly in front of me, grasping the strap in both hands, face flushed. "Come on now. I'll ask you one more time. Where is your homework?"

He began slapping the strap into the palm of his hand. "If you haven't done that homework, you'll be getting another six. And six more for being late today, so where is it?"

A louder murmur ran through the class. Nobody had ever heard of eighteen strokes, let alone twenty-four.

Everyone in the room was watching. Some of them looked frightened, one or two of them tried to smile. Des Reagan, my closest friend, was staring at me, but as our eyes met, he looked away. The murmur grew louder.

Suddenly O'Rourke turned on the class.

"Silence! Anyone who opens his mouth will get the same!" Then turning back to me, he pointed the strap at my face. "You! Right hand."

I put out my numbed hand. He grabbed my wrist and brought the strap down hard across my palm. The pain was intense: one, two, three. Involuntarily, I tried to jerk my hand away.

"Damn you, boy! Damn you! Hold still now! Hold still!" He was struggling with my wrist as he brought the strap down again. My fingers had curled, closing up in a futile attempt at protection. The strap came smashing down across the clenched knuckles. Smash. Smash. Smash.

It was over, my hand felt as if it were broken, the pain was intense. I was starting to feel dizzy, drifting away as if it were happening to somebody else. I looked at him standing there, with the wooden crucifix hanging around his fat neck, his bloated, red face glistening with sweat and his eyes glaring at me with the madness of an enraged animal.

"The other hand!" he snarled at me through clenched teeth, "Put out your left hand!" He was losing control now, shaking with anger.

"No! That's enough. I've had enough!" It was my voice, but it was as if somebody else was saying it.

That tipped him over the edge, and he lunged forward and grabbed for my arm.

"Hold out your hand, boy!" he screamed, "Hold out your hand, damn you!"

I jerked my arm away, but he hung on, and we struggled for a moment, pushing and pulling at each other until suddenly, he snapped and slashed the strap across my face. I exploded in shock.

"Fuck you, O'Rourke!" I screamed, "Fuck you, you fucking bastard!"

"What! What did you say? What did you say?" He attacked me immediately, slashing at me wildly, again and again, driving me backward across the room until I came up hard against my desk. A blow caught me across the side of my face, and I lost balance, falling down between the desk and the raised seat. Then he was on top of me, grabbing at my throat with one hand and swinging wildly at me with the other.

"Fuck you!" I screamed, as I fought to free myself, "Fuck you, you bastard!"

The classroom erupted, the lads screaming hysterically as we struggled on the floor in front of them.

"Damn you! Damn you!" The strap came down again, hard across my face.

I could hear the other kids screaming. Books and papers were being flung up in the air. The whole class was rioting; O'Rourke oblivious to it all.

The strap came down on my face again, shocking me with the pain. Again, it came down, burning the side of my face. He was demented, grunting with the effort of each blow. In a sudden inspiration, I head-butted O'Rourke in the face and, as he jerked backward, I squirmed out from under the desk and made a dash for the door, escaping out into the hallway as he staggered to his feet.

As I ran past the windows of my classroom, I could hear him shouting at the boys, trying to restore order. I felt a surge of rage and turned back. Pulling myself up on the ledge, I stuck my head through the window.

"Fuck you, O'Rourke, you fat, stupid pig!" He spun around, amazed. "Fuck you, you cowardly bastard! You can shove Pythagoras right up your fat arse, you slimy hypocrite!"

He froze, his face distorted with rage. The lads cheered again as he flung the strap at me, but he missed by yards, then he turned and ran out the door.

I took off across the yard, battered but thrilled. Finally, I'd stood up to the bastard. As I sped past the bicycle shed, confident that I could outrun him, it dawned on me that he would take the shortcut through the master's quarters and cut me off at the front of the school! Panic set in again. As I rounded the corner, there was a momentary sense of relief, dashed immediately as O'Rourke burst out through the main doors, moving impossibly fast for a man of his bulk. Flying down the steps three at a time, feet twinkling, cassock flying, as he raced to cut me off at the head of the driveway.

Our paths crossed within a few feet of each other. I was running full tilt and so was he. We were so close as we converged that he stretched out his hand in a desperate attempt to grab me but he missed. His momentum and bulk carried him across the driveway, up onto the grass and then off into a clump of bushes as I fled triumphantly down the long, curving driveway to freedom.

I stopped at the bottom and looked back. O'Rourke had regained the path and had resumed his pursuit, but he was moving much slower now, one hand clutching the side of his chest, the other stretched out before him as if asking for help. As he drew closer, he called out: "Brian stop, come back here, we have to talk."

"Fuck you!" I yelled at him. "You fucking arsehole! You're a fucking disgrace, you fat pig!"

He was closer now and he lunged forward suddenly in a furious burst of energy.

"Come here, you fucking bastard!" he screamed," I order you! I order you!"

I darted off again along the main road by the school, running just fast enough to stay out of his reach. He was panting heavily, gasping for breath. I stayed just out of his grasp, shouting insults back at him whenever he seemed ready to give up until finally, he collapsed down heavily on a low brick wall, exhausted. I went back to within ten feet of him. Bystanders were staring at us, and that made it all the better for me.

"Fuck you!" I told him. "You're a fat, pathetic, slob, you cowardly bastard!"

He was holding up his hands now, unable to continue.

"Stop! Stop now, will you? For the love of God will you stop," he was pleading between gasps. "We can talk this over! Stop it now, please, stop!"

But after years of brutality, I was enraged and kept on screaming abuse at him at the top of my lungs until finally, still clutching one side, he got up and staggered away in the direction of the school.

I was elated. My hands were throbbing, and my face stiff with pain, but I didn't give a damn. It was an honorable battle that I felt somehow that I'd won.

I walked home then, but as I drew closer to the hotel, I began to worry about what I might find there. If my father got started on me, he'd do a lot worse than O'Rourke. As I went through the front door, my mother came out.

"Oh my God, what happened? Who did that to you?"

My father appeared from the front room, clutching a newspaper.

"Why isn't he at school …" he started but my mother stopped him.

"For God's sake, Walter, look at his face."

He came forward.

"Holy mother of Jaysus!" he exclaimed, "Who did that to you?"

"Brother O'Rourke beat me up, he went mad."

"He'll go fucking mad when I get a hold of him," he snarled, "Get in the car."

"Walter!" My mother went to grab his arm. "Don't go up there fighting, for God's sake!"

"No man alive can do that to a child of mine." He was furious. "I'll tell you now, as God is my judge, I'll kill the bastard!" He grabbed me by the arm. "Come on, you."

He strode out the front door, pulling me with him. I couldn't believe it… it was like a dream… this was worth a thousand thrashings. Soon we were speeding up the driveway of St Joseph's. I was never more excited in my life.

As my father banged loudly on the brass knocker, an alarmed-looking Christian Brother opened the door.

"The headmaster will see you in a few minutes," he began but my father pushed him to one side.

"He'll see me right now and fucking well like it!" he snarled as he barged through the door into Kearney's office.

The headmaster was sitting there, talking into a telephone.

"I'll call you back shortly."

He was still hanging up the phone when my father put both hands on the desk and shouted in his face.

"What sort of fucking school are you running here, you useless fucking bastard! My son has just been beaten up by one of your Christian brothers! Well get the bastard in here now and we'll see if he can fight a man!"

Oh Jesus, I could have cheered! I couldn't believe it. In that split second, I forgave my father for everything. I stood there behind him, proudly. I would have gladly died for him right then and there.

"Could you lower your voice?" The headmaster looked totally shocked.

"Lower my voice!" my dad bellowed even louder, "lower my fucking voice! You cowardly bastards beat up my son and all you can say is, lower my fucking voice! Get that bastard O'Rourke in here now, or I swear to God, I'll take this fucking place apart and you with it!"

The headmaster was standing up behind the desk now, hands stretched out before him.

"Mr. O'Raleigh, please! For God's sake, *please, please* lower your voice. You're angry, I know that. I understand that, but you don't know what happened here this morning! You look like a reasonable man. Please, sit down. Just for a few minutes and let me explain what happened. Then we'll get Brother O'Rourke in here for you. I promise you, I will. *Please,* Mr. O'Raleigh, please."

"I want him in here now, do you hear me?" My father had lowered his voice; the conciliatory tone of the headmaster was having an effect. "I want that bastard in here now. We'll see how tough he is when he has to face a man."

The headmaster moved a chair across for my father.

"Please, sit down. Look, I don't blame you for being angry. Why wouldn't you be if you don't know what actually happened here? Sit down there now and let me explain."

My father looked at the offered chair suspiciously for a moment, but then he sat, as Kearney retreated behind the desk.

"Could I get you some tea now, while we're waiting?" The headmaster was smiling weakly. He didn't wait for an answer but turned to the Brother who'd opened the front door. "Brother Cleary, tea and cake for Mr. O'Raleigh. Some of that nice Irish fruitcake we have there." And then to my father, "You're an Irishman yourself. What part?"

My father answered reluctantly. "I'm from Garryowen, County Limerick."

.

"Garryowen!" said the headmaster as if it were the greatest thing since Home Rule. "Well, would you believe that now? Sure, aren't I a Limerick man myself! I know Garryowen well. Sure my own brother was a priest there!" The headmaster seemed delighted and he went on to talk about his family in Limerick, and, as he talked, I felt my heart sinking.

Within fifteen minutes, all traces of anger had left my father's face and they were chatting on about Ireland and all the people and places they knew there. The tea arrived and, as Brother Cleary served it out, there was some joke about him being a Dublin man and they all laughed politely, and then, as the headmaster passed across the cake, he said offhandedly:

"Do you think it might be better if Brian waited outside?"

My father turned to me, but I already knew. I sat on the wooden bench in the long, gloomy hallway. Portraits of the Bleeding Heart of Jesus and statues of the Holy Virgin Mary stared down at me in contempt. I wondered for a moment, should I pray to them but I knew by now, that would be a waste of time, so I just sat there listening to the murmur of voices through the heavy wooden door, coming to terms with the nature of betrayal.

Within a few minutes, I heard laughter and then, shortly after that, O'Rourke came swishing along the corridor, hands sunk deep in his cassock pockets, head slightly bowed, moving quickly. He ignored me completely except for a sideways glance filled with malevolence that didn't quite reach my eyes. Then he tapped on the office door and entered the room in one swirling, gliding movement.

Again, there was the low murmur of voices, then, after what seemed like an age, more laughter.

The door opened.

"Come in." It was the headmaster, a brittle smile corrupting the thin slit of his mouth.

O'Rourke was leaning across in his chair, smiling and talking earnestly to my father and I wondered for a moment if he was a Limerick man, too.

There was a pause then, as they all looked at me, but it was my father who spoke first.

"I want you to apologize to Brother O'Rourke." He was staring at me, and even though I knew I'd been betrayed, I still couldn't grasp what he'd just said. I guess it was one of the few times I ever looked my father in the eye. It wasn't shock, it wasn't anger, just an overwhelming sense of shame and despair that he could so easily cast me away.

"What did you say?" I asked, not wanting it to be true.

"Apologize to Brother O'Rourke. I won't tell you again."

I looked at him for a long moment, wondering who he was.

"No," I told him, "I won't do that."

O'Rourke was looking at me and I could tell by his eyes that he was enjoying himself. My father stood up. "You'll apologize now, or I'll teach you a lesson you'll never forget!"

Nothing in the world could have made me apologize. I had so little left of myself by then that I would rather have died than have taken that final step.

"I'll never apologize," I said as firmly as I could.

The headmaster stepped in.

"Walter, take him home. Deal with this at home. He can apologize another time."

My father hesitated, then gave a quick jerk of his head.

"Wait in the car."

As I left the room, they were shaking hands, the headmaster's left hand grasping my father's arm as if he were a long-lost friend, O'Rourke standing alongside them smiling, and I knew that my school days were over. I walked out and stood by the car for a moment, then decided against it.

.

I was gone before my father came out of the headmaster's office, across the fields by the side of the school, slipping away from St Joseph's College, heading for my old friend, the *Kathleen R.*

Chapter 13

Finding a Job

I spent all afternoon in the fishing boat, dozing on the nets and nursing my bruises. The events with the Christian Brothers, combined with my father's betrayal, had sickened me and I swore I would never believe in anything Christian again. From that moment on I'd be my own man and I'd control my own destiny.

When I returned to the Alexandra Private Hotel that evening, my father was nowhere to be seen. I collected everything of mine that had anything to do with Catholicism - my prayer book, my rosary beads, a catechism and some images of Jesus that I'd had since my first communion - took them all down to the lounge room fire and then sat there watching them burn.

Later on that night as I lay in my bed, I heard my parents' voices and I knew they were talking about me. The following morning, my mother called me aside and advised me to get a job as soon as possible.

"Stay out of his way, he's in a rage. Don't even look at him! Get yourself a job somewhere till after Christmas but stay out of his way, for God's sake."

A few days later, as I was walking back home one evening, I saw a large sign in a butcher's window on Tyldesly Road:

Wanted
Butcher boy for deliveries.

Apprenticeship for right lad
Apply Within

The following morning, I arrived at the shop at 8.00 am. Louis Booth was a short, middle-aged man, with thick grey hair combed back in a quiff from his forehead. He looked clean, neat and disciplined and spoke with a strong Northern English accent.

"What 'appened to tha face, lad?"

"I was playing rugby at school. I got belted."

"Well, just so long as it doesn't 'appen too offen! We don't want ye frightnin' customers! Now look, I'll tell thee straight. If tha works 'ard and does what's right, I'll teach thee everythin' a know. If tha's serious, I'll mebbe take thee on as apprentice an teach thee trade. Now cum downstairs, I'll show ye round."

The cellar was a treasure trove of dead meat. Whole sides of beef hung from heavy steel hooks, the carcasses trimmed with cream white fat, the rib cages strung all in a row like bloodied piano keys. Fat-cheeked smiling pigs with long stiff ears swung from bright steel railings, forelegs stretched out as if in full flight, alert and ready, even in death. Legs of lamb and trays of chops covered the solid timber benches whilst overhead, chains of sausages and black puddings dangled from hooks, glistening smooth and shiny as necklaces.

Louis Booth stood in the midst of it all in his white butcher's coat. Feet firmly planted on the sawdust-strewn floor, hands on hips, his long butcher's knives swinging from his belt like some modern-day Blackbeard addressing his crew. "I'll tell thee now, son. If tha's fair wi' me, I'll be more than fair wi' thee."

Mrs. Booth stood silently, eyeing me up and down.

"Why would ye' want to be butcher's boy if ye' went to St Joseph's College?" she asked suspiciously.

"I didn't like it there. I want to get a job."

She turned away, unimpressed, and climbed up the short wooden steps to the shop above.

"Ye' can start Mundi' mornin." He'd made his decision. "Ye'll get yer own apron 'n' coat but it'll come out of ye' wages. It'll need to be kept clean. Spick 'n' span, now! No excuses. Be ere eight o'clock Mundi' mornin', n' don't be late."

I cycled home furiously and burst into the hotel. My mother was in the dining room, setting out the tables for lunch.

"I got the job, mum! At the butcher's shop, the one I told you about."

"That's grand, son! Well done. When do you start?" She was smiling.

"Monday, he might want me to be permanent! He told me if I work hard, he'll keep me on."

A voice cut in behind me.

"No son of mine's going to be a bloody butcher boy!" My father was standing in the doorway, an open newspaper dangling from his hand. "What's the use of a job like that, for Christ's sake? Sure any bloody eejit can push a bike around Blackpool!"

"It's a start, Walter. He won't get a job anywhere else. It's Christmas in three weeks."

He was glowering.

"How much is he paying you?"

"I don't know."

His mouth twisted in a smile.

"So! You've got a job riding a push bike but you don't know if you're getting paid or not!"

"Of course he'll pay him. It's only for a few weeks, anyway."

He was shaking his head.

"Holy mother of Jaysus, will you look at him! Six years at St Joseph's College and now he's a bloody butcher boy!"

"At least I've got a job," I burst out.

He pointed his finger at me.

"You're to be a carpenter, that's what you'll be! As soon as the holidays are over, you'll be getting a job on a building site. If you're lucky and you're not too bloody stupid, we might be able to get you an apprenticeship." My mother was standing behind him, shaking her head, willing me to be silent. "A butcher boy, for Christ's sake!" He turned to leave. "Six years at St Joseph's and now he's a bloody butcher boy! Holy mother of Jaysus, what's next?"

"I'll never be a carpenter," I said to her, "Never. Not as long as I live. I'll leave here if I have to, but I'll never be a carpenter."

*   *   *

I arrived outside the butcher's shop ready for work at 7.45 Monday morning. It was a cold, crisp winter's day and I stood there stamping my feet, trying to keep warm. A few minutes later, a tall, skinny young man clad in a leather jacket and jeans, came strolling along, hands deep in his pockets, a cigarette dangling from his lips.

"You're new lad, right? I'm Roger. Fuckin cold, innit? They told me ye' were startin' t'day. I finish up Frid'y. He wants me to show ye' ropes. I'm going back te Coventry, big money in factories. That's where am from. Fuck Blackpool, I'm sick a' place."

He was a few years older than me, a hard, crafty face, half-concealed by the sheepskin collar of his leather jacket.

"I'll show ye'all the perks. Ye' cen make some good tips if ye' use yer 'ead. Watch out for er though she's a bloody bitch. E's all right, but don't argue wi' im, e thinks e's still in bloody army."

A car drew up to the curb as we talked.

"Mornin', Roger. Mornin', Brian," Mr. Booth nodded, "that's a good lad. Always be early for me, son. Take him round side, Roger, n' get t'bike out. Show him 'ow te' spread sawdust on floors an' get meat up fe' winder. Come on now, wi' got a busy day 'ead of us."

It was the biggest bike I'd ever seen, a large, ponderous thing with a huge wicker basket hanging over the front wheel.

"Ye'll get used to it, don't worry. 'E wants me t' take ye' round t'day 'n' t'morrer. I'll teach y' few tricks." He was grinning. "There's plenty e' perks Louis Booth knows fuck all about!"

Mrs. Booth was shouting down the trapdoor.

"Roger! Come on, lads! Don't stand down there blatherin'. Get meat up ere quick, come on now!"

We spent the first hour setting up the shop window, sausage and black puddings went with the liver and hearts on the right-hand side, then, down the left, shoulders and legs of lamb, boned and rolled. After that, the chops were arranged in order on the clean white marble, then, in the middle of the window, taking pride of place, thick beef steaks, laid out proudly on stainless steel platters, dressed with sprigs of green parsley and bearing the legend, "British Beef."

As soon as the window was finished, Roger showed me how to dress the floor, scattering fresh sawdust from a Hessian bag across the bare wooden planks. As we worked, Mrs. Booth prepared the orders, weighing and wrapping the meat, printing the addresses on the white bundles in clear black ink before loading them all into the wicker basket.

"Right." Mr. Booth was looking serious. "Take Brian wi' ye' Roger. Introduce 'im to all customers, 'n' make sure ye' point out all places that aren't gettin' delivery t'day, so 'e knows. Off ye' go now lads and don't teach 'im any of ye' bad 'abits. I want ye' back ere as soon as ye' done."

We rode along the promenade together, talking and laughing, sweeping in and out of the lampposts, reveling in the freedom of it all. Then Roger pulled his bike into one of the shelters near Waterloo Road.

"The first and most important stop is right 'ere Brian." He was pretending to be serious. "This is where wi' decide 'ou gets what." He'd propped the big bike up on its stand and was unloading the basket out onto a wooden bench, feeling the packages carefully, squeezing them between his fingers.

"Open this one up." He pulled some folded-up sheets of wrapping paper out of the basket. "Always carry spare paper. It looks better." He'd produced a pocketknife and was hacking off a couple of sausages from one of the orders. "There we are now, some nice pork sausages! Nobody will know the difference. Look through rest e' packages. You can feel sausages. Go on, squeeze 'em. That's right, there ye' go. There's plenty fer everyone t'day, that's good."

Ten minutes later, we were off again, an extra parcel of contraband perched on top of the basket. We raced through the deliveries, tearing up and down the hotel stairs, pausing only in the houses where Roger knew he would get a tip.

"There we are now, Mrs. Lyndhurst, I made sure we put best steak in fe' you. You're me fave'rit customer, luv."

We'd just finished robbing her order.

"Ah, you're a good lad Roger! E's always been good to us, 'as Roger. There y'are now luv, get thi'sen a cuppa tea wi' that."

"Thanks, Mrs. Lindthurst. Brian will look after ye, av' told 'im all about ye. Thanks luv."

Then we were off again to the next hotel, peddling up the street, laughing like mad. We had all the deliveries done by 11 am. The only parcel remaining was the one Roger had made up.

"Cum on," he said, "time fe break."

We pulled up near Bob's Café, parked the bikes around the corner and went in. The place was crowded, the windows steamed up and impossible to see through. Bob's had a reputation as a hangout for all types of shady characters, so just walking in through the door was exciting. Roger went across and handed the parcel to the man behind the counter.

"There y' go Bob! Some good stuff fe ye in there!"

"Ullo, Roger! Well now, what have we got today, eh?" He was unwrapping the parcel. "Oh, that's nice. Sausages and chops! Just what the doctor ordered. What would ye' like son?"

"Just usual thanks, Bob. Bacon egg butte and tea." He nodded in my direction. "This is Brian, e's takin' over job. E'll be lookin' after ye' from now on."

Bob reached across the counter and shook my hand. "Good lad. You look after me and I'll look after you, right? We've always looked after Roger. Isn't that right, Roger?"

As we settled into corner near the jukebox, Roger whispered, "We get free tea 'n' coffee n' a bacon n'egg san'wich. That's what I get any'ow. You get what ye want."

Bob came across with the coffee and put some coins on the table.

"Stick 'em in jukebox, Brian, liven place up a bit."

We spent an hour at the café, talking and playing records, Roger filling me in on all the details. "Now, when wi get back, she'll 'ave a go at us fe' bein' late, she does it all the time. Pay no attention, it's just a bad 'abit she's got. Sometimes I get a leg of lamb out back door but be bloody careful, he's a miserable bugger is Louis, he counts everythin'. Don't ever lift any rump steak. It's 'is baby and 'e knows where every ounce goes. Always give customers plenty e' bullshit. Mrs. Green and Mrs. Lambert are best e' lot. Ye'll get two 'n' six off 'em every week, so be nice to 'em. Mrs. Green's got a daughter called Joyce, she's eighteen; wait till you see 'er tits! She's really somethin', but don't look at 'er too much 'er mother gets jealous. Some of the others are right bastards. That fat old bag in Rawcliffe Street weighs every fuckin' thing, the old bitch. Never touch 'er order. There's a queer in Shaw Road. He'll want to talk to ye'. Just ignore the dirty old bastard. Mrs. Colmslie's pissed day and night, she doesn't know what fuckin day it is. If she asks ye' did she pay last week always say no, cos she'll pay up ag'in. She paid me three times one week! Stick it in ye' pocket. It's a good little job if ye' use yer 'ead, you'll make more money from tips 'n' graft in summer than ye' wages. Don't fuck it up now, 'av worked 'ard on this."

He coached me faithfully all week, introducing me to the customers and teaching me all the tricks of the trade. On Friday morning, we went out on the run together for the last time. After we'd divided up the meat and sausages in the shelter and packed it all away again, he reached into his pocket and pulled out a gun.

"What de ye' think a' that!"

"Wow!" I was impressed. "Is it real?"

"What de you think?" He handed it to me. "There ye go, try it out."

I studied the weapon closely. There were traces of rust on the barrel but I knew how to clean metal. With each pull of the trigger, the hammer rose and fell with a satisfying click, the barrel revolving quickly, presenting the next chamber. There was a small steel ring on the butt of the revolver; I'd seen army people with guns like that attached to their belts.

"Ye' wanna' buy it?"

"Does it work?"

"Course it works, it just needs trigger fixed 'n' some bullets. That shop near Tower'll fix it for ye'."

I stared down at the revolver. It was big and shiny, the steel handle crisscrossed with tiny raised corrugations, a raised sight at the end of the barrel. The gun felt good, sinister, solid, heavy and dangerous.

"How much?"

"Two quid. It's worth a lot more than that! Y'can go back te' St Joseph's 'n' frighten shit out'a that fuckin' Christian Brother prick."

I wasn't thinking about O'Rourke.

"I haven't got two quid."

"You'll 'ave it on Frid'y wi' ye wages. Ye'll get at least two quid."

"No, I can't. I've got to give half my wages to my mother."

"Don't be daft! 'Alf yer wages, why? They own a fuckin' hotel for Christ's sake! You shouldn't give 'em *any* money! Look, ye' can 'ave jacket wi' it. It's a real RAF jacket, like pilots 'ad in war. I'll give ye' gun 'n' jacket for two quid, it's a fuckin' gift!"

The jacket was brown leather with a white sheepskin collar. I'd seen pilots wearing them in the movies.

"I can't give you two pounds, that'll be all my wages. I got to give them something."

"Tell 'em you had to buy ye' coat an' apron, they'll believe anythin'. Tell 'em you don't get ye' first pay till next week. They don't know, parents e' daft, ye' can tell 'em anythin'. Try jacket on."

It fitted me better than him.

"Look ere." He pulled one side of the jacket open. "Look, a'v ripped bottom out 'e pocket. Stick gun in there, see 'ow it fits, see? Ye'll be like Billy the Kid! There ye go, ow's that!"

I wanted that gun.

"OK, the gun and the jacket for two quid."

We shook hands solemnly.

"I want it now."

"Alright, it's yours. If anythin' 'appens, or ye lose it, you still pay for it, deal?"

"It's a deal."

I took the gun home and hid it in my bedroom. The next few days I spent every spare minute cleaning it, oiling and polishing it in the evenings, rubbing away at the metal until it shone.

Roger left on Friday afternoon. I never saw him again. When I turned up for work at 7.45 on Monday morning. I had on a new pair of boots my mother had bought me, a pair of jeans from the Army and Navy Disposal Stores, the RAF bomber jacket with the upturned collar, and the revolver tucked firmly under my left armpit. I was ready to begin my new life.

*   *   *

The Alexandra was open for Christmas that year, packed full of noisy guests from every part of England. The butcher's shop was frantic too and I spent the whole of my days delivering huge parcels of meat to the hotels around Blackpool. I was up early every morning and out the door before my father appeared and I saw little of him over the holidays.

I was my own man at last and I loved the job. I worked hard and the customers liked me. I made more money from the tips they gave me than my wages and I was sure if I worked hard enough, Louis Booth would keep me on for good. Every day, I'd stop off at Bob's for my break and soon the locals accepted me as a regular. Bob always gave me breakfast and money to put in the jukebox and I made sure he got a good parcel each day.

My new life was fantastic. I had more money in my pocket than I'd ever imagined possible and Bob's cafe was humming with excitement from morning till night. Rock'n'roll had just arrived in Blackpool and Elvis Presley had released his first record. Nobody had ever heard anything like it and I played "Heartbreak Hotel" over and over for hours.

The regulars at Bob's were a close-knit bunch and it felt good to have been accepted by them. I would see other lads my age going off to school every morning and I felt sorry for them, it all seemed too good to be true. Then one evening, just after I returned home from work, my father called me into the living room.

"Where do you get to when you're out on that bike all day?"

"All over the place, South Shore, Central, everywhere."

"Do you ever stop off at a café for a break?"

"Yes, sometimes."

"Which one do you go to?" I could feel the trap closing.

"Different ones, it depends on where I am."

"Have you ever been into Bob's Café?" He was smiling.

"No."

"Are you sure now?"

"Yes, I'm sure."

"You bloody liar." The smile disappeared. "You were seen in there two days ago."

"I was delivering some meat, what's wrong with Bob's, it's only a café."

"What's wrong with Bob's? You know bloody well what's wrong with Bob's. It's full of spivs and criminals! Stay out of there, I'm warning you. If I ever catch you in there again, I'll drag you out by the scruff of your neck, do you hear me?"

"Yes."

"Yes who?"

"Yes, Dad."

After that, I changed my routine for a while. Smokey Joe's lay directly across the road from Bob's, but it wasn't the same. None of the interesting people ever went in there, there was no atmosphere and within a few days, I was back at Bob's, playing the jukebox and mixing with the characters my father hated so much.

My birthday fell on the sixth of January. My father came downstairs that morning just as I was leaving for work.

"So," he grunted, "you're fifteen. Come out here, I've got something for you."

I followed him out into the back kitchen. My mother was there, smiling, but I could tell that she was uneasy.

"There you are." He pulled an old paint sheet off a bundle on the kitchen floor. "Happy birthday." A handmade carpenter's toolbox, complete with hammers, chisels, and a handsaw, sat in the middle of the linoleum.

"There you go," he said, "your own toolbox, made by your father. That'll give you a good start in life."

The very last thing I wanted to be in the world was a carpenter. The three of us stood there silently, looking down at the toolbox.

"Go on," he said, "pick it up."

"I don't want it."

There was a long pause.

"Pick it up," his voice had changed.

"I don't want it." I looked across at him. He was standing there stiffly.

"Pick it up." The words grated out like a curse.

"Walter, please, it's his birthday. Remember what the doctor said. You can't afford to get too upset." She turned to me. "Pick it up, Brian, it's your father's birthday present. Go on, pick it up!" She grabbed it herself then, picking it up in both hands, thrusting it at my chest. "There, there you are now, that's right!"

I stood there with the toolbox in my arms, hating them both. He was staring like a madman.

"Calm down, Walter, please. Remember what the doctor said. Just let …" He broke away suddenly and stormed out of the kitchen, slamming the door behind him.

"Get out!" My mother grabbed my arm. "Get out now while you can! Go off to work, you stupid boy! All you had to do was pick it up. For Christ Almighty's sake, isn't he mad enough now without you tormenting him?"

"He can stick his tools," I told her, "I don't want anything from him."

I dropped the box back on the floor, jumped on my bike, and took off up the road.

*   *   *

When I came back home that evening, I had no idea what to expect, but as I pushed my bike into the backyard, I saw him standing on a ladder at the side of the house, painting one of the windows of the lounge room. He must have heard me arriving, but he didn't look up. He just kept on with the painting, working the brush slowly up and down the edge of the glass pane. We sat through the evening meal in a stony silence. The toolbox was never mentioned again.

Chapter 14

Guns

The following Saturday after work, I took a bus to Central. There was a gunsmith there close to the main shopping center, just behind the Blackpool Tower. I waited outside until I was sure the shop was empty then walked in. An old man was hunched over a long-barreled shotgun clamped in a vice on a bench behind the counter.

"Hello lad, what can I do fe' you?"

"I need some bullets."

"Oh, do you?" He was looking me up and down. "What caliber?"

"For a gun," I told him.

"I see. What sort of gun? They're all different, ye' know."

"It's like an army gun."

"Do ye' ave it with ye'?"

I pulled the gun out and placed it on the wood counter between us.

"Hmmm … that's a nice little revolver. Where did ye' get it from son?"

"My dad gave it to me."

"Oh." He was smiling. "That was good of 'im."

He examined the gun carefully, turning it over and over underneath the lamp by his workbench.

"Bullets won't help you much wi' this one, I'm afraid, son. Firin' pin's bin' removed."

"What does that mean?"

"Look 'ere." He pulled the hammer back and pointed with his screwdriver. "See 'ere, pin's gone, see? It's bin filed off." He was staring at me impassively.

"What does that mean?"

"It means it's useless until it's replaced. It's just as well, lad. I'd have to report ye if it wasn't. I should now, in fact. Look son, your Dad didn't give ye' gun. Why don't you just leave it ere wi' me 'n' go on 'ome. Ye' lookin for trouble running round Blackpool wi' a revolver stuck in ye' pocket."

I picked it up.

"Can it be fixed?"

"Aye, it can be fixed, but I won't be fixing it. I'm warnin' you, son, you'll get nowt but trouble carryin' that round Blackpool."

As I left the shop, he called out after me.

"Hand it in at police station, young fella. Save thi' sen a lot of bother."

I ran off up the street as fast as I could, ducking down alleyways until I was well away from the shop.

When I got back to the hotel, I went straight to my bedroom and examined the gun again. I could see what he meant. The part that struck the end of the bullet was missing. I went over it again, oiling and polishing it. I would find a way to fix it.

"Brian!" The handle of the bedroom door was rattling. "Open the door!"

I panicked, pushing the gun under the mattress quickly and stuffing the metal cleaner and oil can in with it.

"Open up, open the door!" He was banging loudly now.

As I turned the key, he came pushing into the room.

"What's going on in here, what are you up to? Why was the door locked?"

"I don't know. I must have locked it."

"Why?"

"I don't know, sometimes I just lock it."

His eyes were wandering around the room. "Where were you after work today?"

"I was up at Central."

"Doing what?"

"Just walking around."

His eyes were still roaming around the room.

"Don't lock the door again, understand?"

"Yes, dad."

He went off and I stood there with my heart pounding. I needed a better hiding place.

The following day when I arrived home, my mother came out to meet me and I knew immediately there was trouble.

"Your father's waiting in the living room, son." She walked with me as far as the door. "Tell him the truth now, don't be afraid. There won't be any trouble if you tell him the truth. He's promised me that."

He was standing by the window, staring out along the road, and I realized he must have been waiting for me to arrive.

"Where were you yesterday evening after work?"

"I went up to Central and walked around."

"Who did you meet there?"

"I didn't meet anyone."

He was staring at me in a different way.

"I want the truth now. Who were you with?"

My mother moved into the room, closing the door quietly behind her.

"I wasn't with anyone."

He went quiet again and just stood there, staring at me.

"I'm going to ask you a few questions and I want you to think carefully now before you answer." He came towards me pointing a finger in my face. "If you tell me as much as one fucking lie, I'll break your fucking back!"

I'd heard the threat many times before.

"Just tell your da the truth, son." My mother was frightened. "You'll be alright, he's not going to hurt you."

He spun on her.

"Keep out of it, Chris!" He turned back to me. "Do you own a gun?"

I was shocked. "You mean a real gun?" I said.

"Do you own a gun?"

My mother was standing behind him, shaking her head and mouthing words. I had no idea what she was saying.

"You mean a real gun?"

"Look at me." His eyes had taken on that mad look. I was beginning to freeze up. "For the last time, do you own a gun?"

"I've got an old broken one. Roger gave it to me when he left."

"Good lad!" my mother exclaimed, "tell your father the truth now, that's all he wants."

"Keep out of it, Chris!" he snarled. "I told you, keep out of this!" He turned back to me. "Who's Roger?"

"He worked at the butcher's shop. I got his job."

"He *gave* you a gun?"

"Yes, no, he gave it to me to borrow. He's coming back in a few weeks and I'll give it back to him then."

"Why was it under your mattress?"

"I put it there."

He exploded. "You fucking eejit, sure don't I know that! Who else would have put it there but you, for fuck's sake! Why, is what I'm asking. Why? You fucking halfwit!"

"Walter, keep your voice down. There are guests in the house! And stop that language, please! It's not his gun, he's told you that!"

"Who's this Roger character?"

"He went back to Coventry. I have to give it back to him when he comes back again in a few weeks."

"So, it's not yours?"

"No dad, honest, it was just a lend, I was looking after it for him."

There was a long silence as he just stood there, staring at me.

"If I thought it was yours, I'll tell you now, I'd break your fucking back."

My heart was pounding.

"It's not, dad, I swear to God it's not."

He stared at me for a long moment. It was touch and go.

"Get out!" I turned to leave. "Come back here." I turned back. "You're not allowed out at night for a month. And stay out of Bob's Café. If I ever see you in there again, I'll drag you out by the scruff of the neck and I'll thrash you to within an inch of your life. Do you understand that?"

"Yes, dad."

"And stay away from Ron Malloy, he's trouble, and that Bracewell character too! Stay away from them all, do you understand?"

"Yes, dad."

"And if Roger the butcher boy wants his gun back, tell him to come and see me. I'll give him his fucking gun back! I'll jam it up his arse and pull the fuckin' trigger. *Now get out!*"

I slipped out the back door and went off along the Promenade.

Christ … how did he find the gun? I wondered. I should have got it fixed and shot him with it.

I left the house, crossed over the Promenade, then wandered along the beachfront in despair. The tide was halfway out and, close to the edge, thigh-deep in seawater, a group of fishermen were maneuvering one of the boats onto a trailer, preparing to pull her up onto the hard sand. I sat down by the sea wall and watched the truck as it reversed out into the shallows.

Sometimes in the summer when the weather was right, the fishermen would take the tourists out for joyrides in the boats. If there was too much wind, they couldn't do it. The boats would be rising and falling and bumping on the sand and there was always the danger of a visitor falling into the water or getting hurt as they were being transferred to the boat.

I didn't like visitors going out in the *Kathleen R.* She was a fishing boat. It always angered me when I watched the tourists struggling on board. They climbed in from the bright red truck that backed out into the sea to where the boat lay bobbing in the water, laughing like idiots, as if the *Kathleen R.* was some sort of ride in an amusement park. Then they'd clamber on board with their dresses tucked up into their knickers to avoid the saltwater, their ridiculous "Kiss Me Quick" hats perched precariously above their sunburned faces as they shouted out orders they'd heard in the movies: "All 'ands on deck!" or "'Oist the mainsail, me hearties!" or "Full steam ahead!"

They had no idea of what the *Kathleen R* was. They'd never seen her out in a blow, ploughing steadfastly towards distant Fleetwood, motor thumping, steadying sail filled. Or the stormy days when she sat stoically on the promenade in her canvas cover, awaiting the turn of the weather.

One day, I was watching them when the ride was cut short. One of the tourists had become seasick. Old Dan slowed the engine and then curved the boat back into the shore, the fishermen waving their arms to the man in the red truck to let him know there was a problem.

He reversed the truck out into the water as far as possible and then the boat was maneuvered around so that her stern came up close by the tray. Rubber tires were hung from the back to protect her rudder and then a gangplank was swung between the boat and the truck. A distraught tourist was sprawled across the seats like a beached whale, a sickly shade of green underneath the red blotches of sunburn. He was frightened and weak and he had to be coaxed off the boat. He was grasping onto the side of the gunwale, panic-stricken. As the fishermen helped him off, he made a grab for the truck but then he froze in fear and got stuck between the boat and the vehicle. He hovered over the water, one hand clutching onto old Dan, the other grasping the rail at the back of the red truck, refusing to let go even when the boat rose and fell dangerously. Finally, after much coaxing, he released his grip on Dan and made a desperate lunge across the void, collapsing down onto the slatted wooden seats like a broken doll. As soon as he was safe, he began complaining.

"Ye' shud warn folk! 'Ow was I t' know? Ye should tell folk! Sea's te rough! Ye' should tell folk it's te rough!"

He sat there forlornly, the waves washing around the axles of the truck, as the fisherman addressed the rest of the visitors.

"Well, what do ye' want t' do? Do ye' want t' go back out, or do ye want t' get off now? It's up to you now folks but either way, there's no refunds."

They always got off. Occasionally they'd argue about money, but they always got off. I'd help the fishermen sometimes, standing with them waist deep in the swirling sea, holding on to the ropes around the gunwale of the *Kathleen R* as they swabbed out the mess.

"Jesus Christ, he made a right bloody mess, didn't he! 'Ou let 'im on board any'ow? Was it you, Tom?"

"You did, you silly bugger, you sold 'im ticket! You should bi one cleanin' up."

"Come on now lads, there's work to be done, day's not over yet. What d'you think Tom, we shouldn't let fat ones on board, should wi? They make a proper bloody mess when they empty out!"

"Mebbe if ye' did your share e' cleanin' up, ye'd be more careful 'ou ye' let on board!"

They'd be laughing and joking with each other as they sloshed out the boat with buckets of seawater.

"Where ye' from lad?"

"Alexandra Road."

"You're a good lad, 'ang on to that rope fe' me now would ye, just fer a minute, there's the lad."

Sometimes they'd take me out for a free ride and I'd sit there in the bow dreaming of the day I would sail her by myself. They never knew about my secret, but that didn't matter, we were all working together on the *Kathleen R*.

"Why do you let them go out in the boat?"

"Money lad, what else?"

"Don't you get enough money from selling the fish?"

"It's not that easy, son. Sometimes you catch fish 'n' sometimes you don't."

His friend was still laughing. "Well ye caught a bloody big one t'day Dan, that's fe' sure!"

Then they'd be off again, pulling old Dan's leg and laughing. I liked the fishermen, but I didn't like them taking the visitors out on those trips. It was wrong, she was a fishing boat.

*   *   *

I waited by the seawall as the boat drew closer across the sands. It was the *Kathleen R* and, as I watched, they towed her up the granite slope to her place at the edge of the promenade. The fishermen worked around her for a while, separating the fish and stowing away all the gear, then they tied down her canvas cover and left, nodding to me as they passed.

I wandered across and walked around her. I hadn't been on board since the day I left school. She was still beautiful, her neat, black planking sweeping gracefully as raven's wings from her bow through to her shapely stern. I stopped by her nameplate. The golden words, *Kathleen R* had faded a little over the years, but they were still clearly visible, etched into the timber for all time.

I ran my finger into the groove, she was as solid and as sound as the day I first discovered her. I stood up on the edge of the cradle, undid the canvas cover and looked inside. In the murky evening light, I could just make out a pile of fishing nets lying damp by the wooden thwarts.

I stood there for a while, staring inside, then I sat down on the edge of the cradle and thought about my father. I was fifteen now, old enough to leave home. If the butcher's job didn't last, maybe I could be a fisherman. Maybe they'd let me go out with them. I wouldn't need much money.

Mum wasn't going to leave him; I knew that now. I'd have to go by myself. She'd been talking for years about how we'd all go to Australia and live with Bernard but what was the point of that if my father came too? We'd done all the paperwork for Australia House and we'd had the interview with the Australian man. They told us we'd been accepted but then my father had put it off for another year.

He didn't want to go to Australia, I knew that. He pretended he was interested but it was only mum that talked about it. It had become just another hopeless dream, something to hang onto so that we could all pretend that things would be alright one day.

Evening was falling across the town as I retied the canvas covers on the *Kathleen R*. I stood there for a while in the gathering dusk, just looking at her, then I collected my thoughts and turned towards home. There was something different about her now, but I wasn't sure what it was.

Chapter 15

The Wake

I came home around eleven-thirty that evening and, as I rounded the street corner, my heart skipped a beat: my parents were sitting in the armchairs in the large bay window of the hotel. I knew that my father was waiting up for me and that meant trouble, and I knew that my mother was there, hoping to keep the peace.

"Goodnight," I called out as I passed the lounge room.

"Get in here!" came the angry response.

It was obvious he'd been drinking.

"Where have you been to, this time?"

"I was at the pictures."

"The pictures finish at ten o'clock! You've been in Bob's again, haven't you?"

He was on his feet now, glaring.

"No, I was just talking with some friends."

"Liar!" he snapped, launching into it, threatening and telling me what he'd do if I ever came home late again, working himself up into one of his mad rages that I knew would end in violence.

"Stop it, Walter!" my mother stepped in, "Don't start again, please." She went to touch his arm but he thrust her away so forcefully that she staggered and fell sideways across a chair, sprawling on the floor as he turned back to attack me.

Seeing my mother knocked down yet again, something snapped in me. I'd known for a long time this moment would come. I was a big lad for fifteen. No match for him perhaps, but I'd had enough.

There was a large empty soft drink bottle sitting on a nearby table and I leapt forward and grabbed it, challenging him with it, screaming into his shocked face.

"Come on, you cowardly bastard, try it on, *try it on!* I'll smash this bottle in your fucking face and ram the rest down your filthy stinking throat!"

Rage born of fear swept aside reason and self-preservation as I screamed at him like some demented animal. He stopped in his tracks momentarily but then he turned suddenly and darted out of the room. I was amazed and looked across at my mother.

"We've won!" I said, stupidly.

"Get out of the house!" She grabbed me by the shoulders, dragging me towards the front door. "Get out while you can! He'll kill you, you stupid boy! He's gone to get something! Get out of the house!"

As we struggled, the bottle fell from my hand, smashing on the tiled floor of the lobby, crunching underfoot as she pushed me out through the front door.

"I'm not afraid of him," I protested, "I'll fight him."

But her fear was contagious, I wasn't so sure now.

"Get out! Get out while you can! Run! *Run!*" She forced me outside, pushing the door closed behind me.

A moment later, he entered the porch, grinning that mad, lunatic, clenched-teeth grin I'd seen all my life in his rages and clutching a wicked-looking claw hammer in his right fist. My mother was blocking his path, grabbing at the hammer as she pleaded with him.

"Don't Walter, don't, you'll kill him. Walter, stop, stop now while you can!" She struggled with him, but he just pushed her aside and stepped out into the front yard.

Just then, Mr. and Mrs. Carpenter, elderly neighbors from a few doors away, came around the corner, arm in arm. I knew I didn't stand a chance and I called out, "Mr. Carpenter, how are you tonight?"

They paused.

"Inside, Brian," my father growled.

"He's got a hammer behind his back, Mr. Carpenter. He's going to bash me with …" That was about as far as I got before he launched himself across the yard, hammer raised.

The Carpenters scattered off quickly, heads down, as I took off over the low brick wall and along the street, terror gripping my heart, his feet pounding behind me. I was running as fast as I could, but my legs felt like lead. It was as if I was in a dream, moving in slow motion. I could sense his breath on my neck as I clawed my way up the street, convinced I was about to die.

The pounding stopped suddenly. Instinctively I bent forward, clasping my arms over my head. The wooden handle of the hammer cracked hard against my knuckles, the weapon skimming past, smashing into a brick wall on the other side of the road, sparks flying. I kept going, as fast as I could. I knew if he caught me at that moment, he would surely kill me.

I ran for a mile or more before ducking into the backyard of a house. From there, out the front, across the Promenade and onto the beach.

*   *   *

I walked along the sands for hours. The truth was out: we'd wanted to kill each other in that room. How could I ever return?

I wandered around for hours until finally, around 3.30 am, I stopped at a public phone. My mother answered. He was asleep, she said, there was no danger.

"Is he standing behind you now, mum, telling you what to say?"

"No, he's asleep, son. You can come home now."

"If he's standing behind you, mum, just say: yes, Brian, yes."

"No, he's not, son, he's asleep. I called the police; they've been here. It's alright now, they warned him. He'd been drinking, he's sorry about the whole thing. I'll walk along the Promenade and meet you."

Walking back along the beachfront towards the hotel, I could see her tall, slim figure in the distance, standing in the glow of a streetlight. My mother was a proud woman and I always admired her. She had her own problems with alcohol, and she had a critical, caustic tongue when she drank, but she was a strong, courageous woman who raised four children alone whilst running one of the best hotels in Blackpool.

I could see she was still shaken when we met. Not so much by the sudden eruption of violence from her husband - she was accustomed to that - but by the level of rage she'd witnessed in her fifteen-year-old son. The pigeons were coming home to roost; he'd trained me well.

* * *

I awoke at seven the next morning, filled with a sense of dread, still grasping the curved butcher's knife I'd taken from the kitchen. What will happen now? I wondered. Should I pack a bag and leave, while I still can, or should I try to talk it over with him? There was no hope of that. The time for talking had long since passed. Maybe I should move to Australia, join my brother? But what about mum and the rest of the family?

As I turned over the prospects, I sensed a slight movement and as I looked up, my heart froze in my chest. The bedroom door was slightly ajar and through the opening, I could see an eye and part of his face. I leapt out of bed as he moved into the room. I was trapped, there was no way out. I raised the knife.

"Get out! Don't come near me! Fuck you! I'll stab you! I'll stab you!" In my panic, I moved towards him, slashing the air wildly. He drew back quickly, and for the first time in my life, I saw fear in his eyes. He held up his hands, palms forward.

"Brian, please, we've got to stop this; it's killing your mother. I'm not going to touch you, I swear. It's over. I promise. I swear to god!"

I didn't believe a word of it.

"Get out!" I was shouting at the top of my voice. "Get out of my room. *Get out!*"

"I'll never touch you again! I swear, I won't." He retreated backwards until he was out of the room, closing the door as he disappeared.

He was right. He never did. He was dead within the week. I was at home when the stroke hit him. He'd been upstairs getting ready to go out to the Red Lion, his favorite drinking haunt. Since our confrontation that night, he'd been sober and on his best behavior.

It was off-season, there were no guests at the hotel. My mother was ironing clothes on the other side of the room and I was sitting in the armchair, reading. I'd heard him coming down the stairs but had chosen not to look up. It had been an awkward few days and an uneasy truce lay between us. Now here he was preparing for another night out on the town. But then I heard his voice, strangely different.

"There's something wrong, Chrissie."

He sounded weak and slurred and, as I looked up, my mother screamed. He was standing in the doorway holding on to the frame, dressed only in trousers and a vest, one side of his face distorted by a series of vicious spasms, disfiguring him grotesquely.

"Brian, help me," he gasped out, "help me, please."

"Quickly, help him, help him!" mum was shouting at me.

I crossed the room to his side and asked cautiously,

"What's wrong?"

When he heard my voice next to him, he let go of the door and fumbled his hands around my neck. For a fleeting moment, I panicked and almost pushed him away. He's going to strangle me, it's a trick! but no, he was pleading for help.

"I can't see, Chrissie! I'm blind. Help me! Please God help me!"

"You'll be alright," I said, "you'll be OK." I'd hardly talked to him in my life. And I couldn't think of anything to say to him now.

He slumped sideways as his legs failed. I tried to hold him up, but his weight was too much, and we began to slide down the wall together, his hands gripping my body, his heavy head resting on my shoulder. His speech was slurred, and I could feel his lips pulling against the skin of my neck as he spoke. I was conscious of his breath on my neck and the overwhelming smell of after-shave. I had no idea what to do and felt embarrassed by the closeness of his body.

"Brian, I'm dying, I'm dying, help me! Oh God, don't let me die! Oh please, help me!" Then he began to pray, the Irish prayer for the dying. "Jesus, Mary and Joseph, I give you my heart and my soul. Jesus, Mary and Joseph, be with me in my last agony." He kept repeating the prayer over and over again as we knelt on the floor, his head on my shoulder, our arms around each other, the only embrace we would ever know, and then, with his voice no more than a whisper, he drifted away toward his death, protesting feebly all the while.

I could hear my mother crying into the telephone, spelling out the address for the ambulance, pleading with them to hurry. Then she came back to him as he lay there with his life ebbing away and took his hands, talking softly, lovingly to him.

"You'll be alright, you're going to be alright. The ambulance is coming now, my love, don't you worry now."

I'd never seen her that way with him and despite what was happening, I pulled away, embarrassed. She stayed there on her knees, talking to him, holding his hands until the ambulance arrived.

I went with them to the hospital, sirens screeching, lights flashing. They rushed him into the emergency ward immediately, but he was dead and gone within the hour. Standing there in the cold, green hospital room, I heard his last rattling breath, a priest mumbling prayers, doctors and nurses fussing about.

It was later, after we returned home, that I became angry. My mother and sister were standing in the lounge room sobbing, their arms around each other.

"Why are you crying?" I demanded.

My mother came across and put her hand on my arm.

"He was your father, Brian," she whispered.

"So what," I pulled away roughly, "I hated him, OK?"

I pushed past her and strode upstairs, and standing there in the dark in my room, I swore to God above that I would never take part in any hypocrisy about his death. He was dead and we were free at last.

The following morning, I awoke early and stood by the window, looking out across the ocean. I was troubled by my mother's reaction and couldn't understand her display of grief.

I thought about him being dead and I realized that I had no emotion whatsoever about it. I wasn't happy, but I wasn't sad either. If I felt anything at all, it was a sense of relief.

When I went downstairs, my mother was in the kitchen, cooking. She tried to smile but there were tears in her eyes.

"How are you feeling, son?" She came across and put her hands on my shoulders, looking into my eyes, searching for an emotion that wasn't there.

"I'm fine, don't worry about breakfast, I'm running late."

"You're going to work?" She was going to start crying again.

"Yes, I'm going to work."

She turned away quickly, dabbing at her eyes as I left by the back door. I didn't want to get involved in any more scenes. It was a bright sunny morning and I rode along the Promenade, wondering what she'd expected of me. He'd tried to kill me only the week before. Why should I worry about him now? My mind kept going back to the hospital and the noise he'd made as he died and I wondered if he'd known at that precise moment that he was dying and, if he had, what had gone through his mind …

… and then I thought of the days all those years before when I used to think something of him, before all the drunkenness and the violence. It was a long, long way back, when I was very young. Memories of him in an English RAF uniform, standing in the doorway of the living room, smiling, and me feeling proud that he was my da, polishing the brass buttons on his tunic, slipping a flat piece of metal with a slot cut in it behind the buttons to keep the white marks off the cloth. Another time in Ireland when I was very young, the memories broken like images through a fractured looking glass, bits and pieces of smells and sights and sounds unconnected to anything known, a river flowing, glistening through a city, standing beside him holding his hand by twisted railings, looking down into the swirling waters, snow-white ducks with yellow beaks and red glass eyes turning slowly in the eddies of a current, smells of Guinness and whisky and big red-faced men smiling down silently beneath thick tweed hats, women tall and thin, elegant and shrill, talking and laughing, cigarette smoke curling from their fingers, pubs and rooms and bars and wooden counter tops and brass ornaments on smoky walls, dark wet overcoats and fires so big you could fall into them, chairs pulled up close, people sitting around, glasses in hands, steaming by the fire, laughing with eyes twinkling and compliments, you're a fine looking lad, rides in buses to things we had to see, voices deep with accents, stairs too tired to climb, breakfast at a round, wide table with stiff white linen

and big shiny knives and forks and table napkins on our knees, mum and dad smiling about our manners, and a farmhouse with a yellow thatched roof and the step at the back door so worn away there was a hollow, chickens and a small pig running in the kitchen, a huge wooden table and a fire you could sit on either side of when it wasn't burning too brightly, potatoes tipped steaming from a pot onto the tabletop with hot bread that was bitter and sweet at the same time, mum whispering 'they're his people', then Bernard holding the chicken's legs so it would stop fighting, standing at the front of the whitewashed farmhouse stroking the jet-black, red-beaked bird with eyes so fierce and independent, and dad saying 'Watch this now' and the bird's head coming sliding off the axe, falling red across the green grass, and a fountain of blood and thrashing feet, Dad's laughing face and fear in Mary's eyes, and not knowing whether to laugh or cry, dinners with stories around the table about grandmother's baby running tipping into the boiling pot and scalding to death and the pig killing Grandma but she should have known better than to get between the sow and the litter, lying half-asleep in the dim light against Bernard's back with the fire crackling warm, with Mum and Dad holding arms around each other, and hoping it would all last, then waking later, being carried up to bed asleep, and in the morning running through the green fresh fields with a horse and the hay stack that was dangerous because Uncle Patrick nearly died of the sun stroke and he was never the same since, and looking in the pig-pen wondering which one had killed Grandma, and the gypsy woman with seven children went to the door in Galway and the rich woman was rude, "Get your piglets off this property now or I'll have the Gardai on you," and then because the woman was pregnant the gypsy woman cursed her and the baby had a pig's head, and the man who was on the wrong side and they took him down to the beach when the Brits left and buried him up to his neck in the sand and the tide came in and when the tide went out he was dead and it served him right anyway,

.

and the holy mass where the priest shouted at everyone and the rivers running shining through the towns, then sitting in the back of Nellie Helly's pub and big round chocolates in a box and Nellie Helly had known my mother ever since she was a little girl and the apple tree and the back of the car at night too tired to speak, their faces talking quietly in the dim glow of the dashboard lights and the click of the indicator when it stuck out from the side of the car, then in the morning old gypsy women standing by the roadside all dressed in black, wearing men's shoes and black shawls and their faces creased and brown and their cheeks going inwards, brown teeth with hands outstretched, an old gypsy woman singing a wailing song outside the white pub and dad singing with her, eyes closed, the gypsies all around him and more Guinness for everyone, and mum laughing and saying he'd drink with the devil himself, but I was proud because the gypsies liked him and I didn't think they would curse us, and the fox on the stone wall in the early morning looking back over his shoulder at us and dad saying, "This way, this way!" and the burst of red fire of sunlight through the fox's coat and his wide, yellow button black eyes piercing back bright and alive into mine, and the fox's mate running off along a gully with her babies like little brown dogs, and walking back down through the rocks to Galway Bay, with the sunlight glittering over the waters, the hotel with big meat sandwiches and black pints of Guinness with creamy white tops, and the dog nudging for food and the old woman with the horse and trap taking us for a ride holding off on the whip and never hitting the horse and a tray and four glasses filled with red raspberry juice that you never tasted anything like it before in your life because she'd made it herself, then the car stopping with no petrol and the Gardai bringing a tin and laughing with Dad and shaking hands, then the ferry again and not wanting to leave because they all liked us, the dirty-black sided boat and the gangplank and steel decks and the lounge room with round tables full of glasses and cigarette smoke rising thickly in a haze, the man with the squeeze box smiling all the time, and playing

and playing and everyone singing, Kevin Barry was a young man and
the cause of libertee, another man with a fiddle dancing and singing
as the boat tossed in the waves, and Peter crying and smelling of sick
and the cabin moving and creaking all night with the little round
window that Bernard saw a fish through, Mum taking off our clothes
when we were asleep, then the gangplank that was shaky and the man
in the taxi who'd never been to Ireland, but he was going to go there
one day ...

"Wake up, for Christ's sake, you bloody idiot!"

A truck was rolling past, horn blaring, just missing my bike,
the driver screaming at me through the side window. I'd ridden
straight through a red light.

By the time I pulled up at the butcher's shop, it was well after
7.30 and Mr. Booth was standing on the steps with his hands on his
hips.   "What time do ye' call this then, lad!" he said, looking at his
watch.

"My father died last night; we were up late."

He looked puzzled.

"Are ye' serious, lad? Ye' dad died last night?"

"Yes, he's dead."

"'Ou's dead?" Mrs. Booth was standing behind him, looking
concerned.

"Brian's dad died last night. What 'appened son? Is ye'
mother alright?"

"He had a stroke, it killed him."

He was frowning at me, as if it were my fault.

"Ye' shouldn't be 'ere lad, you should be 'ome with ye'
mother. Go on, get thy'sen 'ome. Look after ye' ma."

"I want to work," I told him, "my mother's got people with
her."

I went in and started on my daily routine, preparing the meat for the shop window. Later that morning, I heard them talking to my mother and I wondered if they'd rung her just to check on my story.

All morning, I kept thinking about how he'd died. It was hard to believe he was dead. It didn't make sense, one minute we were all living in fear of him, the next thing he was gone. I felt a great sense of freedom when I realized that it was over, but when I thought of my mother sobbing on her knees, I felt guilty.

Several times, Mr. Booth called me in and asked me to do things I'd forgotten, but when I crashed the delivery bike into the back of his car, he'd had enough and he told me to take a few days off.

"Look, lad, yer not all there t'day, and that's understandable. Why don't ye' jus' go 'ome and be with ye' fam'ly."

When I returned to the house, an ambulance was delivering the body. They carried the coffin into the lounge room and placed it in the bay window where my father used to sit, watching, and waiting for me.

His body lay in the front room for several days while people visited to pay their last respects. I stayed out of the way as much as I could, only going home to eat or sleep.

Within two days, relatives began arriving from Ireland and soon the hotel was full of men and women, drinking Guinness, talking about my father and preparing for the wake. The whole thing disgusted me. I'd hated him for very good reason, now I was being told by a group of strangers what a great man he'd been. My mother tried to talk to me several times, but I told her I wanted nothing to do with any of it.

The day of the funeral, there must have been thirty relatives staying at the hotel. My mother had begged me to take part in the ceremony and for her sake, I'd agreed. Alexandra Road never saw a grander funeral. They carried the coffin out of the house as if he were royalty. Then we walked behind the hearse all the way to the church, the relations following on behind my mother and myself.

As the priest droned on, I looked around at the mourners. I knew some of them from the times we'd spent in Ireland and I couldn't help wondering if any of them really believed what was being said.

Then came the long, slow drive out to the graveyard and an endless, meaningless eulogy, entirely divorced from reality. So, this is how it ends, I thought, as I watched the coffin settle on the bottom of the grave.

"The soil son …" she was whispering in my ear.

I had forgotten what she'd asked me to do, and conscious that all eyes were on me as the eldest son present, I reached down, scooped up a handful of soil and scattered it over his coffin.

The only thing I felt at that moment, at my father's funeral, was how dramatic it must have looked, me standing there throwing soil down on his coffin. When it was done, we all turned and walked away. None of us ever went back. He was dead and buried. It was over at last.

Chapter 16

Delinquency

Within weeks of my father's funeral, I was in trouble with the police, and not long after that I was arrested for the first time. I was involved with some guys a little older than myself and we used to steal lead pipes and guttering from church roofs and sell it to a guy who made lead sinkers for the fishermen. A few months later, I was charged with attempted theft of a car and then within weeks of that, I was back in court again, accused of assault.

My brother Peter had become very wary of me when I first began to get in trouble. He was a quiet, serious lad, who did well at school and followed the Catholic religion. We lived in the same house, but we had little or nothing to do with each other.

I hated any sort of authority by that time, the Catholic Church, the Christian Brothers or the police. It didn't matter who it was, if somebody had any sort of authority, I resented them.

Even the gang I was in. When I first joined, they tried to treat me like a kid. But there was a row one night and I got mad with a guy who'd been a close friend of my brother, Bernard. Bob Gittoss had been trying to stand over me and we'd ended up fighting. He was supposed to be something of a hard case so everyone was amazed when I beat him easily in a fistfight one night, overwhelming him quickly with the pent-up rage I had in me. After that brawl, everything changed, and I was treated differently by Gittoss, and the rest of them. I knew from then on that this was the way you gained respect.

A few months later, I was involved in more trouble and finally, after several court appearances, I was sentenced to a year's detention in a probation center for young delinquents.

My mother tried to help me, but after the third arrest, she gave up. I watched her in the courtroom as she took the stand, weeping, unable to hold up her head.

"I know it's difficult for you ..." The magistrate was leaning forward, peering over his glasses, "but your son has been before this court three times in less than a year."

She was looking down at her hands resting on the edge of a timber rail.

"He was a good lad, Your Honor. His father died last year ..." She couldn't go on.

"Take your time, Mrs. O'Raleigh."

She paused for a long moment, struggling with her emotions. Finally, she composed herself and looked up.

"He's   uncontrollable,   Your   Honor.   Absolutely uncontrollable."

*   *   *

I was released from the probation center one year later. All the other lads received time off for good behavior, but I'd been in trouble from the day I arrived.

When I got back to Blackpool, I rejoined my old gang immediately and within months, I was back in court again, this time charged with assaulting two policemen. My mother talked to me constantly about immigrating to Australia. We'd all been accepted before my father's death and she'd kept the application current while I was away.

One morning, just after Christmas, she came bursting into the living room waving a handful of papers. "It's the ticket, son. Your ticket to Australia!"

There was no way around it.

"I'm not going to Australia, mum, you know that."

"Brian, it's your only hope, you're finished here. You have a police record now; you'll never do any good in England."

"I'm not going, mum. This was your idea, not mine."

"There's a ticket there for you now for Australia." She put an envelope down on the table. "March the twentieth, that's only weeks away. If you have any brains left at all, you'll be on board that ship."

I pushed the papers away as she walked out of the room. She was starting to get on my nerves. I'd never had any intention of going to Australia. I'd only signed the forms to keep her happy. I had my own life in Blackpool. I had a circle of friends and I was having a good time. We went out together almost every night, drinking and playing snooker in the pubs along the promenade.

At first, the drink had been a major problem for me. I couldn't stand the smell of the stuff, it reminded me too much of my father. But then one night, I had a drink with an old Scotsman I worked with at the Pleasure Beach and he'd introduced me to whisky.

"Take a drink a' tha, young feller! That'll straighten ye' oot!" The spirits hit me like a blast from a hot furnace and, as I stood there shocked, he pushed a glass of Guinness at me. "Chase it doon wi' tha, laddie!" He was laughing. "Ye shuid see the look on yer face, ye'd think ye'd bin fuckin' shot!"

The smooth, dark Guinness went down easily, calming the fiery spirits. "Jesus Christ," I gasped, "that's fucking dynamite!"

"It is, indeed, it's great stuff altogether!"

I could feel the glow of the whisky way down. I didn't like the taste, but it wasn't as bad as the beer and at least I wouldn't have to stand there for hours forcing down one pint after another. One flick of the wrist and it was gone. It looked good too, tossing it down like that. I gestured to the barman.

"Fill them up again, two whiskies."

"Tek it easy, noo." Jock was shaking his head. "That's powerful stuff, don't get too cocky."

"I can handle it," I told him, "I like this stuff."

The next one wasn't as bad; I knew what to expect.

"Cheers, Bob."

"Good luck, son."

We tossed them down together and then, within half an hour, a deep, warm sensation of confidence began welling up inside me, and I found myself laughing loudly at Bob's jokes. This was followed by a great sense of wellbeing and suddenly, for the first time in my life, I felt like a man.

*   *   *

Once she knew that I'd started drinking, my mother watched my every move. I tried to ignore it, but the constant surveillance soon began to wear me down.

The night I came home from celebrating my eighteenth birthday, she was sitting in one of the armchairs in the front window of the hotel as I rounded the corner.

"Brian," she called out to me as I closed the porch door, "come in here, son."

I put my head around the corner.

"I'm tired, Mum, we'll talk in the morning."

"You've been out drinking again, haven't you?"

"I had a few, it's my birthday, for Christ's sake!"

"You've had more than a few. Look at you, you're drunk."

"I'm going to bed. I don't want to argue with you."

She followed me out into the hallway.

"Brian, you have your father's blood. You mustn't drink, son, not ever. It'll kill you the same way it did him."

I stood there, trying to hang on to my temper. Since my earliest childhood, she'd compared me to my father.

"Don't say that." I turned on her, pointing my finger in her face. "Not ever, do you understand! I'm nothing like him!"

"Don't you dare raise your hand to me! Sure, you're every bit as mad as he was!"

"I'm warning you, mum, don't compare me to him. He was a fucking animal!"

"Don't you dare threaten me. Get out of my house with your filthy mouth. I won't have you here. Go on, get out!"

*   *   *

My probation officer called me in a few days later and said he was concerned that I was mixing with the old crowd again. I knew that mum had been talking to him and I decided it was time to move out.

It all came to a head the following Friday night. A group of us had gone up to Squires Gate for the evening and a brawl had erupted in the dance hall. When an off-duty detective stepped in, I recognized him as one of the police who had arrested me the year before. When he grabbed my arm, I punched him several times in the face, leaving him sprawled on the floor.

When I rounded the corner of the hotel, later that night, I could see my mother's shadowy figure sitting in the darkened bay window.

"They were here an hour ago," she said, "they're out looking for you now. You've gone too far this time. They'll jail you for sure."

"They can't prove anything; it was too dark to identify anyone."

"Well, if they can prove it, you'll be jailed for three years at least, maybe more. The magistrate told you that only last month. They don't like people bashing the police." She was sitting there motionless, staring at me. "You have a free ticket for Australia, son. The boat leaves next week. It's your only hope."

I went out to the kitchen. I had no idea what to do. I'd been charged a few months earlier with assaulting two policemen and the only reason they hadn't jailed me then was because the cops had battered me in the police station and my face was a mess when I'd appeared in court.

Three years in jail, maybe more. I couldn't stand that. I'd go insane. People telling you what to do, every minute of the day. I remembered Jack, the warden from the probation center. I'd hated him from the very first day. I remembered the last time I'd seen him; it was the day of my release and I'd stood by the desk in his office, waiting for the last few insults.

"Well, so you're leaving us today. I'd prefer it if you were to be transferred to a jail somewhere, but you'll get there soon enough under your own steam." He took a few puffs on his pipe, assessing me through a cloud of smoke, waiting for some reaction. "I've just completed the final report for your probation officer. I've told him that you've shown no signs of rehabilitation or improvement whilst you were here." I was staring out the window. "Are you listening to me, O'Raleigh?"

I smiled down at him. "I'm sorry, sir, what was that?"

He exploded.

"You haven't got a hope, O'Raleigh. Not a bloody hope! You'll be back inside within weeks! Your type needs to be behind bars for the rest of your life. You need to have someone watching you twenty-four hours a day!"

"Yes, sir. I'm sure you're right, sir."

His offsider stepped forward.

"Watch your mouth, O'Raleigh, you're not out of here yet."

"I'll be out of here in ten minutes," I told him, "and there's nothing you can do about it."

Jack was on his feet, bellowing.

"Get him out! Get him out of my sight! Get him out of here now!"

*   *   *

There was a loud knocking at the front door, and I looked around the edge of the kitchen as my mother went out through the porch. I could just make out several shadowy figures through the pebbled glass. I moved across the kitchen quietly and peered out the back window. A black police car was parked on the corner near Dick's shop. It was too dark to tell if there was anybody in it.

I could climb over the back wall and get away into Adrian Street. Bobby Schofield would almost certainly hide me for a day or two. I peered around the doorframe again. My mother was standing at the front door, talking to the police. She hadn't let them in. I heard a muffled "Good night, Mrs. O'Raleigh" and then she was walking back down the hallway.

"That policeman you assaulted was a detective, he knows you well, and he has a broken nose. You're not going to get away with it this time. They're out to get you, Brian, you need to get out of Blackpool quickly or you'll be spending the next three years of your life in an English jail." I knew she was right. "Maybe this is the lesson you've needed. I've told you all along you can never take a drink, son. It's the curse of the Irish. You saw what it did to your father."

"Don't mum, please, don't compare me to him."

"I'm not, son, you're nothing like him, but you have his blood. You should never take another drink."

"I won't, mum. I've had enough of it. I don't need to drink."

"They'll be round again in the morning and I can't keep them out forever. The boat for Australia leaves next week. I'll phone Sylvia in London. You can stay with her for a few days. She'll be happy to look after you until you get on board that ship."

Sylvia had worked as a waitress at the hotel for two years running. I liked her a lot; we'd always got on well.

I sat there in silence as mum phoned Sylvia and explained the situation to her. Then she handed me the phone and her Cockney accent came screeching down the line.

"So what you bin up to then, eh! A proper bad little bastard you turned out to be, didn't you! Worryin' your poor old mum like that! I thought you 'ad more sense! You *should* go to Ors'tralia, with the rest of the bleedin convicts! It's the right place for you!" But then she softened. "Come up 'ere t'morrow luv. You don't need any more aggro. Come up to the big smoke, I'll make sure you're on that bleedin' boat!"

I spent the rest of that night packing, moving around the house quietly. The phone rang once, around 3.00 am and I stood in the hallway, listening to her voice.

"No, he's isn't here. He hasn't come home yet. No, that's right. Goodnight, Sergeant. Yes, I'll tell him. I'll call you as soon as he's back." As she hung up, she called out, "I know you're there, son. Come in here."

I walked in and stood by the table. I knew she could get me locked up again with just a few words.

"You thought I was going to turn you in?"

I didn't answer.

"You don't trust me, do you?"

We hadn't spoken for a long time.

"I don't know."

"You never forgave me for what I said in the court that time, did you?"

"It didn't bother me, mum, forget about it."

"Tell the truth son, we were never the same after that."

I didn't say anything, unwilling to hurt her more.

"I meant it for your own good. I didn't know what else to do with you."

"It doesn't matter, mum, it didn't bother me."

"You were never the same since, that place changed you." She stood up and put a hand on my shoulder. "Look, if we can get you out of Blackpool, you have a whole new life ahead of you in Australia."

"I won't be staying there for long." I turned away. "One year, two at the most. I just want to get a few things sorted out, that's all."

"That's grand, son. Just try to keep an open mind. You might like it out there, you never know."

                              *   *   *

The following morning, we took a taxi to Central Station. It was a cold, bleak, winter's day, and a pearl-grey mist was rolling in off the sea, swirling around the shelters on the edge of the promenade.

We stood on the platform without speaking for a long time.

"Give my love to Bernard when you see him now, won't you? And don't forget to write."

"Yes, mum."

"And if you don't like Melbourne, you can always go to live with your brother in Port Lincoln, you know that."

"Yes, I know."

We were like two strangers. I couldn't find a word to say. We'd been drifting apart for years with all the trouble I'd been involved in. The more I drank, the more she compared me to my father and that had caused endless arguments between us.

"Bernard would be happy to look after you till you get on your feet."

"I know, mum."

There was another long pause before she spoke again.

"Brian ..." She hesitated but I knew what was coming. "... did you ever consider going back to the church? You're still a Catholic, you know." I felt a surge of anger, but I didn't want to upset her any more than I had to.

"No, I wouldn't," I told her, "I don't believe in that stuff, you know that."

A train was shunting slowly backward along the platform, and as it came to rest, a whistle shrilled loudly nearby.

"Well, son ..." She was trying to smile but her eyes were full of tears. "... it's for the best. Be a good lad in Australia now, won't you." She reached out to hug me but then suddenly she broke down and fell against me. "Oh, Brian, you have my heart broke." She was sobbing against my shoulder. "I had such high hopes for you. I only ever wanted the best."

I stood there, frozen and mute, not knowing what to say as she clung to on me.

"All aboard!" a voice was booming out close behind us, "All aboard what's going aboard!"

She stood up straight then and held me out at arm's length, her eyes searching into mine.

"Swear to me you'll never take another drink. Promise me that, son."

"I won't, Mum. I've told you that."

"Say it, son, promise me! Say it!"

"I promise I'll never drink again, OK? I promise you."

"Last call, sir. If you're travelling, you need to board the train now."

He helped me up with the bags and then slammed the door shut. She held on to my hand through the open window. A whistle shrilled again close by and then, as the train began to inch forward, she pulled me down towards her and whispered, "Be a decent man, son. For my sake, be a decent man."

.

One week later, I stood on the deck of the *SS Orcades,* staring down at the throng of people below on the Southampton Docks. None of it felt real. The previous week, I'd been roaming around Blackpool with my friends, now I was standing on the deck of an ocean going liner, bound for Australia.

As I stood there watching, there was a deafening blast from the ship's siren and the boat shuddered and shook like some huge sea creature awakening. Then, ever so slowly, she began to inch her way forward through the water. The cheering intensified; people were calling out names, shouting their last goodbyes. A band somewhere was playing "Auld Lang Syne" and a bunch of tipsy passengers were holding hands and singing along.

> *May old acquaintance be forgot*
> *And never brought to mind.*
> *May old acquaintance be forgot*
> *For the sake of Auld Lang Syne.*

As the *Orcades* edged forward, a small group of people broke away from the main crowd and walked along the wharf, keeping pace with the ship until they reached the far end of the dock and could go no further. The older woman with them was crying and the man had his arm around her. Two young women were standing next to me, waving and throwing paper streamers, and I realized they were the passengers that the group below was fair welling. The taller girl had long, dark curly hair and a wide flashing smile. Her sister was pretty too, but the dark-haired girl was stunning. As I watched, she turned, and caught me staring. She flashed a smile, but before I could respond, she turned away to hurl another streamer down to the people at the far end of the wharf.

*   *   *

I awoke early the following morning and went up the steel gangways to the misty deck. There was no sign of England. The ship was ploughing its way through a grey and stormy ocean, whilst overhead dark clouds hurried along toward a distant, threatening horizon. I found my way to the furthermost tip of the ship and stood there, gazing out over the bow at the endless heaving waters ahead of me.

"So, nobody bothered coming to see you off, eh?"

I turned around. She was standing there, smiling her dark brown eyes, mischievous.

"No."

"You can't be too popular then, can you?"

She had a London accent, but her skin had an olive touch to it.

"Where are you from?" I said, "You look Italian or something?"

"I'm English. I'm from Kent."

"You don't look English."

"My mother's people are gypsies."

"So, you're not English, you're a gypsy. You don't have to be ashamed of that."

"You cheeky bugger!" Her eyes flared. "I'm not ashamed of my mum! So what are you then, you're Irish, aren't you?"

"My mother and father are Irish."

"Well, like I said, you're a Mick then, aren't you?"

She had high cheekbones and the wind, coming across the ship's bow, was swirling her long curly hair around her face but her dark brown eyes never once left mine as we spoke.

We stood there for ages until the cold drove us from the deck, then we went down below and had breakfast together. Jean was the most fascinating woman I'd ever met. She had an opinion on everything and we spent the entire day together, talking about everything and nothing, but it wouldn't have mattered what we'd talked about, for I'd fallen in love with her the moment our eyes had met.

We spent that night together. I knew nothing of women, but I knew that this was the woman for me. I was eighteen years old and I wanted a fresh start, away from England, away from Ireland, and away from my past.

Chapter 17

The Orcades

Jean was an awakening. I'd known one or two young women in the year before I left Blackpool but they'd been just brief, casual encounters, one-night-stands with strangers thrown together through loneliness or curiosity. Illusory, uncomfortable affairs in the back seats of cars or on the sands near the sloping edge of the black granite wall at the shore end of South Pier. Fumbling, awkward interludes with aliens of the opposite sex, arms and legs entwining that didn't quite seem to fit, but knowing now that it had started, one had to go on with it. I'd never met a woman like Jean.

She was tall and slim and graceful with a proud almost arrogant way about her, and that night when we came together in her darkened cabin, it was a mystery and a blessing for me. We lay together on the bunk, Jean resting on an elbow looking down at me, her hair falling in ringlets across my arm, her soft, dark eyes half-seen in the dim glow of a candle, my arm around her waist, her hand resting on my chest, all of my bravado gone. If ever I loved a woman, I loved Jean.

I had no notion at all of what to expect, women were as foreign to me as creatures from another world, but not so with her. She'd intrigued me from the very beginning. I was mesmerized by her, lost in her beauty, overwhelmed and undeserving when I was with her, but when we were apart, tormented and torn.

"You're a virgin, aren't you?" She was smiling.

"No, I'm not. I've been with women before." My mind was racing, desperately searching for something to say. "How old are you, then?" I'd regretted it before the words were out of my mouth.

"Why?" she asked.

"You know how old I am." I cursed myself again. I sounded like a child.

We lay there naked on the bed, her hand stroking my chest.

"Don't talk," she murmured, "don't say anything." She leant over me then, kissing me softly on the mouth. "You're nervous," she murmured, and in the dim light of the cabin, I could see her eyes, bright and dark. "Give me your hand," she whispered, "here, touch me here. No, here, that's it, gently. Stroke me there, gently."

I was way out of my depth, hopelessly and helplessly lost.

"You are a virgin, aren't you?" She was smiling.

"No, I'm not. I made love to a girl once, just before I left Blackpool."

"You're a virgin," she whispered again as we came together.

I knew that I wasn't, but I knew what she meant.

We spent all that night and all the following day in the bunk, touching and kissing, whispering together and making love. Her sister, Irene, who shared the cabin, thought it was funny at first, but after the second day, she began to tire of me being there all the time. We didn't care, we made love and talked and then we made love again. Jean taught me things I'd never heard of and led me to places I'd never been.

Occasionally, we'd be driven up on deck by hunger, emerging from the cabin like two starving refugees in search of food. Sometimes it would be daylight, other time's night, it didn't matter to us. In the early hours of the morning, the ship would be deserted, and we'd go all the way forward through the first-class section and then right out to the very tip of the boat where we'd first met. It was our secret place and we'd stand there, our arms around each other, staring forward, without talking, as the ship ploughed its way steadily through the night-dark sea.

We got on well, but she was fiery too, and sometimes when I'd least expect it, we'd clash.

"Your dad sounds like a right bloody nutter!" She was leaning back on a pile of pillows, studying me. "I hope you're not a Jekyll and Hyde too, are you?"

"I'm nothing like him and he's been dead for years, anyway." I was sorry I'd told her some of the things I had about my family, but she'd kept on asking me about what they were like and I had to tell her something. "He drank too much, that's all."

"Bloody Micks," she said, "they all drink too much, everyone knows that. You need to watch yourself."

"I was born in England," I told her, "and I don't like being called a Mick."

"Too bad." She was laughing. "You should have chosen your parents more carefully then, shouldn't you?"

"So what are *you* then? You're half gypsy and half English."

"That's right, I'm half gypsy and half English. I don't have a problem with that. Your problem is you don't know who you are."

"I was born in England, that makes me English."

"That's nonsense, Brian, and you know it. Look at you, your mother's Irish, your father's Irish and your sister was born in Ireland! That makes you a bloody Mick! Like it or lump it, you silly sod!"

"My parents are Irish, that doesn't make me Irish."

"Look …" She was becoming exasperated. "… if your mum was a black African and your father was a black African, what would you be? You'd be a bloody black African! What else? It doesn't matter a damn where you were born, you are what you are!"

"Just drop it." I hated these arguments. Suddenly, out of the blue, we'd be fighting and then, just as quickly, she'd be laughing again, and it would be over. "Let's just forget about it, OK?"

"That's alright for you to say." She wasn't going to let it go. "But you could be a right nutter too, for all I know. You're an ex-criminal, you've admitted that much yourself. I don't know why I have anything to do with you. You've been locked up for a year already and you don't even know who you are!"

I was sorry I'd told her about the probation center and all the other trouble I'd been in. Every time we argued, she brought it up.

"That was nothing," I told her, "that was kid's stuff."

"Well, the law didn't think it was nothing, did they? If it was nothing, why did they lock you up for a year, eh? I could be mixing with a hardened criminal, for all I know." She was smiling. I never knew when she was being serious or not. "You could be a convict, for all I know, being deported to Australia. They probably let you up on deck for a pee and a run around every now and again. I'm just hoping you're not Jack the bloody Ripper! He was probably a Mick too, the way he went on! How would I know?"

Now we were both laughing.

"Oh Christ, Jean, give it a break, would you? I'm starting to think you're not the full shilling yourself."

"Well, there's the difference." She was grinning. "I've never claimed to be, now have I?"

"And cut out the Mick bullshit," I told her, "I'm getting tired of it."

"OK, then, I'll call you Paddy instead."

She was hopeless. I could do nothing with her. One minute, we'd be making love and the next minute, I felt like strangling her. She had no fear of me whatsoever and she knew she could twist me any way she wanted.

But she had me baffled. I had no idea what she actually thought of me and the day before the ship arrived in Melbourne, I tried to pin her down about her feelings.

"Well, what do you think?" I said, "should we get together in Sydney? I'd be happy to move up there to be with you."

She was leaning over the ship's rail, looking at the distant coastline.

"That's up to you, isn't it?"

"Jean, I'm pretty keen on you. I just want to know how you feel about me."

"Do you, now." She spoke without looking at me. "Haven't you worked that out yet?"

"Do you want me to join you in Sydney or not? I need to know."

She was staring fixedly into the distance.

"What do you want to do?"

"I'd like to go to Sydney."

"Well, go to Sydney then, it's a free country."

"Jean, for Christ's sake, look at me! What's wrong with you? Do you want me to come to Sydney or not? Just say yes or no."

"That's up to you." She was still not looking at me. "Knowing your type, you'll probably meet some floozy in a bar somewhere and be off with her within days."

"What's wrong, Jean?" She was like a total stranger, all the feelings and passion from the previous weeks dissipated to nothing in the harsh Australian sunlight. "What's going on? Do you want me to come to Sydney with you or not?"

"That's up to you," She turned away from the rail abruptly. "You'll have to make up your own mind about that."

I stood there in despair as she disappeared down a companionway. I was baffled. It was as if she wanted it to be finished. I couldn't accept that. I knew that I loved her.

I went down to her cabin and knocked quietly. There was no reply. I turned the handle; it was open. Jean was lying on her back in the bunk, a white sheet draped across her body. I sat on the edge of the bed and touched her hair. She was crying.

"What's wrong Jean, what is it?"

She just lay there, staring at the ceiling.

"What is it? Tell me, please."

She closed her eyes and turned her head away slightly.

I bent over and kissed her softly on her neck. Then I kissed her again on her mouth and as I did, her arm wound around my back, pulling me down towards her.

"I didn't want to get involved." Her face was wet with tears.

"I thought we were involved." I was shattered.

"We came to Australia to travel; Irene feels left out."

"Jean, I love you. I want to marry you."

"You're eighteen, Brian. You don't know what you want."

"You're not much older, what does it matter?"

"I don't want to get married. I want to travel."

"We can do that together. Irene can come with us if she wants."

"No." Her voice was firm. "It wouldn't work. She thinks you drink too much."

"She saw me drunk once, for Christ's sake, at the Captain's cocktail party. Everyone was drunk that night!"

"You were rotten drunk, Brian, and you caused trouble all night! You've been drunk three times since we left England! You're always drinking. She's not used to that."

I sat up. "Jean, I love you. I'll stop drinking, that's not a problem. We'll get married in Sydney and then we can travel anywhere you like."

She pulled me back down again, her eyes close to mine.

"Stop talking," she said softly, "I'm not going to marry a Mick. Drunk or sober, they're all bloody mad."

Chapter 18

Travelers

I spent three weeks in Melbourne, long enough to get a job on a construction site and earn enough money for the train fare to Sydney. I arrived at Central Station on a stormy Tuesday afternoon and took a taxi to Jean's address in Kings Cross, turning up on her doorstep just after 2.00 pm. There was nobody home. Directly across the road lay the Piccadilly Hotel. I went across and sat there, having a few drinks, watching out for her along the rain-swept pavement.

She came hurrying down Victoria Street just after five, an umbrella tilted sideways against the rain, a hand clutching her raincoat closed. I crossed the road, waited until she drew near, and then sprang out from behind a phone box.

"Jean!"

She screamed in fright.

"Jesus Christ, you silly bugger, you could have given me a heart attack!"

Then we were kissing. I'd never been so happy to see another human being in my life.

"God!" She pushed me away. "You smell like a bloody brewery!"

"I had a couple of beers across the road. I've been waiting for you all afternoon."

"And you reckon you're not Irish! You'd die of thirst if the pubs ever closed. Did it ever cross your mind to have a cup of tea or something?"

"Never," I said, "I swear to God, it never crossed my mind! If it had, I'd be on my sixth cup of tea by now. Come on …" I grabbed her hand. "… let's celebrate." We ran across the road, laughing like fools, dodging cars in the pouring rain.

The Piccadilly was a dive, but it had a great atmosphere and we spent the next few hours there, drinking, talking and swapping stories of our adventures in Australia. By the time we got back to Jean's place, it was 11 pm and we were giggling like five-year-old's as we rang the bell.

When Irene opened the door, she ignored me completely.

"Where have you been?" she demanded, glaring at Jean. "I was worried sick about you!"

"Aren't you going to say hello to Brian?" Jean asked.

"You must have known how worried I'd be! Why didn't you call me?"

Then she turned without waiting for an answer and stormed off into the kitchen, slamming the door behind her. A few moments later, she was back.

"Where were you?" Then, in a quick aside to me, "Hello, Brian."

"We were across the road in the Piccadilly having a drink. I am over twenty-one, you know."

"That's not the point." Irene was still angry. "You should have let me know."

She calmed down after a while and then we sat around talking, comparing our experiences of Australia so far. She thawed out a little as we talked but it was obvious that she wasn't all that happy to see me.

"Where are you staying?" she asked me, close to midnight. "You can't stay here, there's not enough room."

Jean jumped in. "Don't be silly, Irene, of course he's staying here. I put up with that idiot Craig for long enough in London."

"Where will he sleep?"

"I'll sleep on the floor," I offered.

"No, you won't!" Jean was adamant. "He's sleeping with me on my side of the bed."

"He's not sleeping in *my* bed." Irene was horrified. "Definitely not! I will not sleep in that bed with the two of you!"

"It's not your bed, it's our bed, and I'll have whoever I like on my side!"

"God, Jean, you must be drunk, or you wouldn't be going on like this!" She went off then, disgusted, and Jean and I spent the next hour on the sofa, kissing and giggling. But finally, when we were sure Irene was asleep, we crept into the bedroom and slipped as quietly as possible into the large double bed.

* * *

Irene found a small apartment and moved out a week later. Jean and I were now officially a couple, in love and living in sin. We went everywhere together. I was never happy without her at my side. I was so proud of her, I couldn't believe she was mine. I'd sit there sometimes at night, watching her as she read a book or did a crossword. She had a beauty about her that captivated me entirely. She always walked with her arm through mine and sometimes it was hard to remember what life had been like before we met.

We spent that first year in Sydney. I worked on a construction site and she found a job as a typist. We had plenty of money and we'd go out together most nights, dancing and drinking, enjoying ourselves and exploring the nightlife of the city. Occasionally, there'd be a wild night out at the Piccadilly Hotel, but Jean wasn't too fond of the place and if things became crazy, she'd leave, and I'd join her later at home.

She hated it when there was trouble and sometimes there was. I couldn't always guarantee my behavior when I drank. I'd start off happy enough but as the night went on, things could change. One minute, I'd be discussing something, maybe arguing, and then someone would say one more sentence, or sometimes just one more word, and I'd snap and there'd be a brawl. I was never violent towards Jean, even in my worst blackouts. I loved her and I knew that she would never have tolerated that.

Weekends we'd spend walking along the cliff tops by the ocean or swimming in the surf at Bondi Beach and at nights, we'd lie together on the bed, pouring over maps and making plans to travel. I had to go to Port Lincoln to see my brother, Bernard, but after that, we could go anywhere.

Jean was fascinating to be with. She had an interest in history and mythology and I'd listen to her for hours as she explained about the ancient Greek gods and their legends.

Not long after, Irene met Beala. He was a Hungarian artist and within weeks of them meeting, they'd moved into a flat together. Once Irene was settled, Jean felt secure enough to travel.

*   *   *

We set out from Sydney one Sunday morning in October. Summer had come early that year and it was hot. Irene came to Central Station to see us off and as we said goodbye, she kissed my cheek and whispered, "Look after her, Brian." She was close to tears. "If you get stuck, phone me. Promise?"

The train took us to the outskirts of Sydney and then we waited by the side of the road, resting against two backpacks and a rolled-up tent under the shade of a dusty old gum tree. We were young, we were in love and we were ready to see the world.

The next few weeks, we travelled across Australia, moving from town to town as the mood took us. We'd stay in places we liked for a few days to explore the local countryside before moving on. Once we'd left the city behind, everything was totally different. We took our time, hitchhiking, catching buses and sometimes walking for miles on the lonely roads, enjoying the novelty and adventure of the Australian outback. It was a place I'd only ever heard about and the further we went off the beaten track, the stranger it became and the more we loved it. We made money in some places. Jean would get a job as a typist and I would work on building sites or picking fruit. It was a carefree existence and we met all sorts of characters along the way as we explored a world that we never knew existed …

Small town roads and dusty tracks, heat and endless sun,
lizards sliding through the dust, silent black-faced men.
Hats pulled low to dark brown eyes, horses bolting in the scrub,
Working in an open field, yearning for the shade.

Kangaroos and wombats, snakes and blinding heat,
Hitching at a crossroads in the bush.
Riding in a big white Mac, red rocks and endless plains,
Winding through the shimmering heat, waiting for the rains.

Resting by a waterhole, cigarettes and Billy tea,
lying by a campfire late at night,
Wondering in the silence, resting in its pause,
talking soft and quiet, gazing up at stars.

Camping in a tent outback, silhouettes on canvas walls,
Jean reaching out to touch my lips, her face by love enthralled.
Waking slow and easy, rising soft and quiet,
dry twigs on still red embers, waiting for the light.

Washing in a stony creek as kookaburras call,
knowing this was how it was, unafraid before the fall.
Turning in a rising dawn, as she moves from the tent,
Her face against my shoulder, her heart against my chest.

——

By the time we reached Port Lincoln, it was the week before Christmas. Bernard had jumped ship there a few years before and after marrying a local girl, he'd settled down to raise a family. We turned up at his place unannounced, hoping to surprise him. He wasn't home but his wife, Maxine, made us welcome. She was a friendly woman, about the same age as Jean and within minutes, they were chatting away together like old friends.

"Why didn't you let us know you were coming? Bernie would have been here. I'll call him now; he'll be home soon."

When we heard his car pulling into the garage just after 5.00 pm, I rushed outside. He'd been gone for five years by then. When I'd last seen him, he'd been a tall, awkward youth of sixteen. Now here was this six-foot tall, broad-shouldered man stepping out of a car.

"Bernard?" I hardly recognized him, and we shook hands awkwardly, embarrassed by our strangeness. Jean had come out behind me. "This is Jean. I told you about her on the phone."

After the introductions, Bernard turned to Maxine.

"Could you give us a minute? There's something I want to talk to Brian about." He led me into the lounge room, closing the door behind him. Then he pulled up chairs and sat down across from me.

"How's Mum?"

"She's fine, working away at the hotel."

"Mary and Peter?"

"They're good, Bernie. You know Mary's had a second baby? Peter's at college, he's doing OK."

"That's good, where did you meet Jean?"

"On the boat, coming over."

"She seems nice."

"She is. I really like her."

He paused for some time, staring down at the carpet, and I wondered if there was something wrong but then he looked up.

"What happened the night he died?"

I was puzzled. "Who?"

"You know who. Did you kill him?" He was staring at me.

"You mean dad?" I was baffled. He'd been dead for four years by then.

"You know who." He wouldn't say the word.

"Did I kill him? Why would you ask that?"

"Did you?"

"He died of a stroke; you knew that!"

"Is that what actually happened?"

"Yes, of course it is."

He was staring at me, trying to work out if I was telling the truth.

"I always thought you'd end up killing him," he said.

Maxine put her head around the door.

"Dinner's ready." She paused and looked around. "What's going on, am I missing something?"

"No," Bernard shook his head, "we're just talking about Blackpool. We won't be much longer."

As she disappeared, he turned back to me.

"I just want to know the truth … it was definitely a stroke?"

"Yes, definitely. I was with him when he died."

"Did he say anything?"

"Not much, he was praying. You know that Irish prayer: *Jesus, Mary and Joseph, I give you my heart and my soul.*"

"That would have done him a lot of good, I'm sure."

There was a silence for a while and I sat there waiting, wondering where all this was leading. Then he leant forward in his chair.

"Was it bad?" he asked, "After I left?"

It was pointless lying.

"It wasn't good."

He thought for a while longer then he sat up.

"I never told Maxine about any of that stuff," he said, "OK?"

"That's fine with me."

"I've never talked to anybody about it, what's the point?"

"It's finished," I said, "I forgot about it years ago."

"Good," he nodded, "I feel the same way."

Maxine put her head in the door again.

"This is the last time, dinner's going on the table now."

"We're coming now," he smiled, "don't start."

Later, while we were eating, Bernard brought up Blackpool again. "What happened to Rosemary Baker?" he asked, "Is she still around?"

"Who?"

"Rosemary Baker, you know, she was Miss Blackpool."

"He's got a thing about beauty queens," Maxine said to Jean, "I was Miss Port Lincoln, that's how we met."

"I can't place her," I told him.

"How about Bernadette Doyle, did she ever get married?"

"Bernadette Doyle? I don't think I know her either."

"You must know her. I took her out for a while, just before I left. You'd have seen her at the hotel."

"I don't remember her." He looked disappointed. "Some of your other mates are still around, getting into all sorts of trouble," I said. "Mick Rafter got three years just before I left; breaking and entering."

"Who?"

"Mick, Mick Rafter, your friend."

He shook his head.

"Never heard of him."

"You know Mick, you went to school together."

He shook his head again.

"I can't place him."

I was surprised. They'd been friends for years.

"There were the three of you: Mick, Tony Dagenham and you. Dagenham's still around, I had a drink with him a few weeks before I left. He said to tell you that you could come home now, you've done your time."

Maxine and Jean laughed but Bernard didn't think it was funny.

"I can't place him. How's mum?"

"She's OK, she sends her love." I was baffled. "You must remember Tony Dagenham; he was your best friend."

He was staring at me steadily.

"I've never heard of him, Brian, never."

Jean nudged me. "Forget about it, he doesn't remember, let it go."

After dinner, we sat around the table, going through old photographs and catching up on family news. I mentioned several other people he'd been close to but the response was always the same. It puzzled me at first but finally it dawned on me that Bernard wasn't going to admit to knowing anybody from those early days. He'd excluded them all from his memory, his former life was a closed book, forgotten as if it had never existed.

Port Lincoln's a quiet town set at the tip of the Eyre Peninsula with a population of around ten thousand people. In the previous century, it had been one of the first ports of call for the great, square-rigged sailing ships that set out from England, through the roaring forties, along the clipper route to Australia, seeking grain and wool for the markets of Europe. Wheat had been the foundation of Lincoln's prosperity for generations, but in more recent times, a thriving fishing industry had sprung up with the boats from Lincoln chasing the blue fin tuna that infest the waters of the Southern Ocean across the bottom of South Australia.

Lincoln had the usual small-town prejudices, and if you weren't born and bred there, you'd be regarded for the rest of your life as an outsider. There were only a few exceptions to this, and Bernard was one of them. He'd turned up there at the age of seventeen and after a few youthful clashes with the law, he'd settled down and married into one of the town's oldest families.

A few days after we arrived, I found a casual job on the wharves, loading wheat into boats from around the world. It was hot, exhausting work, slaving away in ship's holds in temperatures that soared over the hundred-degree mark at times. After work each day, the whole gang of us would swarm down to the nearest pub to wash away the dust and quench our thirsts.

Most nights, I'd have a few beers with the guys and then go home to Jean, but sometimes I'd get stuck there and, on those occasions I wouldn't get home until the early hours of the morning.

The casual workers were a wild bunch. None of them were locals. There were men from across Australia and others from around the world. They were itinerants, seeking a casual job for a few months before moving on to greener pastures. Some of them were travelling fast, evading police warrants or trying to stay ahead of maintenance orders from deserted wives. Between them, they spoke a dozen different languages and the only thing they had in common was the love of a drink.

There was trouble at the pub one night. Some local fishermen had been monopolizing the pool table and after a lot of angry words, the place had erupted into a brawl, the locals on one side and the dockworkers on the other. By the time the squad car arrived, a couple of people had been injured. The police interviewed some of us outside the pub, but nobody wanted to press charges, so they let us all go with a warning. I was hoping that would be the end of the matter, but the small-town grapevine was too well established.

A few days later, Bernard called around and took me for a drive into town. There was nothing much said on the way down, but it was obvious that he wasn't happy. We drove along the main street and then he pulled the car into a parking bay close by the town jetty, facing the beach.

"Were you involved in that trouble at the Pier Hotel the other night?"

"There was a bit of trouble," I told him, "nothing much."

"That's not what I heard. What happened?"

"There was a punch-up, those things happen."

He'd switched off the engine was sitting half-turned towards me, leaning back against the car door.

"I heard it was pretty unpleasant. One of the fishermen ended up in hospital for the night. What happened?"

"I don't know, you know how these things are. We were having a few drinks and then some idiot wanted to cause trouble. What do you expect me to do?"

"I'd expect you to walk away. I do business with the fishermen, a lot of them are my friends."

"Look, the guy who ended up in hospital was the guy who caused the trouble. He was refusing to let anyone use the pool table. You know how they treat outsiders here; it pisses people off."

"That's not what I heard. If it happens again, just walk away, OK? You shouldn't be hanging around with those drifters anyhow. They don't belong here. They're responsible for nearly all the trouble in the town."

"Oh bullshit," I snapped, "some drunken fisherman wants to get tough and it's my fault? Fuck him. I'm not going to put up with any shit from these fucking hillbillies."

"Brian, I live in this town, you need to respect that. The police told me that you were the one that caused the trouble."

"Of course they did! What do you expect them to say? They're not going to blame the locals, are they?"

"This is a small town, people talk, you need to watch yourself. You can't go on causing trouble down here."

"You weren't even there. How would you know who was causing the trouble?"

"You're mixing with riff-raff, I know that much. You might have to work with them but you don't have to mix with them socially. Why don't you give the drink a rest for a while? Get yourself a decent job. Save up some money." We were both angry now.

"Is there anything else while you're at it?" I demanded.

"There is, actually. Look, I'm not sure how to say this, Brian, but I don't think you and Jean are good for each other. You need to settle down, mate. Forget all this talk about travelling, it's all just hot air."

It was about the worst thing he could have said.

"Jean's my fiancé, OK? I'm going to marry her." I got out of the car. I was furious. "Don't worry about the gossip, mate. We'll be moving on before too long."

We left Lincoln a few weeks after Christmas. I never talked to Bernard again about what had been said that day, but things were never the same between us. The night we left, Bernard drove us down to the wharf. We were taking the overnight ferry across to Adelaide. Jean and Maxine were talking and laughing together in the back of the car, but Bernard and I hardly exchanged a word. As we boarded the boat, he put out his hand.

"I'm sorry it didn't work out." There was trouble in his eyes. "Think about what I said, you'll have to settle down sometime."

"It was good to see you. Thanks for all your help."

We shook hands then and left them standing there on the dock.

"What was all that about?" Jean was waving down to Maxine.

"Nothing much, older brother stuff. You know, make sure you go to church, wash behind your ears and so on."

I was glad to be leaving Lincoln. It was a beautiful place, but I felt stifled there. We were headed for Adelaide; it would be a fresh start in a new place where nobody knew us, a whole new beginning.

Chapter 19

On the Road

We arrived in Adelaide early the following morning. It was a bright, sunny day and we were both excited to be there. We'd lain out on the deck of the ferry half the night, talking and dreaming about the future.

"We should buy a Mercedes," I told her, "you know, one of those old ones with an open top. We could travel anywhere then. We'd just load it up and off we'd go."

She was laughing,

"A Mercedes! Irene was right, you do have delusions of grandeur."

I was taken aback.

"Did she say that?"

"Yes, several times, but then again she thinks you're crazy anyway."

"What's crazy about getting a car?"

"It's not *getting* the car that's the problem; it's *paying* for the car!" She was looking at me amazed. "How do you intend *paying* for it, for God's sake. You spend all your money on booze!"

"That's bullshit, I drink a bit, yes, but so do you! Everyone has a drink."

"My darling, look at me." She was smiling but she was serious. "You drink like a bloody fish! You drink almost every night!"

"Hang on," I interrupted her. "I have a few drinks after work most days. Everyone in Australia does that! What are you going on about?"

She was shaking her head. "Look, I enjoy a drink too but I can take it or leave it, OK? You've only got the taking part." She was getting angry and I was, too. "You're a Mick, you've got the curse! If you don't realize that by now, you're even madder than I thought."

"Look, let's get something straight, if I decided to stop drinking, I could stop like that, OK?" I snapped my fingers in her face. "I could quit tomorrow."

"Don't get aggressive with me, I won't tolerate it, and your type always talks about quitting *tomorrow*." She jumped up. "I'm tired. I'm going down to the cabin." She turned and headed off along the deck and I got up and ran after her.

"Come on, don't be silly. Let's just forget about it."

"Let go of my arm," she said.

We were standing by the ship's railing. She was staring out towards the land; lights twinkled somewhere on a shore, miles away.

"You're really starting to worry me. You don't seem to have any idea at all of just how much you drink."

"Jean, I'm sorry. Let's not spoil the night."

"You've already done that," she said. "Just leave me alone for a while, ok. I want to be by myself."

She turned and disappeared through an oval doorway, and I went back to where we'd been talking on the mats. I lay there for a long time, thinking about what she'd said and then I dozed off, the ship heaving and rolling gently underneath me. When I came to a little later, I went down below to our cabin and eased open the door. She was lying on the lower bunk, curled up fast asleep like a child, a white sheet draped over her body, her dark hair smothering the pillow, almost concealing one side of her face.

I sat on the edge of a chair, admiring her. She was so beautiful. I undressed, eased myself quietly on to the bunk next to her then reached over and began stroking her hair.

There was a sigh and a slight movement and then her eyes were open. I leaned over and kissed her. Neither of us spoke. Her arm curled around my neck and she kissed me softly on my face and eyes, forgetting the past and forgiving me my sins as we embraced.

"I've decided to stop drinking. I was thinking about what you said. You're right, I do drink too much."

"Shhhh!" she whispered.

"No, I'm serious."

"Shush, honey, shush."

She pulled me down towards her and I came willingly, knowing that this was the woman I loved, knowing that things would be different from then on.

Within hours of landing in Adelaide we found a place to live at Henley Beach, a seaside suburb not too far from the city. The apartment was perfect for us. A colonial style house that we shared with an old man called Amos. He had the upstairs part of the house and we had the whole of the downstairs to ourselves.

Amos was eighty-two and his daughter, Marge, who lived in the house next door, came in frequently to look after him. He was becoming senile, and his memory was so erratic that sometimes we had to reintroduce ourselves when we bumped into him on the stairs.

"Oh hello," he'd say, looking surprised, "so who are you then, friends of Marge?"

"No, Amos, we live here, remember? We live downstairs, you live upstairs, and Marge is next door, OK?"

"Oh yes, of course you do, silly of me, and you're going next door, did you say?" He'd have his hand behind his ear. "Hearing's not the best, I'm afraid. Getting on, you know!"

There was a large white cockatoo in a wire cage just outside the back door and to confuse things even more, the bird would scream out his name several times each day, *"Amos! Hello! Hello, Amos!"*

He'd come hurrying out the back door.

"Coming, Marge! I'm coming!"

Then Marge would come rushing out through the gap in the fence ... "Don't worry, dad, it's just the bird again, don't worry."

"What?" He'd be baffled. "Bird ... what bird? Oh yes, of course, the bird, silly of me."

And then he'd go over to the cockatoo, poking a finger through the wire. "You fooled me again, Percival, you old rascal. We'll roast you one day! Oh yes we will. You'll end up on a plate with potatoes and gravy, mark my words you will."

*   *   *

My promise to Jean lasted just three weeks. I'd had no intention of drinking on that day but, as I left the construction site, a car pulled up alongside me.

"Coming for a beer, mate?" Allen was one of the guys I worked with. I hadn't touched a drop since we left Port Lincoln, but I was struggling with it on a daily basis.

"No, thanks mate, I'm off it."

He shrugged. "I'm only going to have two or three on the way home."

This is ridiculous, I thought, two or three beers couldn't hurt anyone. Jean's not going to worry about that.

"Can you drop me off at my place after?" I asked him.

"No problem, jump in."

The two or three drinks turned into a heavy session, and by the time Allen dropped me back at my place it was well after midnight.

Jean was awake when I crept in, sitting up in the lounge room with a magazine on her lap.

"I'm sorry …" I began.

"Didn't last long, did it? Why didn't you phone? I've been worried sick. I thought you'd been in an accident or something."

"I'm sorry, I should have rung."

She got up. "You can sleep in here tonight. I don't want you in the bedroom."

*   *   *

That was the first time that I'd ever really tried to stop drinking. Over the next few years, that scene was to be repeated in towns and cities across Australia. On some of those occasions, things weren't too bad. But other nights, I'd be brought home drunk by friends, strangers or the police. I was totally irresponsible when I drank and most of the trouble that I was involved in, I caused. I never hurt Jean physically, but the mental torment I put her through was almost certainly worse.

There were some good times too. Jean and I would go out together sometimes on the weekends, swimming in the ocean, exploring the cities or towns we were living in, or going to the movies. Occasionally, I'd manage to stay off the drink for a while and Jean would begin to trust me again, but then, just when it seemed as if things were getting back on track, I'd go off on a particularly heavy bender and wreck everything. Sometimes I'd go for months without getting into any sort of trouble. Other times, Jean would receive a call from the police asking whether she wanted to bail me out or not.

During that period, we lived in every major city in Australia: Sydney, Adelaide, Melbourne, Brisbane, Perth, Darwin and half a dozen other towns in between. At first, we used to tell friends that we were travelling, seeing Australia, but the sense of adventure disappeared along the way and finally, as my drinking grew worse, it became clear that we were running.

We'd been back in Sydney for three months when Jean came to me one evening and told me she was pregnant.

"That's fantastic!" I told her.

"Fantastic?" She looked baffled. "We can't afford to have a child, Brian. We don't have any money. We're not even married!"

At the time, I was working for a company that sold fluorescent lights, door to door.

"We'll get married. And I can earn big money where I am now. The top salesmen make heaps of money."

"Brian, you've been there for two months and you've come home drunk nearly every night. You're not ready to be a father."

"That's not true. Johnny Wilson's told me that he's going to put me in charge of a sales team. He owns the company. Trust me, honey, I'll cut down on my drinking, I promise."

"You've said all that before. I don't want to stay in Sydney. I hate you working with that crowd, they're a bunch of drunks."

"Ok, if you're not happy here, we'll get married and go back to Port Lincoln. You liked Lincoln; we had some good times there."

"You'll have to look after two of us now." She wanted to believe me. "I won't be able to work for a while."

"You won't have to work at all. I'll get a steady job. Bernie will help us until we get on our feet. Lincoln's a quiet town, it's an ideal place to have a baby."

She was holding onto my arm. "Promise me you won't drink as much. Promise me things will be different."

"I promise, darling, ok? I'll cut back on my drinking; I swear to God I will." I put my arms around her. "I love you, Jean. Trust me, I will look after you."

Bernard was delighted when I called him with the news.

"Congratulations, it's about time. You're welcome here, you know that." He paused. "Look, I'm sorry about what I said about Jean that time, I was wrong. You're both welcome here. You can stay with us if you like or I can organize a place for you."

We were married the following week at the Registry Office in Sydney, just across the road from St Mary's Cathedral. It was a quiet affair and three days later, after saying our goodbyes, we boarded a bus bound for South Australia.

Chapter 20

Kathleen

Bernard was waiting for us when the bus pulled into the main street of Port Lincoln. As Jean stepped down, he hugged her for a moment before turning to shake hands with me.

"Welcome back!" He was smiling. "You've made the right decision." He'd organised a flat for us close to the waterfront and he took us there immediately. "Now, you don't have to stay here if you don't like it." He was worried it wasn't big enough. "But it's central and it's a reasonable price."

The place was ideal. It was small, clean and comfortable and from the bedroom window we had an uninterrupted view of the ocean.

"It's great," I told him, "a lot better than I expected."

"I told Mum you were coming back." He turned to Jean. "You can do really well here this time. You could buy a block of land and build a house if you want to. I can arrange finance, that wouldn't be a problem."

We settled back into Lincoln quickly. Jean became more and more pregnant and, as the weeks passed, we spent hours walking together, talking about baby's names and planning our future. I found work immediately with a building company and a few weeks later, we bought an old Ford convertible.

I guess from outward appearances everything looked fine, but I was constantly tormented by thoughts of alcohol. The mornings weren't too bad but, as the day wore on, the idea of having a drink would begin to haunt me and I'd feel more and more uncomfortable. I found it impossible to mix with people unless I had a few drinks, and I was awkward and tongue-tied in company. I craved the ability to go into places and talk and laugh like anybody else. I'd see my friends heading for the pub after work, laughing and joking with each other. It didn't make any sense. Was I the only person in the world who couldn't have a couple of beers now and again?

There were a few slips, but none of them turned out too bad, and Jean always forgave me. I was experimenting, trying to find a way where I could have a few beers and then go home like most of the other guys. Sometimes I'd go for a week or two and not touch a drop. Other times, I'd try to limit myself to no more than three beers a day, or I'd decide that if I only drank beer, things would be OK. Once I got the idea that if I only drank rum and nothing else, I'd be able to control my intake. That was a complete disaster. Once I managed to go for four weeks without touching a drink. Jean was delighted.

"See," she told me, "you can stop drinking if you really want to. All you needed was a good enough reason. Just have a few now and again, Brian, like anyone else." But she had no idea of the turmoil I was going through, and by that time I had no confidence at all in my ability to stay sober.

I managed to stay off the drink for most of the time that Jean was pregnant, but occasionally, just when she was beginning to trust me again, I'd have a major bust. Nobody was more disgusted than I was the following day. I despised myself for my weakness. I'd swear repeatedly that I'd never get drunk again and yet, within weeks, or sometimes days, I'd find myself pushing that decision to one side, rationalising my behaviour with some feeble excuse and walking into a hotel again.

Kathleen was born one afternoon whilst I was at work. I came home that evening to find Jean gone and an envelope pinned to the door. It had the insignia of the Port Lincoln Hospital stamped on the front and I didn't bother opening it. I rushed back out to the car and then drove up to the hospital like a lunatic, turning up in Jean's room still covered in cement dust and bits of concrete. She was sitting in a bed, propped up on a mass of white pillows, a tiny bundle cradled in her arms. She smiled as I tiptoed in, her big brown eyes bright and alive, a joy and a questioning, a pride and a prayer.

"Your daughter." She lifted the little bundle towards me.

"I can't." I drew back.

"Take her."

"I'm too dirty."

"Brian, it's alright, take her."

As I reached out to hold her, the nurse came rushing in.

"Oh no, Mr. O'Raleigh, look at you, you're filthy!" She was laughing. "Go home and get changed, off you go now, go on!"

"It's only dust," Jean was laughing too, "he's a builder."

I kissed Kathleen as the nurse fussed over her, settling her down in a tiny cot beside the bed. When she straightened up, she wagged a finger in my direction. "Now, don't you dare go near her again, do you hear now, not until you've changed!"

Jean and I sat there for hours, talking and whispering together, marveling at this miracle, until finally, at nine o'clock, it was time to go.

"So, we'll call her Kathleen? You're sure you're happy with that?" I asked.

"Yes, Kathleen's perfect. She looks like you already." I kissed them both goodbye and I left.

It was a clear, starry night and when I left the hospital, I drove up to the top of Winters Hill, got out of the car and looked back down over Port Lincoln. The town lay spread out before me, lights twinkling from a hundred tiny windows. In the moonlight, I could see the dark ocean and across the water, the shadowy mass of Boston Island guarding the entrance to the bay. The night sky was filled with a million tiny stars and, sitting there on the grass, I wondered over the miracle of birth. I felt an enormous sense of gratitude. I was married to the woman I loved. She was my queen and my gypsy. She was everything I could have ever wanted in a woman and now we had a child together. I had no idea why I had been so lucky, but I knew as I gazed out across the dark sea that night that I had indeed been truly blessed.

I sat there for a long time on the hill, unwilling to break the spell and knowing that my life would be different from that moment on. We had a baby, a daughter. We had Kathleen. As I sat there, I swore to the gods that Kathleen would not be brought up the way that I had been. She would never see drunkenness in her home. She would never see her mother struck or shouted at. She would have everything she needed, and most of all, from the very beginning, she would know that she was loved.

It was well after midnight when I left there. The stars were still burning softly in the dark night sky, twinkling and dancing, as if they had all come out to celebrate one of their own coming to earth and to witness the joy she had brought. I thanked them and promised that I would never let them down. Kathleen had come to earth into the right family, at the right place, at the right time.

*   *   *

Despite everything I'd been given that day, and although I swore to God, I would never take another drink, within a month of Kathleen's birth, I came home drunk once again. I was so ashamed of myself that I called in to see a local doctor on the way home from work one afternoon. The receptionist told me that he was fully booked until after Christmas, but after convincing her that I was desperate, she squeezed me in on December 24th, his last appointment for the year.

The doctor was an elderly, white-haired man and he sat there, quietly studying me as I explained my problem, then he tested my blood pressure and checked my eyes and lungs.

"You seem to be in good shape." He was smiling. "Your blood pressure is excellent; you're fit and well. Why would you assume that you have a problem with alcohol?"

"Well, I'm drinking a bit too much, doctor. When I get started, I find it hard to stop, and I spend too much money on booze."

"So, money's the problem, is that it?"

"Well, yes, it's part of the problem. I'm married and we've just had a baby. I've promised my wife a dozen times that I'll stop drinking for good, but it never lasts more than a week or two."

"And she's been nagging you about your drinking?"

"I wouldn't say nagging. She's not happy about it. When she got pregnant, I promised her I'd never touch another drink."

"Perhaps that's the problem. The way you talk, it seems as if it must be either all or nothing. Could it be that you've become obsessed with the idea of stopping drinking?" He was smiling. "You're a young man, you're fit and strong, and you work hard. You tell me you're not missing any work, and you obviously care for your family. Don't be so hard on yourself. It's Christmas, most Australians allow themselves one night out a week with their mates. I think you're taking all this a bit too seriously."

"So, you think I'm OK?"

"I think you're fine. You may need to curb your drinking a little, but don't allow yourself to become obsessive. All things in moderation."

I left there feeling elated. My God, I thought, could it be as simple as that? Had the whole situation been blown out of proportion? If I went out just one night a week, and intentionally had a good night out, I could get it out of my system for the week and then leave it at that. All this talk about drinking had become an obsession. This was the solution. I should have gone to a doctor years ago.

When I explained to Jean what the doctor had suggested, she was not impressed.

"And you told him the truth? You told him how much you drink?"

"Yes, I did. I didn't go through every single detail, but I told him that I drank a bit too much."

"A *bit* too much?" Her eyes flashed. "Is that what you told him? My God, Brian, you drink like a bloody fish!"

"This is exactly what he warned me about, Jean. He told me that all this talk about drinking is actually causing the problem. Look, the guys at work have organizing a party at the Tasman Hotel tonight, some of the wives will be there. We'll go together, that will be my one night out for the week, ok?"

"No, Maxine's coming over later. You go, but make sure you're back early. We're going to your brothers place tomorrow for Christmas dinner."

I felt more relaxed heading for the pub that evening than I had in a long time. I parked the car outside the Tasman Hotel and strode inside. It was a relief to know I wouldn't have to keep looking up at the clock all night, worrying about Jean. She'd be happy visiting with Max, and I'd promised her I'd be home before midnight. This was much more civilized, and I wondered why we hadn't thought of it before.

The evening started off well. Some of my mates and their wives were there as I arrived, chatting, telling jokes and laughing. They were a great bunch. When I glanced at my watch a little later, it was 9.00 pm. I could go home now if I wanted to, I thought. I could finish this beer, say goodnight to the guys and go straight home. Jean would be surprised. The doctor was right, once the pressure's off, there's no need to drink. It was all the talk about stopping drinking that was causing the trouble. I felt so good, I ordered a round of double whiskies.

The next time I looked at my watch, it was 10.30. Better get home soon, I thought, just another few …

*   *   *

I came to in the early hours of the next morning, sitting in the front seat of my car, feeling as if I had been punched unconscious. There was a vile taste in my mouth, my head was throbbing, and there was a sharp pain in the center of my chest. As I grappled to the surface, trying to grasp where I was, I realized that I'd crashed the car. Directly in front of me, right at the end of the bonnet, loomed the massive concrete structure of one of the town's wheat silos. I craned my neck upwards, but I couldn't see the top of the tower through the windscreen.

Something was wrong, I couldn't move. Then I realized that the driver's seat had shot forward on impact and locked itself in position, leaving me trapped in between the seat and the steering wheel. I fumbled the car door open, struggled free of the wheel, and fell out sideways onto the grass. I lay there for a moment, then sat up and looked around. It was still dark; the street was deserted. There was a large gap in the wooden fence surrounding the area. The car had run off the road and careered through the fence before crashing into the base of the wheat silo.

I checked my watch; it was just after 4.30am. I had no memory of leaving the hotel. The front of my shirt was torn and covered in blood. I took it off, threw it away, then went back to inspect the car. The front bumper was pushed in and there were a few scratches and dents to the bonnet, apart from that it wasn't too badly damaged. I jerked the front seat back into position, climbed in, and turned the key. It started immediately.

When I got back to my place, I tiptoed through the apartment, eased open the bedroom door and peered in. Jean lay asleep on the double bed. Kathleen was in her cot, pulled up close beside her. I stayed there for a while motionless, watching them, and then I closed the door silently and went back out to the lounge room.

A small Christmas tree stood in the corner of the room. There were parcels in coloured wrappings all around. The tree was covered with tinsel, and bits of cotton wool and multi-colored balls hung from its branches. At the very tip, a tiny angel with a silver wand reached upwards.

There were three envelopes arranged together on the floor; *Kathleen, Brian* and *Jean* printed on them in large, golden letters. I sat there for a long time, trying not to think. It was the first time in my life that I realised there was something desperately wrong with me. And it was the first time in my life that I wondered if it might be better for everyone if I just killed myself.

Chapter 21

On the Road Again

Things went down rapidly from there. I was involved in a fight at the local Golden Fleece petrol station one night and the police were called. Bernard was the representative for the Golden Fleece Company on the Eyre Peninsula and the two men I'd assaulted were friends of his. There were no charges laid but Bernard was not impressed.

The same week, he received a summons for non-payment of an account of mine. The summons should have been made out to me, but it was made out to his name by mistake. He was furious and we had quite a row.

Then I lost my job through a drunken brawl and although I found another one immediately, I knew I was on borrowed time in Port Lincoln. Bernard was completely disillusioned with me by then and I felt as if I was being watched all the time. Jean was tired of it all, too. She hated people talking about us, and when I suggested that maybe we should go back to Sydney, she agreed immediately.

I somehow pulled myself together for a while and got a second job working part-time at night. We saved up enough money in three months so that we could start again in Sydney.

A few weeks before we left, we traded in our battered old car for a better model and I felt we were ready to go. This time, when I told Bernard we were leaving, he didn't try to talk me out of it.

"Take care of yourself, Brian." We shook hands, it was awkward.

I got the car serviced, we bought maps and I tried to put a positive spin on things. But Jean wasn't happy, she knew I was out of control.

"It'll be a new start for us. Sydney will be better this time. We've got a good car and we've got enough money to get a nice apartment."

We left Port Lincoln March 21st. We'd said our goodbyes the day before and we set off that morning just after dawn.

Jean cheered up a little once we were underway. Kathleen was over a year old by then and she played happily in the back seat of the car in a space we'd made for her from pillows and suitcases. By lunchtime that first day, we'd covered almost two hundred miles and we were both starting to feel better. We were on the road again. After lunch, I began to be concerned about the car. Every time we dropped down to fifty or sixty miles an hour, the steering wheel began to vibrate. I had no idea what was wrong but when we pulled into the petrol station of the nearest small town, the attendant pointed to the car.

"Have a look at your front tires, mate. They're completely bald! Look, you can see the canvas on both of them!"

I was shocked. They'd been in reasonable condition when we set off. I told him about the vibration in the steering wheel and he put the car up on the hoist. A few minutes later, he emerged, shaking his head.

"It's your steering rods, they're stuffed. That's what's done it. You've scrubbed out both your front tires. You're lucky you stopped. You were headed for a blow out, for sure. It'll cost you a bit to get your steering rod's fixed, mate, they're not cheap."

We were trapped there in the local motel for days while we waited for parts from Adelaide. After inspecting the back tires, the mechanic told me that he had four good second-hand tires with plenty of tread that he would sell to us cheap. I told him to put them on.

When we left that service station five days later, a third of our savings had been spent on repairs and hotel bills. Now we had to get to Sydney quickly. After that, the trip turned into a nightmare. Everything that could go wrong went wrong. One of the new tires fell apart two hundred miles further on, the rubber stripping away from the front wheel in great chunks, leaving us to limp into the nearest town on completely bald, yellow canvas. The local dealer shook his head.

"Those tires are ten years old if they're a day. The rubber's perished. He must have had them out in the sun for years."

"But they looked fine."

"Sure, they looked fine, but you see what happened when they got hot? They just fell apart. You're lucky to be alive, all of you. Your back tires are the same." We bought four brand new tires and moved on.

The following day, the carburetor failed, and we spent another three nights in a motel, hoping that they would fix it at a reasonable cost. After that, we were both nervous wrecks, listening to every creak from the engine and jumping at every stone that rattled against the underside of the car.

By the time we arrived in Sydney, we were exhausted, and most of our savings were gone. Jean was worried sick, and I was just waiting to see what else could go wrong. Then, as we were pulling away from traffic lights a few miles from our destination, there was a loud clunk and the car slowed to a halt. The engine was still running but there was no movement. I had no idea what had happened. Directly across the road was a garage. I went over and brought a mechanic back to the stalled vehicle. After a quick inspection and a few questions, he made his decision.

"Your back axle's broken, you're not going anywhere in that car."

"Can it be fixed?" I asked.

"Anything can be fixed, mate. All it takes is time and money."

"How long will it take? We've got all our gear in there."

"A week, maybe more, depends on parts."

"OK," I told him, "fix it as quickly as you can. I'll need it for work."

He nodded.

"You'll have to leave some money to cover the cost of the parts."

"I don't have any cash with me," I told him. "Go ahead with the repairs, I'll be back during the week."

He shook his head.

"I'm sorry, mate, I can't touch it until you pay for the parts. You've got South Australian plates. I've been caught before."

We pushed the car into the driveway, and they called us a cab. Kathleen was crying and Jean was exhausted. We loaded everything we could into the taxi and headed for Bondi. A local real estate agent showed us three flats. We took the cheapest, a one-bedroom dump with a dingy bathroom and a kitchen that hadn't been cleaned in years.

Jean was furious.

"Do you really expect us to live here?" she demanded.

"Jean, it's a place to live. I can make money here quickly, you know that. I'm going to phone Johnny Wilson tonight. He'll give me a job."

"Johnny Wilson?" She was horrified. "You swore you'd never work for him again!"

"Jean, we need the money! There's no choice. I can make good money with Wilson from day one. We'll be out of this dump in just a few weeks. Trust me, as soon as we get enough money together, we'll get a decent place and I'll find a better job. OK?"

"Promise me you won't drink while you're with them. Promise me that much at least." She was pleading. "Promise me! Go on say it, promise me."

"I promise I'll never get drunk, OK?"

"I didn't say that!" she flared up, "I said promise me you won't *drink*!"

"I promise I won't drink, OK? Is that what you want, are you happy now?"

"Make sure you stick by it. I'm not going to have my daughter living in a hovel." She put her face in her hands and suddenly, she was sobbing.

I felt absolutely worthless.

"Jean, I'm doing the best I can. How could I know we'd have to spend all our money on the car? You can't blame me for that. Look, things are bad, but they're not going to stay that way. I'll start work tomorrow; we can be out of here within two or three weeks."

"There's something else." She wasn't looking at me.

"What?" I said, "What is it?"

"It's nothing." She was trying to compose herself. "We'll talk about it later."

"What is it? Is it the money?"

"Yes, the money." She was wiping her eyes.

"It's going to be OK. We've had some bad luck but we're here now. I'll be working tomorrow. We'll get a nice place as soon as I get paid. I'll stop drinking, I promise, everything's going to be OK."

She'd turned away, and when she spoke again, her voice had changed. "Brian ... Irene and Beala are coming back to Sydney." She paused. "They want me to go and live with them."

"Live with Irene," I said, "you mean, leave me?"

"Yes, I don't trust you anymore."

"Don't say that. I swear to God, I won't have another drink until we're living in a decent place. I promise you. Trust me honey, one last time. Give me a chance to prove it to you, please."

I talked to her for ages, and finally she relented.

"This is your last chance, Brian. If you come home drunk one more time, I'm leaving."

After she'd gone to sleep, I walked up the road, phoned Johnny Wilson and arranged to meet him at the Shakespeare Hotel the following day.

"Brian O'Raleigh!" Johnny Wilson greeted me loudly as I walked into the public bar, "I thought you'd be jailed for life by now!" There was a laugh from the group at the bar. "When did you get back?" He looked around. "Does everyone know Brian?" There were a few introductions. "Bob, meet Brian. He's one of the best light salesmen you'll ever meet. Don't try to outdrink this lad, he's got hollow legs. Peter, Brian." I shook hands all around. They all looked the same, plastic smiles and worn- out suits. Wilson was gesturing to the barman. "Give him a schooner, Mick, and set them up again for the lads."

"Not for me thanks, John," I interrupted. "Make mine a mineral water."

"You're not serious." He was frowning.

"Yes, I gave it away."

"How long have you been off it?" He didn't believe me.

"For a while. We have a baby now."

"Congratulations! Jean's a wonderful woman. We should have one to celebrate then. Wet the baby's head!"

"No, seriously, John, I'm off it. I have to get back to work, I need the money."

"You can start today if you want. Same deal, six pounds for every light you sell, seven pounds for a cash sale, OK?"

"What time are you going out?"

"After lunch, same as always."

"I'll come back then."

"Stay for a while." He took hold of my arm. "Don't look so serious, have a game of pool."

"No thanks, mate," I told him, "I've got a few things to do. I'll be back later, see you then."

I escaped out the door. I knew they wouldn't be leaving for another two or three hours and I couldn't afford to stay around for that long.

I sat outside reading a newspaper. When they finally emerged two hours later, they split up into three different teams. Wilson and two of the other salesmen climbed into the car I was in. He was slurring his words by then, and as he fumbled with the ignition, I said, "Do you want me to drive, mate?"

He paused, his hand still holding the key as his head swiveled across to look at me. "Now, now, Brian, don't get all sanctimonious with me, mate. I'm perfectly capable of driving after a few beers, as you well know."

"You're pretty pissed, John." I told him.

"Let's not argue now, you never worried about my driving before." Then, addressing the car in general: "There's nothing worse than a reformed drunk, is there." He started the engine but, as he pulled out from the curb, he misjudged the distance and clipped the bumper bar of the car in front. "See," he was grinning, "see what you made me do?" The guys in the back were still laughing as we swerved away up the street, roaring drunkenly as if it were the funniest thing in the world.

I was feeling angry when I knocked on the first door clutching a demo kit under my arm. I'd sworn I'd never do this type of work again.

"Good evening, madam, I'm from the Australian Consolidated Lighting Company. We're conducting an advertising campaign this evening and we've chosen your suburb as it's considered to be one of the better class areas of Sydney."

The old patter rolled off my tongue as if I'd never been away and thirty minutes later, her hand was hovering over a contract for seven fluorescent lights.

"I should wait for my hubby really," she was nervous.

"What's the point?" I assured her. "I'm sure he respects your judgment. You are the homemaker, after all." This was the closing pitch, if she refused to make a choice the sale was dead. "If he was here, what color do you think he'd choose for the lounge room light, the red or the burgundy?"

"Oh, the burgundy, I think. He likes burgundy."

"Very well then, Burgundy it is, and if he happens to change his mind, I'll replace the light myself at no cost to you. There we are now, just sign there, if you would please."

By the time the car picked me up at 9.00 pm, I'd sold twenty-three lights. I'd made more money in four hours than the average person made in a week.

When we got back to the pub, Wilson was sitting on a bar stool surrounded by his salesmen. They were all well drunk now.

"And how did our newly reformed friend perform tonight?" he said as I approached. "Has he lost his magic touch now that he doesn't drink?"

I tossed the contracts down on the table.

"There's twenty-three sales there, John, half of them are cash."

He became serious immediately, sitting up in his chair to examine the paperwork.

"The deposits?" He looked up. "Where's the money?"

I handed him a roll of notes, and he flicked through the contracts, checking to make sure everything tallied. He looked up.

"There's money missing."

The other guys were watching.

"I've taken my share already."

He blinked slowly, like a drunken owl.

"You're supposed to wait till Friday for your commission,"

"I need the money now. I told you that."

"You have to follow company procedure, the same as everybody else. You know that."

"You're pissed as a parrot, John," I told him. "Is that company procedure?"

He stared at me for a long moment, wondering which way to go.

"You're an arrogant bastard, Brian."

"And you're not?" I felt like knocking him off the stool.

There was a pause. It could have gone either way, but then his face broke into a drunken grin and suddenly it was just like old times.

"Jesus Christ," he said, "what can I do with you? Your first night back and you've broken the fucking record! Your old mate Jimmy Delmedge sold twenty-one lights one-night last year but some of them were cancelled, no deposits. You've done well, mate. Don't worry, I'll be looking after you and Jean. I'm not going to have my top salesman living in a fucking hovel!" He raised his hand. "Barman, get this man a drink, give him a beer and a double whisky."

I hesitated for just a moment, then relented. I had one hundred and fifty pounds in my pocket, and I was the top salesman. Jean would be thrilled. I downed the whisky in one go and picked up the beer.

"What happened to Delmedge?" I asked. "Is he still around?"

"Didn't I tell you? He's off the grog, just like you!" That raised a laugh. "No seriously, he stopped drinking a few months back and he stayed stopped. He's got a steady job somewhere. Aluminum siding on houses, I think, a wage plus commission. He met a woman; she's trying to save his soul or something."

"I don't believe it," I said. "How could Delmedge stop drinking?"

"Well he has, I bumped into him recently. He hasn't touched a drop in months." He reached into his wallet. "That's his card, give him a ring."

When the pub closed, we moved on to the Greek Club in Kings Cross and kept on drinking. At one point I looked up at the clock and realised it was 3 am. For a moment I panicked, but then I thought, I don't need to worry, I've got a pocket full of money and Jean's OK. She'll be fast asleep, and when she wakes up, I'll tell her the good news. After that I recall a big Greek guy, and losing an arm-wrestling match, then challenging him to a drinking competition, and glasses of ouzo lined up on the bar, and then arguing with Wilson about something, but after that I don't recall much, just flashes of colour, dark blue curtains and red bottles on a shelf…

Chapter 22

Leaving

When I came to the following morning I was struck at once by the silence. I looked around, the place was deserted, everything was gone. Jean's clothes, Kathleen's cot, the playpen, everything. I stood up and opened my wallet, it was empty. I sat down at the table, sick with fear. A sheet of notepaper lay on the plastic surface, I picked it up. The scrawled lines confirming my worst fears.

Do not try to contact us
I never want to see you again

The next few hours were a nightmare, desperately trying to piece together fragments from the night before. I could dimly remember the Greek club and drinking ouzo, but after that, nothing. I dressed, went up the road, and phoned Wilson, hoping that he might know something. His secretary was cold and abrupt.

"You're fired, Brian. John ended up in hospital last night. He's considering pressing charges. If you come anywhere near the office, you'll be arrested."

"Barbara hang on, can I talk to him?"

The line went dead. I stood there in despair for some time, then I remembered Jimmy Delmedge's card. When he answered the phone, I explained what had happened and told him what I remembered of the night before.

"That's all I can remember, Jim. I was in a complete blackout. I have no idea at all where Jean is."

He was cautious, unwilling to become involved, but finally, when I told him I was desperate to stop drinking, he asked for my address.

"I'll take you to one of the meetings I go to, OK? If you're serious, they can help you. I'll be there at seven-thirty. Make sure you're sober. If you're not, I won't let you in the car."

He knocked on the door that evening just after seven.

"Christ almighty," he said, looking around the flat, "no wonder she left. This place is a bloody disgrace."

We went off in his car then, heading towards the city, weaving in and out of the traffic as he told me what to expect.

"Try to keep an open mind, alright? You might like it and you might not. That doesn't matter. The only thing that matters is that you stay sober."

"It's not religious, is it?" I was a bit nervous. "I'm an atheist. I don't want any bullshit about God. You're not into that stuff now, are you?"

"What did I just tell you?" He'd always had a short fuse. "I just finished saying, keep an open fucking mind! For Christ's sake, you're in more fucking strife than Robin Hood and you're already picking and choosing how you want to get right! Anyhow, it's not about religion, so just sit there and listen! You either want to get sober or you don't."

By the time we arrived, the meeting was already underway, and a tall blonde woman was explaining that when she drank, she sometimes failed to turn up at concerts where she was supposed to be playing the piano. I sat there puzzled, wondering what on earth that had to do with anything. As she talked, I looked around the room. There were people of all shapes and sizes. Some of them looked pretty-well off but others looked like they'd just crawled out of a gutter somewhere. I had a sudden flash of insight and I leaned across to Delmedge.

"Jim, these people are alcoholics!"

"That's right," he whispered back, "and what the fuck do you think you are? A social drinker?"

I stayed silent after that, but as soon as the last speaker had finished and we got outside, I took his arm, "You don't honestly think you're an alcoholic, do you? Is that why you're coming here?"

"Look, O'Raleigh, I haven't had a drink for seven months. That's the longest I've been sober in my fucking life! You make up your own mind what you are, but don't tell me what I am, OK? Now, if you don't like it here, you can fuck off. But if you want your wife and kid back, I suggest you might want to get to some of these meetings. You don't have to call yourself an alcoholic if you don't want to, but if you're going to stop drinking, you're gonna need help."

I didn't believe he was an alcoholic; he was the best salesman I'd ever met, but it was pointless arguing with him.

When we were back in his car, he turned to me.

"Look, I'm sorry if I was a bit abrupt back there, OK? This is important to me. I'm forty-seven and I've fucked up most of my life with the drink. This could be my last chance."

"That's OK." It was strained. "You can do it, mate, we both can. I'll come to the meetings with you if you want. We'll go together."

There was an awkward silence. Finally, he grunted,

"Where are you going now?"

"Bondi. I've got nowhere else to go."

He was shaking his head.

"Get your things together, you won't stay sober for long in that shit-house. You can stay with me for a few days till you get sorted out. But if you have one drink while you're at my place, you'll find your suitcase on the pavement, understood?"

I moved into his apartment the following morning and spent the rest of the day trying to contact Jean. I phoned Irene several times, but she refused to talk.

"I don't want you phoning here. Give me your number. If Jean wants to talk to you, she'll call you."

"Irene, tell her I'm sorry, and tell her I've stopped drinking."

"Use your head, Brian, leave her alone for a while. Let her get over what happened. If you have stopped drinking, consider her for once. Please don't keep phoning, you're only making things worse for yourself."

Jean called three days later and agreed to see me. We met on a Sunday afternoon in the park by the fountain, directly across the road from the registry office where we'd been married just a few years before. I was waiting on a bench when she came along the pathway through the trees. She was wearing a long flowing summer dress with buttons all the way down the front and she hadn't brought Kathleen. As she approached, I stood up, but she held out her hand.

"Don't touch me, please."

There was a difficult pause and we both just sat there, staring out over the fountain.

"Where's Kathleen?"

"She's with Irene."

"Why didn't you bring her?"

"It would have confused her too much. Besides, how was I to know whether you'd be drunk or not?"

"Jean, I don't know what happened that night, I was in a blackout. I have no recollection of anything. Do you believe me?"

"It doesn't matter what I believe. I don't want to talk about it, it's degrading."

"I know, but it'll never happen again. I've stopped drinking, I haven't had a drink since that night."

She flashed me a quick look.

"It's a bit late for that. I've believed you too many times before. I'm not going to come back to you. It's over. I've made up my mind."

"Look, I don't expect you to believe me yet, but I have stopped drinking. I'm living at Delmedge's place ..."

"Delmedge!" she burst out. "And you're trying to tell me that you're sober!"

"Jim's sober, Jean, he hasn't had a drink for over seven months. Honest to God, you wouldn't know him. He's got a lovely flat near the harbor. He's living with a woman there. She's a doctor, his whole life has changed."

She held up her hand again.

"Look, let's get something straight. I'm not the slightest bit interested in any of your drunken friends, OK? And I couldn't care less how long it is since Jimmy Delmedge or any of the rest of them had a drink. I don't have conversations like this anymore. I mix with normal people now. We have dinner every evening and the police never come around. Do you understand? I'm not interested in talking about a bunch of drunks." She was glaring out across the park. "When I think of how we've been living for the last few years, it makes me really mad. And after what happened the other night, how could I ever trust you again?"

We both fell silent then and I sat there, not knowing what to say. She was right; there was no point in arguing.

"So why did you come here then?" I said.

"Two things, I didn't want you coming to Irene's place, and I need you to sign some forms."

She dug into her handbag for a moment, then thrust some papers at me.

"If you want to do something decent for once in your life, you'll sign these."

"What are they?" I was glancing through them. "Immigration papers?"

"They're for my passport."

"Why should I have to sign them?" Then I saw Kathleen's name and I understood. "You're going back to England?"

"Yes, I'm going back to my family."

The words hit me hard, shredding whatever hope there was left.

"You can't take Kathy away from me, Jean. You can't do that."

She turned on me.

"Take her from you! Listen to what you're saying! You're out almost every night of the week drinking, and you think I'm taking her from you? You're living in a fantasy world. You're a drunk. You've destroyed everything we ever had, but I will not allow you to destroy my daughter."

"Our daughter, she's my daughter too, you know."

"Wrong, Brian, she's my daughter. You deserted her a long time ago."

We both fell silent, and I sat there, sickened. Was this how it was all going to end?

"Jean, listen to me, please, just for a few minutes." I was trying to hold on to my emotions. "You're right, I've made a mess of everything. And you're right, maybe it is too late." I felt an absolute despair as I said the words. "But if I can prove to you that it's different this time, if you see it with your own eyes, if I stay sober for six months and get a proper job, would there be any hope then?" The question hung there forever. I couldn't look at her. "If you see that I'm genuine this time, if I get you a really nice place to live. You can't take Kathleen away from me, with you both gone ..." My voice choked off. I couldn't continue.

We sat there for ages, each of us struggling with our own demons. Finally, after an age, she spoke again. "I'm leaving in two months. I need you to sign those forms. We've already booked the boat, but …"

"Jean!" I burst in, but she held up her hand again.

"Wait!" She was trying to get something out. "Listen to what I'm saying! If you have stopped drinking, *if you have*, and if you are going to stay stopped this time." She paused again, not sure of whether to go on. "If you come to London, get your act together, stay sober for at least six months, get a proper job and a decent place to live. *If you can do all of those things,* I'll consider getting back together." I felt a sickening despair as she spoke but then I realized there was hope there too. It was something, a thin reed, a possibility. She went on. "But you must sign those papers. If you don't, I'll go to court and get custody of Kathleen immediately. It won't be hard, not with your track record." I don't know how long we sat there in silence but when she spoke again, her voice was quieter.

"There's something else."

"What?"

She wasn't looking at me, her gaze directed across the park and into the trees.

"What?" I said again, "what else?"

She turned to meet my eyes.

"I'm pregnant."

"Oh, Christ, Jean!" I was stunned. "Why didn't you tell me! You can't leave now!"

"God, you're so stupid sometimes. I *have* to leave now!" And suddenly she was crying. "I can't trust you anymore, don't you understand? You've broken every single promise you ever made! I can't risk Kathleen with you, you're totally irresponsible! I'm pregnant, I have to go! I have no choice."

I sat there feeling utterly degraded. She was right, I knew that. I'd broken every single promise, how could I expect her to trust me?

"Can I see Kathleen before you go?" I could hardly get the words out.

"You'll sign the papers?" she asked. "If you don't, I'll go to a lawyer on Monday morning and you'll never see either of us again." She was staring at me. "Well, what's it to be, will you sign them or not?"

"Yes." I sat there, absolutely defeated. "Can I see her?"

She scribbled an address on a card.

"Irene and Beala are going away next weekend. Come over to the flat on Saturday morning after ten." She paused. "If I even suspect you've had a drink, I won't open the door. Bring the papers with you. You'll need a JP to witness your signature."

*   *   *

Two months later, I stood by the ship's side at Circular Quay. Jean had her arm around me, there with tears in her eyes. We'd spent the last few nights together, making love and talking of the future.

"You're a different man when you don't drink," she'd whispered,

Lying there with Jean in my arms, Kathleen asleep in her little bed, I knew that I'd been given yet another chance.

"Jean, you don't have to leave now. You know it's going to be alright. I haven't had a drink in over two months. I don't even want to drink. Why don't you stay?"

"I can't, Brian, you know that. I'm pregnant. I can't take that risk. We'll start afresh in England. We've been through all this. Please, don't spoil our last night."

She was right. It was just fear. I had to prove that I could, to myself as well as to her.

But there were things that I hadn't told her. Jimmy had come home drunk three days before. There'd been a terrible row and his girlfriend had moved out. He was driving us to the boat the following day. I couldn't let her know that he was drinking.

The following morning, my stomach was in a knot from the moment I woke up. Nothing seemed real. Jean kept herself busy, packing and unpacking her cases, handing me things for me to keep and chatting on and on about nothing, trying to avoid the tears.

Delmedge turned up on time. He didn't look too bad, but he was jumpy and I could tell he was hung over. Jean was so upset she didn't realize anything was wrong, and he drove us down to the quayside without incident.

Jim said goodbye to Jean and then he left us there alone. Suddenly, there was nothing to say.

"I'll be back soon, Jean. I'll send you money every week."

She'd buried her face in my shoulder and I could feel her sobbing.

"If you're coming on board sir, you need to board now," an official was indicating. I walked up the gangplank with them and watched as he examined the tickets. "I'm sorry sir, you can't come on board."

I held Kathleen then for a long time, trying not to let her see my tears.

"It's for the best," Jean was whispering, "you'll be home in no time."

Then we kissed, and they were gone. I walked back down the gangplank, turned and looked back. Kathleen was standing motionless, watching me from between the ship's railings. Jean was standing behind her, trying to smile.

A few minutes later, the ropes were cast off and the tugs began pulling the ship away from the wharf. Jean had picked Kathleen up and they were both waving to me. A few minutes later, there was a blast from the siren and the ship began to move forward steadily, out into the deeper waters, heading for the ocean.

I felt absolutely worthless. My pregnant wife and my baby daughter were sailing away to the other side of the world because of my drunkenness.

"Well, how are you feeling now, eh?" Delmedge was standing next to me. "It happened to me too, you know. Two of my wives pissed off." He was a bastard when he drank. "Well, what are you going to do? You can't stand there weeping all day, man! I'm going for a drink. I'll see you over there."

I stood there, watching the ship until it disappeared around the curve in the harbor, then I followed him across the road into the Orient Hotel. The barman was pouring Delmedge a whisky as I walked in.

"Buy your own drink, O'Raleigh," he snapped. "You're not going to blame me for getting you back on the piss."

I never did blame him, I ordered and paid for it myself.

*   *   *

I came to the next morning, just on dawn. Hot, hung over, sick and sorry and lying across the front seats of Delmedge's Mini Minor. Something was licking at my face and I could hardly breathe. I sat up, confused, and as I did, I became aware of a terrible stench. The interior of the car was like a garbage tip. Open jars of jam and pickles had been tipped out on to the seats. Pieces of bread and half-eaten meat were scattered everywhere, and a large slab of butter was melting on the dashboard. Above all, there was an overwhelming stench.

I dimly remembered stealing Delmedge's car with the idea of driving it to Melbourne and stowing away on the boat with Jean … and I vaguely recalled emptying out a fridge somewhere, but I had no idea where.

There was a movement by my side. A large white dog was pushing its way between the front seats. It was distressed and had been licking my face, trying to get my attention. Brown lumps clung to its coat and I realized that it must have defecated the previous night in the back seat. As I opened the door, the dog jumped out and, without a backward glance, took off up the road. I had no idea at all where I was, so I staggered away from the car and along the empty streets until I found a taxi. When I got back to Delmedge's place, my suitcase was already lying on the narrow strip of grass outside his front door.

Chapter 23

The Nakuta

The marriage had lasted five short years, swept away in a torrent of alcoholism and broken promises. Jean was four months pregnant when she left and in the months that followed, I tried everything I knew how to stop drinking, desperate to rejoin her and Kathleen.

When willpower failed, I went to see doctors, psychologists and even a hypnotherapist. I tried one drinking program after another, but nothing worked. As the months wore on, I became more and more depressed and by the time my daughter, Sharon, was born, I was in despair.

I had a drink with a seaman one night who told me I might be able to work a passage back home and for weeks after, I roamed Sydney's waterfront, inquiring on every ship I could get aboard.

I met Jack Ryan in a waterfront pub. He was the chief cook on the *Nakuta,* a small cargo vessel running between New Zealand and Australia. After the hotel closed that night, we went on board for a few more drinks and then, in a drunken inspiration, I decided to stow away. After saying my goodbyes to Jack, I wandered around the ship until I found a place to hide. The laundry wasn't the wisest choice, but I was drunk, so I buried myself in the dirty sheets on the floor and passed out.

I woke up hours later, wondering where I was, and peered out the door. The corridor was empty, so I climbed up the steel ladder and wandered around on deck. There was no sign of Australia; the *Nakuta* surging and rolling gently as she ploughed her way eastward under a starry sky. It was 3.00 am. I returned to my hiding place and spent the rest of the night sleeping fitfully as the boat steamed her way steadily across the Southern Ocean.

Next morning, in the cold light of dawn, I wasn't so sure how sound my plan had been. It would take days to get to New Zealand and I needed to eat. After deliberating for some time, I went back to Jack's cabin and knocked quietly. There was no answer. I tried again. A man stuck his head out of a cabin across the hallway then disappeared just as quickly without a word being said. I opened Jack's door, went across to the figure snoring in the bunk and shook him awake. He came to, hung over and confused.

"We didn't sail?" he asked, blurry-eyed.

"Yes, we sailed."

"So what the fuck are you doing on board?" He was wide awake now.

"I fell asleep in the laundry," I told him. "I didn't wake up till now."

He swung his legs over the side of the bunk.

"Christ almighty, that's my job fucked! If they catch you in here, I'm gone!" He thought for a moment. "Has anyone seen you on board?"

"I saw a guy in the corridor. He came out of the room across from you."

"Fuck!" Jack was despairing. "That'd be the steward. He's a poofter, he'll give me up for sure!"

"Look, I'll go up and see the captain and explain what happened. I'll tell him I was drunk and fell asleep. That's the truth anyhow."

"OK, it's worth a try but don't mention my name, whatever you do. This is the best job on the coast, I can't afford to lose it."

I left him sitting there and walked out onto the deck. The *Nakuta* was rolling along gracefully to an easterly swell, ploughing her way steadily through moderate blue seas. I stood on the foredeck for a while, staring at the ocean and getting my story together, then I walked toward the bridge deck. As I clambered up the ladder, the heel of my right shoe jammed in one of the steel rungs. I tugged at it unsuccessfully then bent down and jerked at it hard. The heel tore off flush with the sole. Christ, that's all I needed. Now I was hobbling. After a moment's thought, I jammed the other shoe in the same hole and tore the heel off that one too. At least I was even now.

I was jittery and nervous from the hangover and I lost courage outside the bridge deck. I went back down the ladder to reconsider my position. There were warrants out for my arrest in various parts of Australia. They were for minor things like unpaid fines and an assault charge I'd been dodging for months. I searched through my wallet. I'd blown all my money the night before so I tossed it over the side, along with any papers that could identify me. As I sat there pondering my next move, a burly seaman in a white apron came bursting out of a doorway nearby. I watched as he strode to the ship's rail and hurled a bucket of scraps over the side to the seabirds shrieking and wheeling around him. He smiled at me on the way back in.

"Good morning sir, lovely morning."

He disappeared through the hatchway. Moments later he was back again. "Could I offer ye a cup of coffee?" He had a pirate's face and a broad Scottish accent.

"Thanks."

"In you come! Welcome to Jock's on the Rocks Blue Water Café!" He was grinning. "Will ye be having some breakfast wi' us as well? We're the only decent restaurant for miles."

I couldn't help laughing.

"Don't call me sir, please. My name's Brian."

"Well then, Brian, what's it te' be? Ye' cen have bacon, sausages, eggs, any fucken' way up or doon, toast, jam, you fucken name it and Jock will be fucken' delighted to cook it up for ye. It's noo off'en we have a gentleman on board."

He clattered around the galley talking incessantly as I just sat there, pondering what to do.

Minutes later, he handed me a plate loaded with food.

"So what brings you on board sir, or Brian, or Sir Brian, if you like?"

"I got drunk last night and I woke up in the laundry here this morning."

"Oh, Jesus Christ almighty ..." He banged a saucepan down on the stove. "... you're a fucken' stowaway, and here's me treating you like a lord's bastard! Jesus Christ, McLeod won't be too happy wi' yee! He's the skipper. He's a Scot too, so he's a fucken' mad bastard, but he's better than most of them. Look laddie, eat your breakfast, you're gonna need it. Go on, eat it up while we decide what's best for ye."

He fussed around the kitchen as I ate, throwing questions at me now and again.

"Are you in any trouble wi' the law in Aussie?"

"There's a couple of warrants out for me in New South Wales, nothing serious."

"Nothing we canna handle?"

"No, minor things, fines and an assault charge."

"On the police?"

"No, a publican."

"Ah, dinna worry aboot tha' laddie, they'll probably gi' ye' a gold medal for that one. So you're pretty clean?"

"Yes."

"Alright then. When you're done here, go up above to the bridge and talk to the skipper. Tell him you don't know how ye got on board and ask him te' turn the ship aroond and take you back. Dinna' take any shit from him. He's no gonna turn her aroond noo but he may think you're genuine."

After breakfast, I climbed the stairs again and walked through a steel door into the bridge. The whole of the forward side of the room was made up of windows looking down along the full length of the *Nakuta*. There were two men in there. The one sitting at a desk was wearing a peaked cap and a black uniform. The other was standing by a steering wheel, staring out over the ocean.

The man behind the desk stood up abruptly as I entered and walked across to shake my hand.

"Good morning sir. John Reynolds, Second Officer."

"Good morning."

"Lovely day, sir."

"Yes, indeed."

We stood there, side by side, staring out across the wide blue ocean. I was wondering how to start the conversation, but he eventually broke the silence.

"Have you had breakfast yet, sir?"

"No, not yet."

I was weakening.

"Follow me, if you would."

He led me back down to the galley.

"Jock, look after Mr. er …"

"O'Raleigh."

"Yes, look after Mr. O'Raleigh, would you, cook? Nice breakfast and all that!" Then he was gone with a nod and a smile.

"Well!" Jock was standing there with a grin on his pirate's face. "What would Sir Brian Baroo like this time, besides a jug a'whisky, that is?" We both burst out laughing; it was ridiculous. "Would I be correct in assumin' oor little secret is still intact, laddie?"

"Yes."

"Ah well, they'll wake up sooner or later."

He made me another coffee and after we'd talked for a while longer, he opened the door. "Look, ye might as well get it over wi', Brian, off you go now."

Reynolds was smiling as I walked back onto the bridge.

"Enjoy your breakfast, sir?"

"Yes, thanks, it was fine."

We stood there again, side by side, silently gazing out over the ocean until finally I mustered up enough courage.

"Where's the ship going to?"

"New Plymouth, sir."

"And when do you expect we'll arrive?"

"Tuesday morning, if everything goes alright."

There was a long pause; I could almost hear his brain cranking over.

"Friend of the Captain's?" He was still smiling.

"No."

He turned toward me.

"You're with us as a passenger?"

"No."

The smile had disappeared.

"Could I ask you what you're doing on board?"

"I have no idea. The last I remember; I was drinking at the Bell's Hotel. I woke up in the laundry here this morning."

He spun around immediately.

"Coombs get this man off the bridge. Escort him down below to the galley. Jock's to keep an eye on him until the skipper calls him up. Is that clear?" He turned back to me. "You're a stowaway. Consider yourself under arrest. Do what you're told and you'll be treated fairly. Now, get off the bridge before the old man turns up. He'll make mincemeat of you if you're here when he arrives."

Coombs took me down below in disgrace and charged Jock with my safety. An hour later, I was called up to the captain's cabin.

Coombs led me into the dark wood-paneled room as if we were entering the gates of hell.

"This is the stowaway …" he began.

"Get out."

The skipper was a short, thickset, red-haired Scot. He sat behind a heavy wooden desk, looking like a time bomb about to explode.

"Your name?"

I'd decided against lying. Jock had said it would only confuse things further. "Brian O'Raleigh."

"What are you doing on board my ship?"

"I have no idea. The last I remember; I was drinking on the waterfront."

"You don't look like a drunk." He was studying me intently, trying to decipher the story.

"No, I'm not, I'm a married man with two children." It sounded pathetic. "I want you to turn the ship around and take me back to Sydney."

"Do ye now?" He fell silent, assessing me. "Who did ye come on board wi'?"

"I don't know."

"You came on board with the chief cook, Jack Ryan."

"I don't know."

"You were seen leaving his cabin this morning."

"I didn't know where I was. I went around banging on doors when I woke up. Look, all I want to do is get back home to Sydney."

He questioned me for a while longer but finally, he seemed satisfied. "You're headed for New Zealand, like it or not. What happens to ye from there on is up to the police." He pressed a button and Coombs reappeared. "Give him the guest cabin. He's free during daylight hours. Lock him up at night. Now get out, both of you."

*   *   *

That night as the *Nakuta* sailed on, I lay in my bunk wondering what was going to happen to Jean and the girls. I knew that my drinking was completely out of control and I doubted now whether I would I ever be able to stay sober. I had so much to lose and so little to gain and yet I just couldn't seem to stop drinking. The pattern was always the same. The day or so after a bender, I'd feel sick and disgusted with myself. I'd be full of shame, guilt and remorse and I'd curse myself for being a weakling. The second day, I'd be convinced that I'd learnt my lesson and that would bring a little hope. I wouldn't have even considered touching a drink when I was like that. The smell alone would have been enough to put me off. On the third day, I'd be feeling better physically. The shakes would have stopped, and my appetite would have returned. At that stage, I would make a decision that I would never drink again. That always felt good. The decision felt a little shaky though and I'd decide to follow it up with some sort of plan. Maybe if I exercised this week instead of drinking. Or, I'll go to the movies or maybe begin some sort of educational course. On the fourth day, I'd be feeling jumpy and ill at ease with myself, uncomfortable talking to people at work and uneasy in social situations. Soon after that, I'd begin wondering if I was exaggerating the whole thing. At least when I drank, I could mix with people and relax. Maybe it wasn't as bad as I was making out. Before long, I'd begin to feel envious of people who could have a few drinks and I'd begin to wonder if I was supposed to spend the rest of my life feeling nervous and uptight. Would I never be able to have a few drinks? What about my social life? What about meeting new friends? Was that all finished?

Day five, the demons would begin to nag. Why can't I have a few drinks, for Christ's sake? Everybody else is drinking. What am I supposed to do? Be a fucking hermit for the rest of my life? I'd see other people laughing and chatting through a hotel window and I'd feel like a leper. What's going on? Am I the only alien on the planet?

I'd begin to get angry with myself, then I'd become jumpy. The idea of having just a few quick drinks would start tugging at my brain. Just have a few, for Christ's sake, just a few. Maybe even half a dozen but no more, just enough so you'll feel alright. What's wrong with that? Have a few with your mates, have a good meal and then get an early night. Just break the pattern, you can do it. Willpower, that's all it takes.

But then, the other side would start. You can't drink, you know that. You're hopeless when you drink. Once you start, you can't stop! Sometimes I'd argue like this for a day or two, the madness getting worse by the minute, filling my waking thoughts with a desire to try it just one more time.

Sometimes I'd say, "No, definitely not!" but then, still convinced that I'd meant it, I'd walk straight into the nearest pub and without a second thought, stride over to the bar and order a beer. As I stood there at the bar waiting for the drink, the voices would come up in me again: "What are you doing? You swore you were off it, remember?" But the answer was even quicker, "Fuck off! I'm having two or three beers, OK? Fuck off! Let me enjoy that much, at least."

Within just a few minutes, I'd feel the change, coming up from way down below. A confidence, a courage, an ease and a pleasure, and the next thought would be, that's it! That's just what I needed. Just a few more and I'll feel OK, I'll feel human again.

An hour and six or eight drinks later, the voice of reason would give it one last, feeble try. "You've had your few drinks. Shouldn't you be going home now?"

But then a darker voice would intrude.

"Who has the right to tell you how many drinks you can have? Fuck off, OK? Leave me alone."

And that was it. After that, it was on. After that, anything could happen. Dr. Jeckyll had left the room, Mr. Hyde had arrived.

.

*   *   *

When we arrived in New Zealand, the police were waiting for me on the wharf. I shook hands with the captain and thanked him, then they handcuffed me and led me down the gangplank.

The following day, I appeared in court, charged with illegal entry. The judge sentenced me to three months in jail but ordered that I was to be deported as soon as possible. I spent the night in the lock-up at New Plymouth and the following day, they drove me to Auckland Airport where I was escorted on board an aircraft then flown first class back to Sydney. The Australian Police were supposed to pick me up on arrival but, since I had no luggage, I just walked straight through the Customs area without stopping and off out into the street.

I decided to leave Sydney after that and, in a stroke of luck, I was offered a job on a dry drilling rig, way out in the bush. No alcohol allowed on site and three hundred miles from the nearest pub. I worked that rig every day for three months without a break, and by the time the job was completed, I'd saved enough money for my fare back to the UK.

Chapter 24

England

The first thing you see of Blackpool, coming in by road, is the Blackpool Tower, a pale, plagiaristic, inelegant imitation of the Eiffel Tower, looming up over the distant rooftops like a warning to unwary travelers. I'd hitchhiked from London and my last lift was with a Yorkshireman, bound for the Lake District on business. When he dropped me off on the outskirts of Blackpool, I went over to a phone booth, leafed through the directory and, wondering what sort of reception I would get, I dialed my sister's number.

"Hello, Mary speaking."

"It's Brian, Mary, how are you doing?"

"Brian … Brian who?"

"Brian, Mary. Brian O'Raleigh."

"Brian's in Australia. Who is this?"

"It's Brian, Mary. I'm back."

"Oh god, it's Brian!" she said loudly, "It is you! Oh Brian love, where are you? We all thought you were dead. Where are you, love?"

"I just got back. I'm up on the main drag near the turn off to the M1. There's a pub right across the road from the phone box."

"I know where you are. I'll pick you up straight away. Now don't you dare move, alright? I'm coming to get you right now."

Fifteen minutes later, a car pulled off the highway, horn honking and lights flashing.

"Oh, Brian, we had no idea where you were, you silly bugger!" She was almost in tears. "Why didn't you write? I didn't believe it was you; your voice has changed so much. I thought it was some bloody Aussie, pulling my leg."

As soon as I closed the door, she took off at speed.

"Where are we headed?"

"I'm taking you straight to mum's place. You can stay there for a week or two till you get sorted. She moved, you know, we rented the hotel out. She's trying to sell the place. Didn't you know?"

"No, I had no idea. How's Peter?"

"Peter's in Birmingham luv, he's still at Uni. Where were you? Why didn't you write? We didn't know if you were dead or alive; we were worried sick about you."

Mary had phoned to let mum know I was back and, as we pulled up outside her place, I caught a glimpse of her at a window, holding the white lace curtain slightly to one side, a concerned look on her face. I hadn't written to her for years. The front door opened as we approached and there she was.

"So, the wanderer returns!" she greeted me. "God almighty, we thought you were dead and gone. Why in God's name didn't you write?"

"It's a long story, mum."

"I'll bet it is." She kissed me on the cheek and then held me out at arm's length. "You're the image of your father, God rest his soul. Does Jean know you're back?"

"Let him in the house, mum!" Mary was pushing past her. "Come in love, I'll make you some tea." She was upset and trying to hide it.

Mum led me into the lounge room and then turned around.

"Let me have a look at you. Put that case down over there. There we are. You look grand." She was looking at my suitcase. "Where's the rest of your luggage, in the car?"

"No, mum."

"It's coming on after you?"

"No, that's it mum, just the one suitcase."

"You're travelling very light, m'boy." She was never short on humor. "And I suppose you're full tilt into the drink and drugs by now, eh? Jean said she never knew you sober."

"It wasn't that bad. I've never touched drugs. I drink a bit."

"Um," she said, "that would be the Irish 'bit' I'm sure! Do you have any money to your name?"

"No."

"God forgive you." She was shaking her head. "Eight years in the land of milk and honey and you come back home with one suitcase and no money. Ah, what are we going to do with you?"

Mary had reappeared with a tray.

"Leave him alone, Chris, for god's sake, he's tired. You didn't know if he was dead or alive an hour ago and you're nagging him already."

"Ah, pay no attention to me, sure it's grand to have you home again in one piece. We can thank God for that much at least. Sit down there now and I'll pour you a cup of tea."

We sat there for a while, talking and catching up on news. The Alexandra Hotel had been leased out for two years and was now up for sale.

"You know that Jean divorced you now, don't you?"

"No, I didn't know that."

"Oh yes, it would be well over a year now. The poor woman had no choice. Sure Jaysus, nobody knew if you were you dead or alive! What in God's name happened to you?"

"I don't want to talk about it, not yet. I want to get settled in. I'll call Jean later."

"Leave him alone, Chris," Mary stepped in again, "can't you see he's tired?" She turned to me, "Come on love, I'll take you up to your room."

.

That evening, I took a stroll around to the South Shore Hotel. A lot of the old faces were still there, drinking beer and playing snooker. I didn't stay for too long. The place felt alien to me. I'd travelled too far, and I'd seen too much. I was a foreigner there and they knew it. I didn't bother saying any goodbyes. I just slipped out the door, crossed the road and then walked along the promenade, remembering my childhood and the *Kathleen R.*

*   *   *

The following day, I phoned Jean. When she heard my voice, there was a momentary silence, then she came back, cold and hard.

"So, you're back."

"Yes, I arrived two days ago. I'm coming up to London in a day or so. I want to see you."

"We thought you were dead."

"No."

There was a pause and then she said, "I can't talk now. Call me when you get to London, but I don't want you anywhere near the house."

*   *   *

Two days later, I stood outside a café in Orpington and watched as a small red car pulled into the parking lot. Jean stepped out and hurried across.

"We'll go inside." She walked past me without touching and chose a table at the rear of the café. As soon as we were seated, she glared across at me. "Well," she demanded, "what do you want? What have you come back for?" She was angry. "We thought you were dead. Does your mother know you're alive? You're the most self-centred bastard I've ever met in my life! Why didn't you write? Come on then! Couldn't you even have sent a postcard?"

"I'm sorry …" I began.

"Oh nonsense, I'm sorry! What does that mean? You have two children. I didn't know what to tell them. They think their dad's a sailor! Sailing around the world all the time! What do you want anyhow? Why have you come back? Why didn't you just stay dead? That would have been better for everyone."

I didn't say anything. There was no point.

"Well," she demanded again, "why did you come back?"

"We're divorced?"

"Yes, we're divorced! You disappeared, remember? What did you expect? Did you think I was going to spend the rest of my life waiting for you? You didn't really think you were going to come back here and just start up again, did you? Even you couldn't be that stupid!"

"How are the children?"

"You stay away from my children. I don't want you anywhere near them. Where were you? Were you in jail or something?"

"I've been drinking, Jean."

"Oh, is that it? I've been drinking! Not much of an excuse, is it?"

"No, it's not."

We sat there for a while then, just staring out the window. Then she turned to me again. "I don't want you hanging around here, OK? I don't want to see you again."

"You've met somebody else?" I said.

"That's none of your business."

"I want to see the children," I told her.

"Well you can't. You should have thought about that two years ago when you were carousing around Australia, having a good time. It's too late. They don't know you and they don't want to know you."

She was glaring out the window as she spoke, refusing to look at me, there were dark shadows under her eyes.

"You don't look well. You're not sick, are you?"

She paused for a long while and then turned to look at me.

"Ron's dead, he was killed in a car crash last week." The sentence shocked me. I'd never met her brother, but I knew how close they'd been. She was staring at me now, stony eyed. "The wrong people die, Brian; people like you should die like that."

The words struck me like a blow, crippling me inside. I couldn't meet her eye after that, and I knew that I had to get away from there.

"I'm sorry, I had no idea."

"You've never had any idea, never."

"Look, this is no good for either of us." I stood up. "I'm leaving, but I do want to see the children. I'll call you next week."

As I turned to walk away, she said,

"You're not wanted here, Brian. I divorced you two years ago. Stay away and don't try to contact the children. I forbid it. If you come anywhere near the house again, I'll take a court order out against you. Stay away from us, we never want to see you again."

That evening, on my way back to a small B&B in inner London, I stopped off for a few quick drinks. Six hours later, I caught a taxi back to my room. When I awoke in the morning, I knew that it was all over. There was no hope of me ever sobering up, and Jean and the children were gone for good.

Chapter 25

Israel

A few days after the meeting with Jean, the Six Day War broke out in the Middle East. Egypt had amassed an army near the Suez Canal whilst Syria, Jordan and Iraq had moved troops into battle positions on Israel's borders. The Israelis appeared to be in a hopeless position, the odds were stacked against them.

The English newspapers said that people from all over the world were offering to fight there. I'd read a lot of books about Israel over the years and when I saw the headlines, I decided to volunteer. It felt like a chance to redeem myself, an opportunity to do something decent for once, and if I died fighting there, at least it might have some sort of dignity to it. I phoned my mother to tell her I was going.

"Israel! What has Israel got to do with you, for God's sake?"

"I just want to get involved, mum. It seems worthwhile."

"So now you're going to head off to some God-forsaken place where you're likely to get shot, are you? Is that it?"

"I'll be alright, there's a lot of people volunteering."

"There's a lot of Jews volunteering, you silly boy! It's none of your damn business. Those Arabs would shoot an Irishman just as quick as they'd shoot a Jew, and so they should! You have no business going over there at all!"

"I'll be OK, mum. It's not a big deal. The papers are exaggerating the whole thing."

"Have you met up with Jean yet? What does she think of all this?"

"It's over between me and Jean, it's finished."

"Is that what this is about? Is that why you're running? Oh god, you're no sooner back than you're gone again to some place worse than before!" She stopped talking and I waited, not knowing what to say. When she came back again, her voice had changed. "Come back to Blackpool, son. You can live with us here as long as you like. Come back home, son, please."

"I'm going to Israel. I've made up my mind. I'll write to you."

There was another long pause.

"Don't you dare go anywhere near the fighting. Do you hear me now? You're no good to anyone dead. I'll tell you now, if you go and get yourself killed, I'll never forgive you. Not ever, do you hear me now?" There was another silence then that went on forever and when she came back, she was struggling to speak. "I love you my boy, always remember that, I do love you." And then there was a click and she was gone.

*   *   *

I tried to book a flight to Israel that day, but it was impossible. Most of the airlines had cancelled their flights due to the fighting and the rest were totally booked out, so I went down to the London docks and boarded the *Venus*, a rusty old cargo steamer bound for Tel Aviv.

The following morning as I sat in the dingy little dining room sipping a cup of black coffee, a swarthy looking seaman with a huge beard who doubled as a waiter approached my table and pulled out a chair.

"You have company."

A small, dark-haired woman about my own age was standing next to him.

"Is it OK if I join you?" she asked.

"Yes, sure," I said.

As soon as she sat down, the waiter took her order and disappeared in the direction of the galley.

"You've made quite an impression on Blackbeard," I said. "It took me half an hour to get served."

"You're Australian?" she asked.

"No, but I lived there for a while. Where are you headed?"

"Tel Aviv."

"Don't you know there's a war on?"

"I'm Jewish. You're not, are you?"

"No, I'm Irish."

"So why are you going to Israel?"

"Too much Leon Uris, I suspect."

"You've read *Exodus*?" she asked.

"Yes."

"I did too. I was going to Israel anyhow, so when the trouble started, I tried to volunteer but I couldn't get through to the consulate. All the phone lines were jammed. A friend of mine told me about this company."

"Not much of a friend," I told her. "We'll be lucky to survive the *Venus,* never mind the Arabs."

Carol was a schoolteacher from a Jewish family in Sydney and we got on well from the beginning. She'd led a sheltered life, but she was interested in travel and wanted to see as many countries as she could in the two-year break she was taking from Australia.

*   *   *

A day or so later as the ship nosed its way through a bright blue Mediterranean, past tiny islands topped by ancient white crusader forts, an announcement in broken English came booming out across the foredeck:

"The war in Israel is over. Israel has been victorious!"

There was a scattered cheer from some of the passengers, but I felt cheated. I'd wanted to play a part. I'd wanted to do at least one decent thing in my life.

By the time we arrived in Israel, Carol and I had decided to travel together, and we found work and accommodation on a kibbutz. The lifestyle was healthy. We worked in the fields by day and on the weekends, we swam in the sea off Tel Aviv, spending our evenings exploring the old city of Jerusalem.

After three months on Kfar Masarick, we moved to Tel Aviv. The cost of accommodation was high in the city and so, when we were told we could apply for a new immigrant's flat that would be a fraction of the normal cost, we were thrilled. There was only one problem: both of us had to be Jewish.

"Don't worry about that," I told Carol. "I'll tell them my mother was a Jew."

"You can't do that! It's obvious that you're not Jewish. Nobody will believe you."

"Who cares? A guy from a kibbutz told me that if anyone claims to be Jewish, they must accept that. It's in their constitution."

We turned up for the interview at the Jewish Agencies head office in Tel Aviv at nine o'clock on a Monday morning. As we began filling in the forms, we were interrupted by one of the staff. He had an English accent.

"Mr. O'Raleigh, I'm sorry, somebody should have explained to you. Both partners need to be Jewish to be eligible for New Immigrant status."

"We are both Jewish," I told him. "What's the problem?"

"Oh, I'm sorry," he looked flustered, "my mistake."

"There you go," I winked at Carol. "I'm a Jew now, your family will be delighted."

After filling in the forms, we sat there for ages, waiting for them to be processed. An hour and a half later, we were called back up to the counter.

"I'm sorry it's taking so long." He was obviously embarrassed. "We're having a slight problem with your surname." He grinned weakly. "It's very Irish, isn't it?"

"Why wouldn't it be? My father was Irish! My mother was the Jewish part of the family and that makes me Jewish under Israeli law, doesn't it?"

"Yes, it does. We were just wondering whether you had any proof of your mother's Judaism."

"Christ almighty," I said without thinking, "I don't believe this. All of my life, I've been abused and called a Jew boy and now, when I finally come to Israel, you're telling me I'm a bloody Goy! This is outrageous!"

"Mr. O'Raleigh, please, there's no point in getting angry. I'm just doing my job." He was shuffling papers in his hands. "If you could just fill these forms in, I'm sure we can resolve the matter quickly."

He disappeared again.

"Why don't we let it go." Carol was getting nervous. "They're not going to believe you, it's not his fault."

"Don't worry," I told her, "we're nearly there."

The forms were mostly to do with my mother, and I decided to stick with the truth as much as possible so that I wouldn't have too much trouble remembering the details. As soon as I finished, he returned, took the forms and advised us that there would be a further wait.

"Why don't you go off and have lunch?" He seemed more relaxed now. "You'll be seeing a Mr. Haim Goldstein at 3.00 pm. That gives you plenty of time."

We arrived back at the agency around 2.30 and were immediately ushered into Goldstein's office. The room was large and had no windows. The walls were white, and a large fluorescent light shone high overhead.

Goldstein was sitting at a large, rectangular, wooden desk, a portrait of Haim Hertzog frowning down at us from the wall behind. He was a large man, strongly built, with sharp intelligent eyes and the biggest nose I'd ever seen in my life.

He stood up and came across, a broad smile on his face, and as he thrust out his hand, I guessed he was American.

"Brian O'Raleigh, and you're Carol Sandler, right? Great to meet you both." He didn't wait for a response. "Sit down, please. Now, what seems to be the problem?"

"They didn't tell you?" I said.

"They told me that you're claiming to be Jewish."

"I am Jewish," I told him.

"Wow." He was grinning. "You could have fooled me! I'd have taken you for an Irishman anywhere, even without the name!"

"Look, Haim, I've gone through all this stuff outside and I don't feel like going through it again, OK? It's pretty bloody insulting."

He nodded in understanding and then picked up a file from his desk and began scanning the pages.

"Why did you come to Israel, Brian?"

"I wanted to fight for Israel."

"Very noble of you." He smiled. "And how about you, Carol, what brings you here?"

"Same thing." She was nervous. "We just wanted to help in some way."

"And your mother and father, they're both Jewish?"

"Yes, my mother's Polish, my father was from Latvia."

"You follow the Jewish religion?"

"No, we aren't a religious family."

"OK, Carol, that's fine. Now would you mind waiting outside while I talk to Brian. We won't be long." He waited until the door had closed behind her before turning back to me. "Look, I'm going to be frank with you. I've looked at the forms you filled in and we're not satisfied that you're Jewish." I went to protest but he raised a hand. "No, wait, hear me out. Now I don't know why anyone would want to claim to be Jewish, but it's pretty obvious to everyone who's spoken to you that you're not."

"Look, Haim," I cut in, "I'm not the slightest bit interested in whether you think I'm Jewish or not. I know who I am, and I know what I am. All I want from you people is my new immigrant status, OK?"

"So that's what it's about." He raised his eyebrows. "That's all you want. To be classified as a new immigrant?"

"Yes, that's all."

He thought for a moment.

"Look, I've lived in this country for twenty-three years. I'm an officer in the Israeli Intelligence Service." He smiled. "Now, whilst I don't doubt for a moment that you're sincere in your affection for Israel, I do not believe that you're a Jew."

"Like I said, Haim, I'm not interested in what you believe. I'm here to claim my new immigrant status, that's all. Nothing else really matters."

He thought for a moment.

"That would entitle you to cheap housing, wouldn't it? Is that what you're after?"

"I'm not after anything. I have a right to be classified as a new immigrant; you know that."

"You said your mother was Jewish, is that correct?"

"That's right; it's all down there on the forms."

"And what is your mother's first name?"

"I've already told you, Christine."

As soon as I said it, it dawned on me.

"Do you know the meaning of Christine?" He was smiling again. "It means *of Christ*."

"So, she was born in Ireland!" I was indignant. "Everyone there's a bloody goy! Her parents were ashamed of being Jewish, so what! That doesn't make me any less of a Jew!"

"Brian ..." He was shaking his head. "... I like you; I think you're a good man. You've come over here to help us and I respect that, but don't go telling me you're a Jew, that's insulting my intelligence. You don't look like a Jew, you don't talk like a Jew, and you don't think like a Jew. Be honest, please, for my sake. Don't worry about the papers, I'll fix all that. Just tell me the truth, you're not a Jew, are you?"

"Haim," I leant across his desk, "all of my life, I've been an outsider. Always, wherever I went, sooner or later, somebody would realize that I was a Jew and throw it in my face. Now finally, I come to Israel, to our homeland, and you of all people want to tell me that I don't belong here?"

He sat there for a long time then, studying me as if I was some sort of puzzle to be solved. Then he leaned forward conspiratorially, lowering his voice. "My friend, I'm going to tell you something that I've never told to any other living soul." He paused. "And I'm going to ask you to swear that you will never repeat it to anybody. Will you promise me that?"

"Yes," I told him, "you have my word."

He looked across the desk at me for some time before continuing. "My mother and father were both Christians. I'm not a Jew either." He stayed silent for a long moment, letting the statement hang in the air, then he went on. "I've always admired Israel. I've always believed that the Jewish people had a right to their own homeland." He was speaking very earnestly now and I was trying not to look at his nose. "I decided a long time ago to dedicate my life to Israel so I came over here, just like you, and told them that I was a

Jew. I've been here ever since." He nodded as if pleased with himself. "Well, what do you think? You're the only person in Israel who knows that, but I know I can trust you with my secret."

I paused for a long moment as if deep in thought.

"Haim, I'm very touched by what you've just told me. You're the sort of Christian that I respect and admire. I can only guess at the hardship that you must have endured living here, like missing Christmas and Easter and all those other things that the gentiles love to do. And even though it may not seem like much, I would like to thank you on behalf of the Jewish people, for your dedication and service to our nation."

I stood up and put my hand out across the table. He stared at me for a long while, but when he finally spoke, all he said was: "Get out."

Chapter 26

Swinging London

When we returned to England, we found a small flat in Earls Court directly across the road from the Kings Head Hotel, one of London's most popular watering holes. The clientele there were mostly Australian, but there was always a cross-section of other nationalities present and on any given night, you'd be rubbing shoulders with Irish, Spanish, English, Germans, French and Canadians, swilling down drinks in a bar so crowded you had to fight your way to the counter to be served.

The pub was a crossroads for a hundred different nations and notions; passionate Anarchists from France debated politics with concerned Communists from Poland, long-haired American Flower Power people argued the toss with drunken Australians and, as the Irish contingent kept up an endless barrage of rebel songs, Belgian and English mercenaries on leave from Mad Mike Hoar's Wild Geese units in the Congo, squandered their blood money on Scotch Whisky in their own tightly held corner of the public bar. To me, it was paradise regained and I slotted back in like the return of the Prodigal Son.

I found work as a steel-fixer on a major construction site just outside of London; it paid well but we worked like slaves to earn it. Carol got a job teaching so we had money to burn and virtually every night, I was out on the town drinking, singing and, when the occasion arose, brawling in the pubs and clubs the length and breadth of Earls Court.

The Kings Head had a colorful reputation and you never knew who you were likely to meet there. One night, the buzz went around that the Cray twins were in the lounge and sure enough, when I stuck my face around the corner, there they were at a table like two lord's bastards, surrounded by a motley collection of spivs, sycophants, beefy bouncers and big-breasted bottle blonds. I didn't bother introducing myself. The Cray's were the most notorious criminals in London and, shortly after, they were jailed for life on numerous counts of murder, robbery and extortion.

Another evening, Richard Burton and Elizabeth Taylor turned up with a film crew in tow. Burton was already well on the way and after tiring of sitting in the Lounge with Taylor, he came into the Public Bar and joined in the revelry as we sang ribald versions of 'The Irish Rover'. Liz was not impressed and finally, she sent her minders in to redeem her inebriated partner.

A few weeks later, Burton's show aired on national television as 'Kangaroo Valley SW5'. Unfortunately, the opening shot after each commercial break, was of me standing on a bar, a pint in one hand, a mike in the other, singing at the top of my voice. The following day, Jean called. I'd tried to contact her several times and I'd left my number with her mother, but this was the first response I'd had.

"So, you're making a fool of yourself on national television now. You do get around, don't you!" She was furious. "My whole family watched that show, Brian. It was bloody disgusting! You're a hopeless alcoholic, a stupid, irresponsible drunk! Don't ever try to contact us again, do you hear? We're legally divorced. If you come anywhere near this house, I'll take a court order out against you. Stay away from us, do you hear? We never want to see you again."

Chapter 27

Padraig's Bar

The craic was good at Cricklewood
Especially at the Crown

Pat Doran - an Irishman I'd met at the Kings Head Hotel, had invited us to Roscommon that year for the Christmas holidays and we met up with him at the Castle Inn in the center of Dublin on Christmas Eve. Pat was an old friend of the landlord and after the closing bell rang, the doors were locked and the private session that ensued went on until well into the early hours. Carol enjoyed it at first, but as the night wore on, I knew she was getting frustrated, so I wasn't surprised when she ambushed me on the way back from the Gents.

"How long are we staying here?" We were in a small corridor off the main bar. "We're supposed to be meeting Pat's parents tonight. You promised you'd control your drinking. This is not a good start."

"What do you want me to do?" I said. "Pat's a friend of the owner. We're just having a few drinks. Come on Carol, it's Christmas Eve, don't spoil things, please."

*   *   *

It was 3.30 am by the time we arrived in Roscommon. Pat's older sister, Siobhan, was still awake but his parents had been in bed for hours.

"They waited up till after midnight." She was standing, arms folded in a pink, patchwork dressing gown. "We thought there may have been an accident."

"No, nothing like that. We ran into some old friends in Dublin. Come on, Sib, you know what it's like."

"You should've called, Pat. You had us worried sick."

It was awkward for a moment, but after Pat introduced us, she softened and showed us to our room.

"If you need more blankets, you'll find them in the wardrobe. If there's anything else, just ask."

As soon as the door closed behind her, Carol began.

"That was really embarrassing." She was rummaging through her rucksack, refusing to look at me. "We should have called, it's the least we could have done." She looked up. "I hope this isn't going to turn into another of your drunken weekends. I didn't come here to watch you and Pat making fools of yourselves. I came here to see Ireland, not to watch you two get drunk!"

"Don't be silly," I told her, "we'll be heading for Galway in a few days, then the Aran Islands. But it is Christmas, Carol. We will be having a few drinks."

It was 4 am by the time we got to bed but I was awake again at seven, a throbbing hangover dragging me up from a fitful night's sleep. Carol was curled up, motionless, on her side of the bed so I eased myself out from the blankets, dressed quietly and went in search of Pat.

"How are you feeling?" It was a silly question. He was sitting on the edge of the bed, his head cradled in his hands.

"Same as you, I'd imagine." He looked up, squinting out the window. "What time is it?" Then, without waiting for an answer, "I need a drink and there'd be none here. My mother's a Pioneer, she won't have it in the house."

"So, what do we do?" I asked. "Is there any place open nearby?"

"No, everything's closed on Christmas Day, but we'd probably get a drink at Padraig's. He lives above the bar. I usually go there if I'm desperate." He looked up. "Is Carol up?"

"No, your mother's in the kitchen but the rest are still asleep. Come on," I told him, "we won't be gone long."

When we left the farmhouse, there was still no sign of Carol, so we told Pat's mother we'd be back in an hour and jumped into the car. A hundred yards along the lane, a group of horses blocked our path and, as we slowed to avoid them, a posse of red-faced children, no shoes, bare-arsed, and wearing nothing but thin vests and toothy grins surrounded the car. They were holding up a small, dead bird in what looked like a shoebox. "Give us a penny to bury the wran! Give us a penny to bury the wran!"

It was a freezing cold morning, hoar frost thick on the ground.

"They're the traveler's kids." Pat was searching his pockets. "You know, gypsies. It's an old tradition here. Do you have any change?"

In a field nearby, a large mobile home stood perched on a high piece of land, surrounded by smaller caravans and a few tents. At the bottom end of the pecking order, tiny canvas humpies like hessian igloos stood forlornly by side of the road.

"Ah go on now, mister!" The leader of the pack couldn't have been any more than ten, fierce blue eyes and a wicked grin. "Show us some paper money or we'll curse the both of ye!"

"Away with you now, you little blackguard! St. Stephen's Day is not till tomorrow. I should put my boot up your arse!" Pat was laughing. "Be grateful we stopped at all, next time we'll go right over the top of ye'. There ye' go!" He tossed a handful of change in the air and as they scrambled for the coins, we made our escape. "They're the McDonalds," he explained as we made our way along the winding lane. "They're here every Christmas; they're not a bad lot."

As I looked back at the gypsy camp, I caught a flash of Siobhan standing by the farmhouse gate, arms folded, staring after us.

Padraig's bar was comprised of one long room divided down the center by a dark brown, mahogany bar-top that stretched from the wall at the far end to within fifteen feet or so of the front door where it curved in a graceful arc into the varnished timber wall on the right-hand side. At the other end of the bar the room swelled out into an area with assorted tables and chairs, a presumptuous wooden plaque over the fireplace declaring this to be the 'Ladies Lounge.' Swinging low overhead in this hallowed area, three dusty chandeliers hung incongruently from a centuries old wooden beam that supported an off-white, smoke-stained ceiling, whilst all around the varnished oak paneled walls were festooned with swords, cutlasses, old muskets and flintlock pistols. Crossing the threshold of Padraig's bar was like stepping back in time into a medieval pirate's den.

"Morning lads." Padraig was a tiny little man with impossibly bright blue eyes, large, triangular ears that stuck out at right angles to his head, a tousled mop of straw-colored hair, and a childlike grin. Pat had told me that he'd inherited the bar from his father but that he drank so much, he'd been forced to take a job with the local council to help support the place. "It's a little early to be knocking on my door now, is it not?"

"Ah, come on now, Padraig.' Doran walked past him into the bar. "Sure Jaysus, it's Christmas and my head's fit to burst. We're just after a drink or two to settle the nerves."

"Well get in here quick before the Gardaí sets eyes on you." He stood aside to let me pass. "And don't ever go knocking on my front door again Pat; you should know better. If he catches me open on Christmas Day, he'll have me robbed blind with free drink."

As Padraig locked up behind me, I wandered around the bar, admiring the various swords and pistols. I'd never seen such an array of weapons outside of a museum.

"Are they genuine?" I asked.

"Some of them are, sir, the rest are plastic copies. It's hard to tell one from the other. I've had this place for thirty years and they were here before me." He pulled down an ancient steel cutlass with an ornate brass handle. "This is the favorite, every Yank that comes in here makes me an offer but it's not for sale. It's from the Spanish Armada, or so I was told."

"Never mind the history lesson." Pat was waiting by the bar. "You can tell him all that over a pint. Set 'em up, Padraig, and have one yourself."

A few minutes later, the landlord was back. "There you go, lads, two pints of porter!"

"What about yourself?" Doran looked up, surprised.

"Not for me thanks, sure I haven't touched a Guinness in over a month now."

"Get yourself a whisky then." Pat looked concerned. "Have whatever you like."

"I'd love to, but I can't. Sure, didn't I take the pledge just four weeks ago? The wife was leaving me if I took another drink. You know how it is."

"Ah, come on now," Pat persisted, "she couldn't possibly mind you having a drink or two on Christmas Day!"

"Ah, but that's not the way it is with me, as well you know. One or two turns into three or four and the next thing I know, I'd be blind drunk again! No, I don't trust myself. I've failed too many times."

"Padraig, I'm not saying you need to get back on the drink!" Doran was frowning. "All I'm saying is that you're entitled to have one or two; it is Christmas after all." He pointed up at the top shelf. "Now, hand me down that bottle of Scotch." As Padraig reached for the whisky, Doran went on, "There you go, now put up three shot glasses on the bar." Padraig obeyed without a word. "There you go now." Pat filled them to the brim, pushed one at me and the other at Padraig before raising his glass. "Two drinks for the Christmas, two and no more. Sláinte!" I raised my glass. "Sláinte!" Padraig stared at us both for a long moment, then he grabbed the glass and held it high. "What the hell. Sláinte!" He tossed it down in one gulp.

"That's more like it. Jaysus, you had me worried there for a moment!" We were all laughing now. "Those priests would have your balls in a bag if you let them, sure they're worse than the women!"

Two hours later, as we sat chatting with Padraig, there was a loud banging on the front door. "It's Siobhan and Carol." Pat was peering out from behind the curtains. "They don't look too happy."

There was another loud banging.

"How do they know we're here?" I said.

"Siobhan knows I come here, and they'd have seen the car."

We stood there still and silent, like burglars caught in the act, but finally they gave up and we watched from the rear window as they strode back up the hill to the farm.

Every now and again, there'd be a discreet tapping on the back door and by noon the pub was crowded with locals enjoying a hair of the dog. Three gypsies from the McDonald's camp had joined us; the older man had a leg missing but it didn't seem to bother him as he swung around the bar on an old-fashioned wooden crutch like Long John Silver from *Treasure Island*.

"So, how's your Da these days, Pat? I haven't seen him in an age."

"I think you know why, Finbar." Pat was smiling. "That horse you sold him was blind as a bat; he was only any good for the knackers' yard!"

Long John looked shocked.

"Now that's not true and you know it. That horse had perfect vision the day your father took him off me! Didn't I beg him not to buy the beast, sure wasn't it my favorite horse?"

"Well, his perfect vision had him wandering up the middle of the highway and straight underneath a ten-ton truck three days after you sold him! So perhaps the poor beast was so depressed with you leaving him he decided to end it all. Could that be what happened?"

There was laughter all around but then suddenly, Padraig was calling out a warning. "Pat!" He was staring out the rear window. "You're in trouble now! Siobhan and the little woman are back down the hill!"

We joined him at the end of the bar. Carol and Pat's sister were careering down the long winding slope on a pair of old bikes and minutes later, when they came pushing in through the back door, it was clear they'd made some decisions.

"Brian ..." Carol's voice was loud enough for the whole bar. "... Siobhan and I are going to Roscommon. You're welcome to come with us if you like, but we're not going to sit around waiting at the farm while you and your friends get drunk down here."

We were the center of attention now, the locals enjoying the unfolding drama.

"Will you join us for a drink?" Pat offered hopefully.

"No, I will not, but your mother would like you both to be there tonight for Christmas dinner." Then turning back to me. "We're guests here, Brian, try to act like one."

"You're wasting your breath." Siobhan took her arm. "There's no way you'll get them out of here now." Then, turning to her brother: "You're a bloody disgrace, Pat! Mum and da waited up half the night and now you're back down here again, drinking! Come on, Carol, just leave them to it."

By 5 pm, the bar was crowded to capacity. The fiddler had been joined by a wild looking woman on a bowran drum and an old man with a flute, and they were all going strong.

"Airplane Johnnie's arrived." Pat had reappeared by my elbow. "I told you about him in London."

I followed him to the far end of the room where he introduced me to a small group of men clustered around a fire.

"This is Fergal, our local butcher ..." We shook hands. "... and this man here is Sean Flaherty, better known as Father Flaherty. He's in civvies today so you don't have to worry too much about your language, and ..." He turned and pointed to an elderly man with mischievous eyes and snow-white hair. "... and this old reprobate is widely known - both here and across the pond - as Airplane Johnnie, you'll find out why later. And last, but not in any way least, we have Judge Michael O'Rourke, our most famous son and guardian of law and order in our little village. Judge O'Rourke's the man you'll be answering to if you get up to any mischief while you're here!" Then, in an aside to the landlord, "Whisky all round Padraig, this one's on me."

The judge was a tall, thin, bitter-looking man of around seventy or so with a pepper and salt goatee beard and hard, piercing eyes. Pat had warned me on the way across not to mention that I'd been born in England as the judge was known for his extreme prejudice against all things English.

"Slainte!" Airplane Johnny was holding up a glass. "Slainte, Brian, and to you, too, Pat, sure it's grand to have you back home."

We chatted away for a while, swapping stories and laughing, but all the time I could feel the judge's eyes on me and finally, he addressed me directly. "I can't place your accent, sir." He was smiling a cold, bleak, smile. "Where would you be from?"

"I was born in Australia," I told him. "Both my parents are Irish."

"From what part?" He was still smiling, but it looked more like a grimace now.

"My father was from Garryowen, County Limerick, my mothers from Galway. My sister was born in Galway, too. I was born in Sydney."

"So, you're an Australian citizen?"

"I have dual nationality, but I consider myself Irish, not Australian."

"Good man!" he declared emphatically. "Keep the faith! And so you came all the way over from Australia to spend Christmas in Roscommon?"

"No," I told him, "I've been living in London for the past year or so, sort of a working holiday."

"London?" He didn't sound too impressed. "Now there's one place I've never had any desire to visit. A cesspit is what it is, by all accounts. The Queen, Harold Wilson, homosexuals, drug addicts, criminals, pimps and gangsters. And what about those Cray twins!" He was frowning. "They nailed a man to a door, according to the newspapers! Did you know that? Now what sort of a man does a thing like that? Then they murdered that other fellow … what was his name? McVitie, that's it, Jack the Hat McVitie. Now you might well say that he wasn't the nicest type of person himself, but that's hardly reason enough to be nailing a man to a door now, is it?" He looked back at me. "So, what sort of people are they?" He was staring at me intently. "The Cray twins?"

"I'm not sure what you mean," I said.

"Well, it's a simple enough question," he went on, "you just said that you've lived in London for the past year."

"Yes, I have, but London's a big place. I just know what I read in the papers."

"But you must have some idea. What are they like as men I mean?"

"They'd be hard men," I told him. "I guess everyone knows that. I saw them in a pub one night, that's the closest I ever got to the Cray twins."

"So, what will happen to them now?" He was staring at me fixedly. "Will they hang them?"

"I think the death penalty was abolished in England ..." I began.

"Hanging's too good for them!" he exploded suddenly; his frosty demeanor shattered by a sudden burst of rage. "What they really need is a good kick in the arse!"

"Ah, come on now, Michael, don't be worrying yourself about the Cray twins." Pat was gesturing to the barman. "Another round if you would, Padraig." Then, turning back to the group: "Johnnie, tell Brian the airplane story. He thinks I made it up."

"Ah now ..." Johnny was shaking his head. "... sure Jaysus that all happened donkey's years ago."

"I'd teach them a lesson they'd never forget!" The judge wasn't done. "It wouldn't be jail I'd be giving them, oh no! I'd hang them up by the balls outside the Post Office and I'd flay the skin off them with a horsewhip! We'd see how tough they were then!"

"Come on now, Johnnie." Pat was keen to change the topic. "You can't be making a liar of me now. Tell us the story."

"No, I will not. I've told that story so many times, it has me tired just thinking about it. Ask Fergal." He nodded to the butcher. "He was there, and besides, I need to see a man about a horse."

As Johnny disappeared in the direction of the toilets, the butcher took up the story.

"Well, I was there alright and it's not the sort of thing you'd forget in a hurry. Now, you probably all know that when Johnny was a younger man, he was landlord of a pub just outside of Roscommon. But he was also something of an amateur pilot and he owned his own plane. The story has it that he got it off a Dublin man who owed him money. Well, John had always had an interest in flying so he took lessons and got the license and everything. It was just a bit of a hobby at first, like another man might breed horses, but when he took over the pub, he began to get requests. You know, people would be having a drink and somebody would mention the plane, and the next thing, they'd all want to go up for a ride. Most of them would have forgotten by the next day, but some of them would come back and occasionally, John would take one of them up for a spin. Well, that's how it got started. There was no money involved; it was all just part of the craic. Every now and again, some Yank would turn up asking to see John, then they'd tell him that their cousin, Joe, or Richard, or whoever it was, had been up for a ride and could they go up too, and sure enough, the next thing, they'd be off over the fields and up in the plane. Well word got around and before you knew it, it seemed as if every Yank who ever came to Ireland had to have a ride in Johnnie's airplane! Of course, it all became too much after a while and in the end, he was refusing nearly all of them. It was only if he knew you him well, or maybe if you caught him in the right mood, he'd take you up for a spin." The butcher looked around solemnly as if wondering whether to go on or not. "Unfortunately, on the day in question, this particular Yank was very persuasive."

"You were there, Fergal?" I asked.

"I was, of course. I was there when the Yank and his wife arrived. They came in around 11 am, as I remember. He was some big shot from Chicago, shaking hands and buying drinks all around. His wife was a peroxide blond with those big, white, tombstone teeth the American women have. She'd seen better days, but she was a nice enough sort of a woman. Well, it didn't take the Yank too long to get around to the plane. It seems that a cousin of his had been up with Johnny the previous year and he was hell-bent on doing the same. Well, if John said no once, he said it a hundred times; you see, he hadn't been up in the plane himself for months. But the Yank was a likeable enough sort of a man, you know, telling jokes and putting up whisky for the lads, so finally, I suppose Johnnie just felt obliged."

"Foolish decision." The judge was shaking his head. "There's no getting around that, it was a foolish decision."

"Ah come on now." Fergal didn't want anyone spoiling the story. "Sure, Jaysus this all happened years ago, and haven't you done worse fucking things yourself?"

"Hold on now, boy." The priest was well drunk, a warning finger poised in mid-air, an owlish grin slipping sideways on his pale face. "Go on with the story, if you must, but it is Christmas Day, so be mindful of your language."

"Stay out of it, Sean." The butcher prodded him with a finger. "You don't pull any weight around here in your civvies, boy! Think yourself lucky to be getting free drinks on Christmas Day, you bloody hypocrite!"

"Ah, you're an awful man with a drink in you, Fergal."

"And you're not?" Fergal snorted before continuing. "You see, the problem was that by that time, John was four sheets to the wind himself. Now it wasn't the first time he'd gone up in that condition - some say he never went up sober - but this day, he was well and truly drunk!" Fergal held out his glass and Pat topped it up. "Now the plane was an old dual wing, two-seater; you know, the type with open cockpits. Now Johnny had been flying for years by then and it was said that he could make that machine sing if he was in the right mood. But that was years before when he was a younger man and by this time, his skills had probably faded somewhat. Well, as it happened, the field out the back of the hotel was too short for a runway, so we used to sling a rope around the plane's tail and then we'd have the tractor drag her backwards up the hill." He gestured out the window. "Once we got her far enough up the slope, Johnny would crank her up, rev the engine for a few minutes and then I'd get a log underneath the rope and, on his signal, I'd chop through it with an axe and off she'd go, boy, like a bat out of hell!' He made a sweeping motion in mid-air. "Well, that day was no exception and up she went, smooth as could be. The Yank's wife was delighted, taking pictures and waving as Johnny zoomed around, waggling his wings and giving them all a thrill. To this day, I'm not sure why he decided to get into all the fancy moves. He hadn't done any of that stuff in years. Some say he'd had a few too many, others thought he might have taken a shine to the Yank's wife and was trying to impress her. Whatever the reason, he went into a long, steep dive and as he was pulling out of it, he decided he might as well loop the loop! Well, the next thing, the Yank's wife was screaming "Look, look, something's fallen off the plane!" and sure enough, as we stood there watching, a bundle came flying through the air and straight into a ploughed field less than half a mile from where we stood! 'What was that?' the wife was asking, 'Is the plane alright? Is it safe?' Well, the plane was safe enough and so was Johnny, but the husband was not, of course. You see, it was him that fell out the plane!" There was a roar of laughter all around and even the judge allowed himself a smile as Fergal went on. "The poor man went in so far, we had to fetch shovels to dig him out!"

"Don't believe a word of it, Brian." Johnny was back. "Sure, they'd tell you anything to keep the craic going; they're desperate men altogether."

When Carol and Siobhan reappeared, Pat and I were standing on a table in the middle of the room singing *The Black Velvet Band*. The 'hair of the dog' imperative of early morning had morphed into a full-blown session and the whole place was swinging. As soon as we finished the song, we joined the girls at a table by the bar.

"God, look at the two of you!" Siobhan was shaking her head. "You'll be sick as brown dogs tomorrow, and don't be looking for any sympathy from me." Then, as an afterthought: "Have you eaten today?"

"I was told that Guinness is good for you," I said.

"I'll remind you of that in the morning," she came back.

"Pat's mother wants to know if you're going to be home for dinner." Carol wasn't happy either. "It's almost seven o'clock, Brian."

"Don't worry," Pat assured her, "you can tell her we'll be up there shortly."

"It's the same every year," Siobhan said to Carol. "He comes home for Christmas and we see less of him then than when he's away."

"Have a drink while you're here." I waved to Padraig. "Come on girls, loosen up a bit."

Carol stood up. "If you get any looser, you won't be able to stand. Come on home, Siobhan, we won't get any sense out of them now."

The pub was packed and a tall man with a bushranger's beard and wild eyes was slashing out tunes on a fiddle as we joined the revelers by the fire. Everyone was having a great time and when Padraig made an announcement that Doran was going to sing *Soldier Laddie,* the fiddler swung into the tune immediately.

Now one morning in July as I went walking through Tipperary
I heard the battle cry from the mountains overhead
As I looked up to the sky saw an Irish soldier laddie
He looked at me quite fearlessly and said
Will you stand in the band like a true Irishman?
Will you go and fight the forces of the crown
Will you march with O'Neal through an Irish battlefield?
For tonight we're going to free old Wexford town!

There was a roar of approval as the song came to an end but before it had faded, the Master of Ceremonies was pointing a bony finger at me.

"Your turn, Brian." Padraig was grinning like a drunken leprechaun, a dirty white towel around his neck, his insane blue eyes wet and shining, a tumbler of whisky on the bar in front of him. "Come on now, up on the counter and give us a song!"

"Come on, Brian," Doran jumped in. "Give us *Captain Farrell*!"

It was an old favorite from the *Kings Head* and, as I clambered up on the bar, Padraig made his announcement.

"Listen up, everyone, listen up!" He was waving his arms and shouting over the din. "Brian's going to give us *Captain Farrell*, better known as *Whisky in the Jar*!

The fiddler kicked in immediately, followed at once by the wild woman on the bowran…

As I went over roving on Killgarry Mountain
I met with Captain Farrell and his money he was counting

As I sang, I pulled a cutlass and a pistol off the wall and shook them in Padraig's face.

I first produced my pistol then I rattled forth me rapier
Stand and deliver boy, I am the bold deceiver!

"Holy Jaysus!" Padraig was loving it. "A man's now forced to defend himself in his own establishment!" And the next minute, he was up on the bar like a miniature Errol Flynn, flourishing a sword he'd grabbed off the wall. "On guard!" he screamed as he took a swing at me. I blocked the blow and kept on singing. It was as if a signal had gone off and within seconds, the locals were pulling swords and pistols off the walls and brandishing them at each other.

He counted out his money and it made a pretty penny
I stuck it in me pocket and I took it home to Jenny
She swore and she lied that she never would deceive me
But the devil take the women for they always lie so easy

Musharingam durumadah
Whack fall the daddy oh!
Whack fall the daddy oh!
There's Whisky in the jar!

The whole place was in an uproar, women screaming and laughing as men fought mock battles in the crowded room. Everyone was having a great time, but as the song went on, I realized that things were getting out of hand. Padraig had jumped off the counter and was now fencing with the one-legged gypsy behind the bar. Long John had a crutch in one hand and a sword in the other and as I watched, Padraig give him a hard crack on the side of the head with the flat of his sword. The blow shocked Long John who then lashed out with his crutch, but Padraig grabbed it and tried to jerk him off his feet. This infuriated the Gypsy who immediately took a swipe at his tormentor's head. Padraig attempted to block it but his sword was a plastic copy from Japan and Long John's, a steel cutlass from the Spanish Armada which sliced straight through the replica and chunked firmly into the landlord's forehead, and Padraig slid down behind the bar like a sack of potatoes off a donkey's back.

"Keep it going, lads!" The fiddler was roaring over the din. "Keep it going, sure the craic's fierce altogether!"

But then suddenly, over all the chaos and confusion, a high-pitched screaming brought the mêlée to an abrupt end.

"Stop! Stop! Will you stop for the love of Jaysus?" A huge, fat woman, her hair encrusted in a net and curlers, had emerged from the back of the hotel and was screaming at the top of her lungs. "Stop it, you mad bastards, stop it!" She was furious. "That's it! There's no more drink to be had here tonight! Go on, get out, all of you, get out, and you!" She was pointing a quivering finger at Pat. "You're to blame for this. Padraig hadn't had a drink in a month!" And then, turning back to the revelers: "Do you not have homes to go to?" She was pushing the reluctant locals out the back door. "Go on, Martin, on your way, and you too, Father. On your way home, Pat, your own mother wouldn't know you! And you too, mister, sure you're worse than the rest of them!"

As we passed by the traveler's camp on the way home, I spotted an old woman in a black shawl, crouching low over a small open fire in one of the canvas humpies. A turn of the head, as if she had known we were coming, a mouth shadowed by unspoken words, glistening eyes peering out from a smoke-shrouded face, slowly stirring a soot blacked pot, like one of the witches from Macbeth.

*   *   *

The following morning, I woke early, head throbbing, mouth dry, trying to piece together the events of the previous evening, and in desperate need of a drink. Carol was still sleeping, so I dressed quietly, crept into Pat's room and shook him awake.

"I need a drink, Pat. Do you think Padraig would be willing?"

We parked the car outside the pub and approached cautiously. The handle turned easily, and my hopes rose as we stepped inside. Padraig was standing motionless in the middle of the floor, a long-handled broom clutched in both hands. His forehead swathed in white bandages that came down to an eyebrow on one side and a little higher on the other, a clump of black hair jutting out above like a bird's nest. A slash of crimson, perhaps three inches long and angled slightly to one side, indicated the location of the sword swipe. His left eye was invisible behind a swollen, purple lid, but his right eye was alive and glowing with an almost palpable hostility as we faced each other across the barroom floor.

"Good morning, Padraig ..." Doran was attempting a smile. "How's the head?"

Chapter 28

Mandy

Three days later, Pat dropped us off on a highway a few miles outside of Roscommon. It was midday, he was heading back to London, we were planning on hitchhiking to Galway, and from there, by ferry to the Aran Islands.

"You'll be heading south," he pointed. "Galway's less than fifty miles from here."

"Thanks for everything, Pat." We shook hands. "Safe home."

"See you when you get back to London. Try to stay out of trouble; you're a mad bastard, O'Raleigh."

And then he was gone, waving as he went. Things had been strained in the car on the way down. We'd stayed at Pat's place for three days and I hadn't drawn a sober breath in all that time. Carol was furious and she'd just sat there, glaring out the window.

We'd been up late the night before, arguing quietly in our room after everyone else had gone to bed. She was disgusted with my behavior and wanted to cancel the rest of the trip and return to England.

"Look," I told her, "I made a fool of myself but it's not the end of the world, OK? We'll head off to Galway tomorrow morning. I've stopped drinking now. I won't touch another drop in Ireland, I promise you."

"You destroyed the Christmas holidays and not just for me. Mrs. Doran was in tears on St. Stephen's Day. That man had eight stitches in his head and you seemed to think it was funny! You're insane when you drink, absolutely insane."

"Hang on!" I protested. "It wasn't my idea that he get into a sword fight with a tinker. What did he expect?"

"Maybe not, but everyone agreed that you started it! You're crazy when you drink. Wherever you go, there's trouble!"

She made me promise that I wouldn't have another drink in Ireland. I was suffering from the worst hangover I'd ever had in my life and the very last thing I needed was an argument, so I agreed.

*　　*　　*

As soon as Pat disappeared, we set off towards Galway, tramping along the grass verge by the side of the road. The weather was bleak, sullen grey clouds rolling low over rain sodden fields, driven on by a bitter westerly wind that tugged at our anoraks and brought tears to our eyes. Carol had wanted to hitch immediately but I was feeling sick and shaky from the drink and I didn't relish being forced into inane conversation with total strangers.

"Why do you drink so much?"

We were sitting in a graveyard by an ancient stone church, unwrapping sandwiches Carol had prepared at the farm.

"I don't know," I told her. "When I go out, I'm convinced that I'm only going to have a few, then something changes and I can't stop."

"Do you ever think about me? Doesn't it cross your mind that I'm waiting for you somewhere, not knowing what's happening?"

"No," I said, "once I've started, it's like nothing else matters. I always think that you'll be alright anyway." It sounded pretty lame. "Look, I'm sorry, I really am, but can we talk tomorrow? I'm really strung out. I hardly slept last night."

"Promise you won't drink again while we're in Ireland. Promise me!"

"I promise," I said. "I promise I won't."

The first car we flagged after lunch pulled over to the side immediately.

"Where to?" he asked.

"We're heading for Galway."

"Jump in quick," he said, "before you freeze to death! I'm a Galway man myself, we'll have you there in no time." He held out a hand. "John Kildare."

"Brian O'Raleigh." We shook hands. "And this is Carol."

"So, where are you from?"

"We're Australians," I told him. It was easier than going through the pedigree.

"But you're Irish by the look of you?"

"Yes, my mother's from Galway, my father was from Garryowen."

"So, who's your mother then? Do I know her?"

"She's a Stewart, from Salt Hill."

"I know the Stewarts," he said. "What's her name?"

"Christine Stewart, she's Jack's sister."

"Sure, Jaysus I know Jack well! Didn't I have a drink with him just before the Christmas? We do bit of work for them occasionally. Do they know you're here?"

"No," I told him, "my Uncle Frank may know. My mother called him last week."

"Frank," he looked surprised. "You mean Frank the Yank? That's what we call him here; he spent most of his life in America. He'd be too old to be your uncle, would he not?"

"Well, he's my mother's uncle, actually. We just call him that."

"That would be right, I never met your mother, but I knew that Jack had a sister in England. That must be her."

"Yes," I told him, "I was born in England. I went to Australia when I was eighteen."

"And you?" He was looking at Carol in the rear vision. "Are you one of us?"

"No," Carol told him, "my family's from Russia."

"Irish and Russian!" He was laughing. "Now there's a nice mix for you."

*   *   *

An hour later, we were slowing to a halt outside a large two-story building set in landscaped gardens.

"That's the Yank's house right there now." He was pointing. "But he's not home by the look of things." It was 4 pm and the light was fading. "I better wait here to make sure you have a bed for the night."

We knocked on the door several times but the place was in darkness so we gave up and returned to where John Kildare was waiting in the car.

"No answer, we'll have to book into a hotel. Are there any reasonably priced places nearby?"

"Look, I can't take you there tonight, but you could book into the youth hostel in Kinvarra in the morning. It's a nice enough place and it's cheap. But tonight, I'll take you to a little B&B close by. It'll cost you a few pounds but it's clean and you'll get a good breakfast in the morning. Just make sure you tell her you're married; she's a fierce Catholic."

Miss Flynn kept a neat two-story bed and breakfast place on the outskirts of Galway and John made a point of taking us to the front door to introduce us.

"Mr. and Mrs. O'Raleigh, Miss Flynn, I hope you can look after them both. They're good friends of mine."

As we followed Miss Flynn up a tight, narrow staircase, she stopped suddenly and turned. "No offense to you now, but you are married, are you not?"

"Yes, we are, Miss Flynn," I told her, "we were married two years ago in St Mary's Cathedral in Sydney. Bishop Michael Murphy himself married us."

'Oh, God bless you both, what a wonderful thing to be married by a bishop!"

I awoke the following morning to the sound of rain pattering softly on the small square panes of glass of our bedroom windows, the wind whistling at the gables, the distant muffled roar of the ocean, ominous black clouds surging low over a mist-shrouded horizon.

"There's tea and toast there for you now, if you like." Miss Flynn's voice came softly through the bedroom door. "Breakfast's any time from eight till eleven. It's a terrible day outside so there's no rush."

We sat up in bed, drinking tea and discussing our options. Neither of us felt like traipsing around Galway in the rain, searching for relatives, so after a late breakfast, we packed out rucksacks and caught a bus into Galway. We spent a couple of hours wandering around the city center, fighting with a windswept umbrella and sloshing through muddied pools, but it wasn't much fun so by 2 pm, we decided to head out to Kinvara. We backtracked to the city center and, after getting directions from a surly, rain-washed Guarda, we eventually found our way to a rickety old bus parked outside the railway station. As we approached, two old men wearing overcoats and scarves watched with appraising eyes.

"Good day to you, sir." The older of the two was smiling up from beneath an old tweed hat. "Could I be of any help to you?"

"We're looking for the bus to Kinvarra."

"Then look no further, you're standing right next to it."

"Thanks," I told him. "Do you know when it leaves?"

"I should sir, I'm the driver."

"So, is it leaving soon?"

"Yes indeed," he nodded, "we'll be heading off in no time."

"Great," I said, "can we get on now?"

"You can of course. Put your bags up in the rack above."

We got onboard, stowed our rucksacks, then sat there for a while, talking. The driver and his friend were still smoking their pipes and chatting by the wall, so after another few minutes, I went back out.

"Excuse me," I said, "will the bus be leaving soon?"

"It won't be long now, sir." The driver was knocking out his pipe on the stone wall. "Just make yourself at home."

Twenty minutes later, we were still sitting in the back seat, waiting. Carol was beginning to worry, so I went out again.

"Look," I told him, "we need to get to Kinvarra before dark. When does the bus actually leave?"

"It's due to leave at 4 pm or thereabouts." He was smiling up at me.

I looked at my watch it was 3 pm.

"Why didn't you tell me that before?" I said.

"Because you didn't ask, sir."

By the time we arrived at Kinvarra, it was almost pitch dark, just a sliver of moon peering out occasionally from behind heavy, sullen clouds, the wind buffeting at the bus as the driver gave us directions.

"There you are now." He was pointing a finger down a darkened lane. "Doorus House is just along the road."

"I can't see anything," I told him.

"That because it's nighttime, sir. In the daytime here, you can see for miles."

.

We stared at each other for a long moment.

"How far is it to Doorus House from here?" I asked, hoping I'd phrased the question correctly.

"Oh ..." He was smiling again. "... it would be an Irish mile or more."

We walked for twenty minutes before spotting a light directly ahead and moments later, we were approaching a white, two-story building surrounded by tall, dark trees and shadowed gardens. Apart from a tiny light over the porch, the building was in utter darkness. As we arrived at the entrance, a fluttering sheet of white paper, held in place by a large brass lion's head door-knock, caught my eye.

Welcome to Doorus house.
I'm up at the hotel for a drink. You can join me if you like.
If not, go in, sign the book and make yourself at home.
Jack Bevan.

The heavy wooden door swung open at my touch and I fumbled for a light. We were standing in a hallway, a flight of stairs rising up to the right. On a small wooden table close by the entrance lay a leather-bound guestbook and, opening the cover, I turned to the last entry:

Date. December 2nd 1967.
Name. Yoshiro Katamari
Country. Osaka, Japan

I pondered that as we explored the building. The first door on the right carried a simple plastic sign stating: *Private.* The door on the left led to a comfortable sitting room with the remnant of a fire still smoldering in the grate. We discovered the kitchen and, as I brought the fire back to life, Carol made tea and cut the fruitcake we'd bought in Galway. After supper, we explored upstairs. To the left was a large dormitory bearing the legend *Men* in gold letters on the door; to the right, a smaller room marked *Women.*

"We'll kip in here," I said.

"No." She was always on the side of law-and-order. "You'll have to sleep in the men's dorm."

"No way," I told her, "its bloody freezing! Don't worry, if anyone turns up, I'll move."

We went to bed around 10 pm. We'd borrowed extra blankets from a linen cupboard and, as we snuggled up together in the women's dorm, I was hoping for a decent night's sleep. I drifted off quickly but was woken around midnight by the sound of tires crunching on the gravel driveway. Carol was sitting up in bed.

"Go back to sleep," I told her. "We'll talk to them in the morning."

A car door slammed and then we heard a loud male voice.

"Out of the car bitch! Come on, get out of the car!" He sounded like a Welshman. "Come on, you're not that drunk, get out!" Oh Christ, I thought, more trouble. Another door slammed and I could hear feet crunching towards the entrance. "Get inside, go on! I'll black your other bloody eye if I have to! You made a complete fool of me there tonight, Mandy. Two drinks and you turn into a slut. I can't take you anywhere!" I got out of bed and tip-toed to the top of the stairs. Peering over the banister, I could just make out a man's black shoes by the office door.

"Don't say another word, bitch. You're a bloody disgrace! Go on, get inside!"

I was praying to God he wouldn't start hitting her. Carol was standing next to me, shivering. She looked frightened.

"Don't get involved," she whispered, "it's not our business. We don't know these people."

I didn't answer. The last thing I needed was to get involved in a drunken brawl with a total stranger.

We could still hear his voice through the closed door but it wasn't as loud now.

"You're a disgrace, Mandy! Go to bed, we'll talk in the morning."

I was up at six the following day. I'd spent another uneasy night, but the hangover had just about run its course and I was starting to feel more normal as Carol and I sat on the bed, discussing our options.

"If it gets too unpleasant, we'll just pack up and find another hostel," I told her. "Look, you stay here, I'll go down and check things out."

When I got to the foot of the stairs, the office door was wide open and peering in, I saw a middle-aged man standing by a stove, cooking, the smell of bacon filling the air.

"Good morning."

"Oh!" he jumped, "I didn't know we had guests. You didn't sign the book?"

"No," I told him, "I'll do it now."

"Don't bother, do it later." Then, turning back to the stove, "Can I offer you something … a cup of tea, coffee?"

"No thanks," I told him, "I have my wife with me. She's still asleep."

"Well, I hope we didn't wake you last night. We were up the road having a few drinks. Got home after midnight. Did you hear us come in?"

"No," I assured him, "we didn't hear a thing. We were fast asleep by ten o'clock; we didn't hear anything."

"Mandy!" He yelled it out so suddenly that I jumped. "Come in here and get your breakfast, you horrible little slut!"

Christ, I thought, this bastard's raving mad! I was turning to leave when Mandy appeared. She was a small, fat, cocker spaniel with a large black patch over her right eye, wagging her stump of a tail furiously as Jack Bevan shoveled piles of bacon onto a dish on the floor.

For the next ten days, gale force winds accompanied by torrential rains enveloped the entire West Coast of Ireland. All ferries to the Aran Islands were cancelled and we were virtually prisoners at Doorus House. Whenever there was a lull in the weather, we worked in the orchard with Jack, walked along nearby beaches huddled underneath borrowed umbrellas, explored Dunguaire Castle that stood nearby, or hiked in bright yellow oilskins in the Burren, an ancient rock formation that held the ruins of prehistoric fortresses, ancient standing stones and long abandoned dwellings.

In the evenings, we sat before roaring log fires as the wind howled through the trees outside, read books from the Doorus House library, wrote letters to friends and listened to yarns from Jack, who was, it turned out, something of a seanchaí. It was a welcome respite from the madness of the drink, an escape from the chaos of London, a glimpse of what a sober life might look like, and an inkling of a future that we both hoped might be …

Chapter 29

The Battle of Grosvenor Square

When we arrived back in England, the world appeared to be on the edge of profound and cataclysmic change. The war in Vietnam was raging and nightly newscasts depicted men, women and children being slaughtered by the indiscriminate bombing. The use of Napalm and Agent Orange had sickened people worldwide and, in the USA, public opinion had turned firmly against their involvement in Vietnam.

In London, the peace movement was shifting into top gear, rumors of a major anti-war demonstration were on everyone's tongue, Joan Baez's evocative, *Blowing in the Wind* was the new international anthem and Scott McKenzie's voice was everywhere belting out *On the Streets of San Francisco*. Anarchy was in the air.

There had been other demonstrations, but word on the street was that this one would be big. A few months prior, sickening photographs of a Viet Cong prisoner being summarily executed had been splashed on the front page of every international newspaper. The unidentified victim, hands strapped behind his back, shoulders hunched, eyes tightly narrowed in anticipation of death as General Nguyen Ngoc Loan held a revolver an inch or two from his right temple and blew a 45-caliber hole clean through his brain. The second photograph showed the man's knees buckling, his body curving and falling away as a jet of blood spurted upwards like a fountain from the other side of his head.

Those graphic images of callous slaughter sickened millions worldwide, and people who'd had little or no involvement in the peace movement till then, were instantly galvanized into action; it was a call to the heart, the catalyst that polarized people's thinking about the war, and from that moment on there, was no middle ground. You were either for it, or you were against it.

I'd never taken part in a demonstration before but on the seventeenth of March, Carol and I headed off into Central London to hear Vanessa Redgrave and Tariq Ali deliver speeches denouncing America's involvement in Vietnam. It was the biggest anti-war rally London had ever seen and as soon as Ali finished talking, the whole crowd began moving as one towards the American Embassy. Both Ali and Redgrave had given impassioned speeches and feelings were running high as the crowd approached Grosvenor Square. A dozen different political groups were represented. The Anarchists had a large following, as did the communist Party, but the main bulk of demonstrators were just ordinary people disgusted with America's involvement in Vietnam and angry about the British and Australian Governments craven support of it.

As the demonstrators surged along the streets, the Anarchists began chanting 'Ho, Ho, Ho Chi Min! Ho, Ho, Ho Chi Min!' and soon the whole crowd had joined in: 'Ho, Ho, Ho Chi Min! Ho, Ho, Ho Chi Min!' The mood was electric and, as we neared the embassy, the crowd became even denser, to the point that, even if you had wanted to turn back, it would have been impossible. The only thing you could do was to move forward with the mob, holding your hands against the people in front to avoid falling down and being trampled. As we moved closer to Grosvenor Square, I tried to drag Carol out of the pack, but it was impossible, people had already squeezed themselves into every nook and cranny to avoid the mad crush. Some had found refuge in doorways; others were perched up on window ledges to escape the surging mob. The atmosphere was euphoric, everyone was laughing and chanting as we were propelled forwards into the square itself.

As soon as I saw the set up outside the embassy, I knew there was going to be trouble; the place was arraigned like a battlefield. Hundreds of uniformed police stood shoulder to shoulder, commanding the ground outside of the embassy. They were drawn up in unbroken lines, stretching all the way across the front of the building. Behind them, like covered wagons from some old Wild West movie, stood a long line of Black Marias, large windowless vehicles usually deployed to carry riot control units to violent demonstrations.

There was a stillness about the scene that was chilling. They announced on the news later that day that there were 1,000 police and 20,000 demonstrators - but the rally organizers claimed 100,000 and that would have been closer to the mark. But whatever the numbers, you could tell that the place was about to explode and explode it did.

As we came to a stop directly in front of the embassy, the chanting grew louder, 'Ho, Ho, Ho Chi Min! Ho, Ho, Ho Chi Min! Americans out! Ho Chi in!' The crowd was surging this way and that like an angry, teathered beast; one minute, we'd all be forced sideways a few tottering paces and then, involuntarily, the entire crowd would surge back the opposite way, people cursing, elbows in your ribs, fists in your back, toes trampling, pushing and shoving, women screaming and holding up young children to save them from the crush. It was a madhouse, made worse by the knowledge that the whole situation was now clearly out of control. We were two or three rows back from the front line of police and I could see the fear and confusion on their faces as they fought to control the burgeoning crowd.

Then people behind us started to pelt things. It was harmless enough at first, flowers, water bombs and bits and pieces of rubbish, but then suddenly, directly in front of us, a milk bottle smashed into a young constable's face and he went down, blood running from a gash over his left eye. The police line broke at once and, as his comrades knelt to help him, the crowd surged forward through the gap.

It was as if somebody had pressed a button. I saw a uniformed officer make a signal with a baton towards the line of Black Marias and immediately, two vehicles at the center moved out of formation. As they did, the gap was filled by mounted police who immediately charged the demonstrators, truncheons flailing right and left. The people who weren't bowled over by the thundering horses were clubbed down by the cavalry as they charged deep into the demonstrators.

The scene was chaotic. What had started out as a peaceful demonstration had spontaneously exploded into a pitched battle. Some of the mounted police overestimated their abilities and rode so deep into the crowd that the mob closed behind them, cutting off their retreat. These unfortunates were immediately set upon by demonstrators, enraged by the wanton brutality of their actions.

One of the horses came down directly in front of us, dragged off its feet by the screaming mob, legs flailing, head rearing up, eyes dilated in terror as the crowd dragged its terrified rider from the saddle and began beating him viciously. Within seconds, he was hoisted from the ground like a broken doll, helmet and truncheon gone, people pulling at his arms and legs, men and women alike punching at his head and face as his captors strove to tear him apart.

The horse staggered up and away, but the young cop was helpless. It was a sickening scene, but the violence had been instigated by the police and now he was paying for it. Carol was in tears but there was no way out. The best I could do was to try to keep her upright and stay away from the baton charges.

I was still struggling to get her out of harm's way when I realized that a Pakistani guy directly in front of me was waving a foot square piece of broken security glass. The shattered glass was held together by the wire reinforcing and, as I watched, he lashed out at the hapless policeman with it. As he brought his arm back for a second go, I caught his wrist from behind and twisted the glass out of his hand. I had no sympathy for the police, but this was going too far. As he turned, he threw a punch at me and we ended up wrestling with each other in the midst of all the surrounding chaos. "He's a cop!" he was screaming to no one in particular. "He's a plain clothes copper!" It could have turned nasty but suddenly, there were horses everywhere as mounted police arrived in force to rescue their mate.

I don't know if the cops realized what was happening, but in the melee that followed, one of them pointed a truncheon at a sobbing Carol and screaming at me, "If you think anything of that woman you'll get her out of here now!"

The mob was beginning to thin as the demonstrators dispersed across the square. Smoke still swirled around small pockets of resistance, but the main engagement was over. The golden eagle stood intact above the American Embassy … the battle was lost, but the point had been made.

_____

Chapter 30

Earls Court Police Station

When I lost my job in late October because of the encroaching winter, I knew there was almost zero chance of getting started elsewhere. I tramped around London for weeks afterwards, but the weather remained bleak and all major construction companies were already operating with reduced staff. Occasionally, I'd find a few day's casual work on a building site somewhere, but I was drinking more than ever, and an edge of lunacy had crept into almost everything I did.

I was borrowing money, mixing with mercenaries from the Congo, brawling in bars, and hanging out with all types of petty thieves and conmen, and as I slid further and further downhill, I dragged Carol with me. But then one night, totally out of the blue, it all came to a sudden and violent end.

Ray Harding, an old friend, had offered me a job demolishing a disused house not far from Earls Court. The agreement was that, if we finished the job within ten days, there'd be a sizeable bonus, and with four Glasgow lads, one Jamaican, Ray and I operating twelve-hour shifts, we tore the whole place down in a week. The work was hard and dangerous, but the money was good and when he paid us off at 5 pm that Friday, we all headed up the road to the Kings Head to celebrate.

The Scottish lads insisted on drinking whisky with beer chasers and by the time the pub closed, the Jamaican couldn't stand, so we loaded him into a taxi and sent him home before heading off up the road in search of more drink.

The *Yodeling Sausage* was a licensed restaurant on the main road close to the Earls Court Police Station. It was a popular nightspot with live music and we often went there after the pubs had closed. The restaurant was busy when we arrived, but they organized a table for six near the front door and soon, we were singing along with the rest of the crowd. Everyone was having a great time and we were all taken by surprise when a drunken Australian suddenly punched Ray in the side of the head and sent him sprawling on the floor. I was sitting in a corner booth, with my back against the wall, and by the time I got out, Ray was back on his feet, punching the daylights out of his opponent.

The fight had barely ended when the doors burst open and there were uniformed police everywhere. At first, they treated the whole thing as just another barroom brawl, but when the ambulance medicos told them that they were having trouble reviving the Australian, they marched us all up to the police station for further questioning. I wasn't too worried: Ray had been attacked and he'd defended himself. But when I noticed the arresting sergeant talking to two plainclothes detectives and pointing across to where I stood talking to Ray, I realized that they were taking it seriously. A few minutes later, one of the detectives gestured to me.

"You," he motioned with his head, "come with me."

I followed him through into the interrogation room where his mate was waiting. Through the glass partition, I could see Ray near the front desk, still arguing with some uniformed police.

"So what happened there tonight?"

The older detective was sitting on the edge of a desk, notepad in hand.

"You tell me," I said.

"You're in big trouble, Harding. The Australian guy you assaulted is still unconscious. If he dies, you'll be charged with manslaughter, maybe murder."

The police were pushing Ray and the others towards the revolving doors. I was hoping he'd take the hint and disappear.

"Your Australian mate caused the whole thing," I told them. "You should have arrested him, not me."

'So, what happened? Let's hear your version of it."

"It's pretty simple," I told him. "The Aussie assaulted the wrong guy."

As we were talking, the arresting officer arrived back in the room.

"Where's Harding?" he said, looking around.

"This isn't Harding?"

"No, Harding's the big guy, this one wasn't involved."

They ordered me to leave then rushed outside and grabbed Ray who was still arguing with a group of uniforms in front of the station. We tried to follow them back in but were stopped by the police just inside the revolving doors. There was a lot of pushing and shoving but when a fat old sergeant punched one of the Scottish lads in the face, it was on for young and old.

The police drew their truncheons, and as we tried to force our way into the station, they kept beating us back. One of the Scottish lads grabbed two dustbin lids and we went back at them again, kicking and punching as they rained blows on our shields. One young cop caught me a glancing blow with a truncheon, but I wrestled it off him, and whacked him with it several times before his mates could drag him free. The whole place was in an uproar, but it was never going to last for long. Reinforcements were rushing in from the back of the station as we jammed dustbins in the revolving doors and fled off up the street and into the night.

.

The following afternoon, I received a call from Ray's roommate, the police had been to his flat. The good news was that the Australian guy had regained consciousness, the bad news was that they'd issued a warrant for my arrest.

They released Ray two days later. He'd been beaten pretty badly in the police cells and his face was a mess, but the Australian guy had admitted that he'd instigated the brawl, so the police had no option but to drop the charges. Ray called me the following day.

"You need to stay away from Earls Court, Brian. They have an artist's impression up in the station and it looks exactly like you. They're determined to get you, mate."

I lay low for the next few days, hoping it would pass, but then Pat Doran told me that two detectives had called in to the Kings Head with a pretty accurate artists impression drawing that was being circulated around Earls Court. The description read: *Name - Brian Slater alias Brian King – Nationality - Irish/Australian – 5 foot 11 inches tall - solid build - florid complexion - wild staring eyes.*

"I'm not too happy about the wild staring eyes bit," I told him.

"You think this is funny, Brian?" He was staring at me. "You'll get four or five years for this, maybe more. You need to get out of England now, while you still can."

I talked it over with Carol. We'd already considered returning to Australia overland, so when Jack Swarby, a Jewish travel agent we'd met in Israel, offered us a good price on two tickets to Istanbul, we accepted.

Carol stayed in Earls Court to sort out the visas whilst I lay low in Blackpool. I returned to London for the last week but, a few days before we were due to leave England, Swarby called around to our flat.

"The cops are onto you, Brian, don't ask me how. They were at the office today; they know you're booked on the tour."

I'd made a few enemies in London and it was obvious that someone was informing on me.

"Give me the address where you'll be staying in Calais," I told him. "We'll get a ferry across and meet up with the bus there. If the police call again, tell them I cancelled the trip."

We left London the following day, took a ferry across to Calais and met up with the bus there. Then, after leaving the tour in Istanbul, we hitchhiked through Iran, Afghanistan, Pakistan and India before catching a plane across the Indian Ocean, back to Australia.

Chapter 31

A Vision

Within months of arriving back in Sydney, the cycle began again … drinking, losing jobs, drinking, hangovers, drinking, police, hangovers and more drinking. I wondered why Carol stayed sometimes, the situation was clearly hopeless. It was as if we were bound together somehow, her strengths filling in my weaknesses, and my lunacy pulling her out of a quiet, conservative existence into a world full of madness, excitement and danger.

But then one night, I awoke abruptly from a deep sleep. I'd dreamt that I was standing on the quayside of some unknown town, talking to a man who was trying to sell me a sailing boat. 'She's a lovely little boat.' We were staring down at a yacht tied up alongside the stone jetty. 'That little boat will take you anywhere in the world!' This is the solution; I was thinking in the dream. I'll live on board my own boat. When things get too bad anywhere, I'll simply up anchor and sail away.

The dream was so powerful that I couldn't get back to sleep, so I got out of bed and sat in a chair, staring out the window. A boat, this could be the solution! My own boat! We could go anywhere we wanted; nobody would even know where we were. When I travelled, I didn't need to drink. I knew that. This was the solution! It was 3.00 am but I couldn't keep it to myself. "Carol, wake up, it's important, wake up!" I told her of my dream as she sat up on one elbow, staring at me. "A boat, a yacht, we'll live on board! I'll stop drinking. We can sail anywhere in the world. It'll be fantastic!"

"Go back to sleep, Brian, you've been dreaming. Go back to sleep, OK?"

"No, this is important! We can go anywhere in the world! We'll be free, independent!"

"We can't even pay the rent. How are we going to buy a boat?"

"Go back to sleep," I was sorry I'd woken her; I didn't want her spoiling my dream. "We'll talk in the morning."

I got up, dressed, then sat at the kitchen table drawing pictures of sailing boats and conjuring up visions of life on the high seas. This felt right. This was the solution. I knew it in my heart.

The first rays of light were threading their way through the darkened streets as I left the house and walked down toward Rushcutters Bay, early morning joggers slipping through the half-light in shorts and T-shirts, pained expressions and panting breath. A light breeze was rustling through the leafy trees as I walked along by the low stone wall that surrounds the harbor, and as I drew near to the marinas, the air was filled with the tinkling and clinking of ropes and rigging, tap, tap, tapping against the masts of a hundred yachts that swung and bobbed restlessly at their moorings. I spent the whole day there, entranced, wandering around talking to the men working on the boats, asking them a million questions, eager to learn as much as possible about the chances of crossing an ocean in a boat. By the time I left, I was hooked, completely and irreversibly. I wanted to sail a small boat around the world.

My next stop was the Kings Cross Library. After fossicking around for hours, I found just the right book. *A Long Sail to Haiti* by Frances Breton became my Bible, and his little boat, the twenty-four-foot, *Nengo,* became my hope and inspiration.

When Carol came home that afternoon, I dragged her down to the marina and pointed out the types of boats I thought would be right for us. She was completely baffled by it all, but she hadn't seen me so animated for years, so she went along with it. We talked it over for days and eventually, Carol began to get the boat bug, too. Money was the problem and I knew the only way I could raise sufficient funds was by getting a big-paying job, so I applied for a job operating earth moving machinery in a small mining town, way out in the back of beyond.

*　*　*

Dampier was the most depressing place I'd ever been, a grim, dirty, dusty, isolated, iron ore mining town on the north-west coast of Australia that existed only to plough iron ore out of the ground and ship it off to Japan. Carol got a job there, teaching at the local school, and we estimated that, with our combined wages, we would be able to save enough money to build our boat within eighteen months.

We stuck it out for almost a year, but after an accident where I damaged the cartilage in my right knee, I was forced off work for three months and eventually had to throw the job in. It disrupted our plans, but we'd already saved enough money to begin building our boat, so we packed up and headed for Queensland.

I'd already purchased plans through the mail for a twenty-four-foot sloop from a boat-building yard in Brisbane, and as soon as we arrived, we began construction. I thought at first it would take a year or two, but the progress slowed as my drinking became worse and eventually, we both began to wonder if the boat would ever be finished. Carol was sick of it all by then and one morning as I sat in the lounge room, hung-over and depressed, she came in and stood by the door. "I can't live like this anymore," she began, "your drinking's killing both of us. I've been talking to my sister. My family want me to move back to Sydney."

"Don't be silly," I told her, "the boats nearly finished. Another few months and we'll be there. Then we can get moving again. We can go anywhere we want, anywhere in the world. Don't give up now, not when we're so close."

"You've been saying that for three years now, and I've been stupid enough to believe you."

"Look, the boat will be finished in twelve months, don't give up on me now. As soon as it's launched, we'll leave. You know I've never liked Brisbane. We'll move to Sydney or wherever you like. Once we get sailing, it'll be different. That was the whole idea."

She shook her head. "It's no good, I'm sick of it. I have no friends and we never go anywhere. All you talk about is the boat and when you're not working on the boat, you're drinking."

"Carol, I know it's gone on for too long, but don't give up on me now, please. We're almost there. Just hang in for another few months. We'll put a time limit on it, OK? If it's not finished by the end of this year, we'll sell it as it is and forget about the whole idea. How's that?"

But she'd heard it all before.

"I'm sick of it all, Brian. If you don't stop drinking, the boat will never be finished."

Chapter 32

Sobriety

Things came to a head two weeks later. I'd been out on a particularly heavy bender, and as I rose to the surface that morning, stiff and confused, I had no idea at all where I was. I was cold and cramped and it took me a while to realize that I was lying in the forward cabin area of the boat. She was propped up in a cradle by the side of the house and I must have crawled up there for some reason after coming home drunk the night before.

Images of the previous evening flittered in and out of my consciousness, unwanted scraps of memories that revolted me. I vaguely recalled arguing with a bunch of bikers at the Wynnum Hotel and I remembered the sound of bottles smashing. There'd been a fight, but I couldn't recall the outcome. My head was throbbing badly, and the side of my face was swollen and sore. I dimly recalled Carol shouting at me, but I wasn't sure what it had been about.

I drifted off back to sleep and when I came to again, the pale light of dawn was just beginning to filter down through the open hatchway. I lay there, sick and sorry, feeling like death, a dirty old canvas tarp pulled up under my chin. I'd always dreaded the dawn. You're finished, I thought, you're fucked. I lay there in despair, drifting in and out of consciousness, unwilling to face another day.

My head was throbbing, my neck was stiff from leaning against the hull all night. As I lay there, motionless, staring listlessly at the inside of the boat, memories of the *Kathleen R,* my old refuge from childhood, came back to me. She hadn't crossed my mind in twenty years, but it dawned on me as I lay there that this boat looked almost the same. They were about the same length and their construction was similar, heavy ribs spaced every foot or so, supported by solid stringers that ran fore and aft the entire length of the hull.

I drifted off again, wondering where the old fishing boat was. Could she be still working somewhere? Or would she be a forgotten wreck, sunk on her moorings or washed up on some lonely beach?

When I woke again, it was just after 8.00 am and I sat there, looking around the boat, thinking of the years of work we'd put into her. Any normal person would have built her in a year or two. It was hopeless and I knew at that moment that I would never finish her. I would never launch her. Somebody else would … but not me. It was a sickening realization and it hit me hard. She was to have been my salvation. I climbed over the back of the cockpit, got down from the cradle, and crept into the house. All was silent, Carol had already left for work.

I sat in the living room for hours, hung over and dreading the thought of Carol coming home, dreading the look in her eyes. I wandered aimlessly around the house like a zombie, every thought was despairing, there was no way out. I stood in the lounge room, staring at a map of the world that I'd stuck on the wall. Pencil lines from more hopeful days traced wide arcs across oceans that I would never sail. There was some scribble down in one corner.

Most men lead lives of quiet desperation.

Thoreau. I'd written it there one night when I was drunk. What would he know of this? Then, further down, another scrawl.

We build our character on the debris of our despair.

I sat there for more than an hour, staring at the words then I picked up the phone and called the operator. "I need help," I said.

"What sort of help?"

I paused for a long time, unable to form the word that would tie me to my father.

"Hello, are you still there? What sort of help do you need?"

Finally, I choked it out.

"I'm an alcoholic. I need help."

"Hold on, please. I'll connect you."

I'd dreaded this moment for years. I'd have done anything to avoid this final humiliation.

"Hello, Central Office, how can I help you?"

I couldn't bring myself to say it again.

"I think I may have a problem with alcohol."

"Well, you've called the right place then. My name's John. I'm an alcoholic. Would you like to tell me your name?"

"Do I have to?" Suddenly, I felt panicky. I had no idea who this guy was.

"No, of course not." He sounded cheerful. "So, you're not travelling too well, is that right?"

"I've got a few problems. I probably drink a bit too much."

Why had he asked for my name?

"Have you ever tried to stop drinking before or is this your first time?"

"I contacted your Sydney office once, a few years ago."

I was feeling jittery, wondering what I was getting myself into.

"Did you get sober that time?"

"I got sober for two months, then I busted. I didn't like the meetings, all that talk about God."

There was an abrupt laugh at the other end of the phone.

"A lot of us feel that way when we first arrive. Don't worry, it's a God of your own understanding."

"I'm not interested in any sort of God. I don't believe in that stuff."

"That's fine," he said. "You get to choose your own concept of God, one that makes sense to you."

Why was he going on about religion?

"Look, I don't want anyone telling me anything about God, OK? I had a gut-full of that stuff when I was a kid."

"I understand where you're coming from," he sounded amused. "I used to feel the same way. But like I said, you choose your own concept of God."

For a fleeting second, I felt a glimmer of hope, but then, just as quickly, I pushed it away.

"You think this is funny?" I said. "I phoned up to ask you about drinking. I'm not interested in listening to all this shite about God!"

"Take it easy, son." He was speaking quietly now. "Don't get on your high horse, I'm only trying to help. If you …"

"Well don't preach to me about God then, OK?" I cut him off. "I'm a fucking atheist." I was starting to get some of my energy back. "I phoned up to see what you people did, that's all. If I wanted to talk about God, I'd have phoned a fucking priest, and if I want to have a drink, that's my business, so don't fuck with me, OK?"

"You're right, son, it's entirely your business." His voice came back calm and quiet. "But I'll tell you something. I haven't had a drink for twenty-three years, but I never once knew anyone get sober talking the way you do. If you want to stop drinking, I'll do anything I can to help you, free of charge. But if you don't want to stop drinking, then you've probably dialed the wrong number." He paused. "Maybe you should go back out there for a while, have a few more drinks, see how you go. Is that what you want?"

Suddenly, I was frightened. I'd made a mess of the whole thing already. There was a long silence and I could feel the moment slipping away. Distorted remnants of pride were almost choking me but finally, in desperation, I managed to say, "Can you help me?"

"That depends." His voice softened. "If you want to stop drinking, I may be able to help you."

He told me his story then. He'd been alcoholic from an early age; he'd abandoned his wife and children and he'd spent years in prisons around Australia. I listened as he recounted a tale that probably would have been shocking to most other people and then he gave me an address just a mile or so from where I lived. "There's a meeting there tonight at 8.00 pm. Try to stay sober today."

After hanging up, I sat there, mulling over the conversation. This is probably pure bullshit, I thought, some sort of watered-down Christian crap. There'll be Catholics there for sure, hiding in the wings, waiting for me to weaken so they can drag me off to some fucking wacko church.

I wandered around the house aimlessly. Then it struck me, if I'm not going to have another drink after tonight, I might as well have my last few today! That cheered me up immediately.

By 6 pm, I was drunk. My small amount of cash had run out and I went from pub to pub looking for someone to borrow money from. Nobody was interested, I was too well-known. Ernie, my last hope, hadn't arrived at the hotel and I'd gone around to his house only to be confronted by his angry wife and four little children.

"No, he's not here. I threw him out last week. I'm divorcing the bastard. He's a parasite, like you. You're all bloody parasites!"

She slammed the door so hard in my face that it nearly knocked me off the front steps. I walked off down to the main street. I knew where the meeting hall was. I looked at my watch: it was 8 pm. I paused for a moment. I wasn't too drunk. I wasn't staggering. Maybe I could con a few dollars at the meeting.

I walked up the stairs to the hall, the door was closed but a small blackboard propped against the top step bore the inscription:

"The meeting has been moved to the library across the road. Please join us there." I was furious. I'd come here to give myself up and now they'd moved the meeting. I crossed the road. A nunnery lay on the other side and a sign stood against the gate:

Sobriety Meeting 8.00 pm
All are welcome

I stopped at the gateway, agonizing as to whether to go in or not, and then, as I stood there, a small figure appeared out of the dark and an Irish voice inquired: "Is it the meeting for the alcoholics you're looking for?"

She was tiny, covered completely in black, except for a flash of white linen above her forehead. I started back, alarmed.

"You've got no right to talk to me like that! Do you go around asking everyone if they're alcoholics?"

She ignored my bluster and, tugging gently at my arm, led me up the pathway. "Come on inside. You've come this far, don't stop now."

I was getting emotional. I could never face kindness unaided by drink. "I made a mistake. I'm at the wrong place." I tried to pull my arm away, but she clung on.

"Come in here now. They're nice people."

Oh Christ! I knew if she kept going, I'd break down.

"Let go of my arm," I told her. "I'll go in if you let go of my arm."

"Promise me … promise me you'll go in?"

"I promise, but not with you. I'll go in, but not with you."

We were outside the library now and through the open door, I could see people sitting around a crowded table, peering out at us. She stopped at the entrance.

"I'll pray for you. Now in you go."

She waited until I stepped into the room and then she slipped away as quietly as she'd come. The people at the table were staring at me. I pulled myself together.

"You bunch of poofters aren't going to stop me sailing around Cape Horn, OK?"

One of the men got up. "You can sail wherever you want, mate, but you'll probably have a better chance of getting around Cape Horn if you're sober." He pulled back a chair. "Sit down, please."

I stayed there for an hour, listening to their stories. Some were worse than mine and, as I listened, I began to feel a little better. When I left there later that night, I was still drunk, but for the first time in a long time, I felt the first, tiny, glimmerings of hope.

The lights were on when I arrived home. I knew Carol would be sitting up waiting for me, and I knew she'd be angry. As I walked in through the back door, a frying pan hit me in the face and knocked me down.

"Wait!" I shouted, "Wait, I've stopped drinking, I'm sober, everything's alright!"

"You bastard," she screamed. "You're drunk again, look at you!" As I struggled to my feet, she took another swing, belting me across the other side of the head. I saw stars and exploded.

"Stop it! You mad little bastard! I've given away the drink and you're still fucking crazy. I'll fix you!"

I strode into the bedroom and pulled a double-barreled shotgun out from under the bed. Carol heard me loading it up and, as I came back out into the lounge room, I caught a flash of her foot disappearing out the back door. I tilted the gun high and fired both barrels through the lounge room ceiling. The noise was deafening. The shotgun had no wooden stock to it and the steel frame jerked backwards, tearing open the skin between my thumb and forefinger as the thrust from the gun knocked me over backwards onto the floor. As I lay there, stunned by the blast, two thoughts, both as clear as crystal, went flashing through my brain. The first: '*You're crazy! This is not an act. You are fucking crazy!* The second, like a message from above, just before I passed out: '*You have to stop drinking for yourself, not for anyone else, for yourself.*'

When I awoke the following morning, I was still lying on the floor. Carol had put a blanket over me as I slept and I lay there, staring up at the holes in the ceiling, shaking badly from the drink. I thought back to the night before. Ian, one of the men from the meeting, had invited me to a barbeque and I fished through my pockets looking for the piece of paper he'd given me. The address was only a few streets away. When Carol woke up, I told her about the invitation, and she agreed to come with me. There were two large bottles of beer left in the house. I drank them quickly to calm the shakes, then we walked along the road to Ian's place.

That was the beginning. I was thirty-three. I felt like an old man. I was penniless. There were warrants out for my arrest in various states of Australia. I hadn't worked for three years and, apart from Carol, I didn't have a friend in the world.

I went to the meetings every evening for the next few weeks. The people were friendly and understanding but I knew I couldn't last there for long. When they got up to speak, they all spoke of a 'power greater than themselves' as being central to their recovery, and it was obvious to me that they were referring to God.

The meetings helped me stay sober for the first few weeks and gave me a breathing space to get my head together. But I was incredibly depressed. I woke up each morning, wondering whether I could make it through that day without drinking. I had no faith in myself whatsoever; I'd failed too many times before.

Within a few weeks of stopping drinking, I found a job on a construction site. It was the first job I'd had in three years and it was hard work, digging out foundations by hand in the ferocious summer heat. I was in bad shape physically after years of alcoholism and the work nearly killed me. The boss was a tough, wiry little Australian guy by the name of Archie Linning. Archie was burnt black and wizened from years in the blazing sun and I knew he was watching me from the minute I started. On the second day, he approached me just before knock-off time. He was blunt.

"How are you doing?" he asked.

"I'm doing OK." There was obviously more to it.

"Are you a piss-pot, son?"

I looked up, angered.

"I don't drink, mate. What's your problem?"

"Bullshit!" He was grinning. "You're either a piss-pot or a junkie. I'm an ex drunk, so don't try and fool me."

"I stopped drinking three weeks ago."

"Well, you still look pretty crook to me. Look, I'm going to give you two choices. Either you come with me tonight to a meeting at the Royal Brisbane Hospital, or you can find yourself another job. You're no good to me the way you are. Think it over."

On the way home in the truck, I asked him what the meeting was about.

"It's for alcoholics who want to stay off the piss," he said. "Come and have a look. It can't do you any harm. It's kept me sober for four years and I was the town drunk."

"Is it religious?" I asked, but Archie just grinned.

"If it was religious, you wouldn't get me anywhere near the place. I'm an atheist, mate. I'll pick you up at your place at seven-thirty, OK?"

Chapter 33

Pavilion 4

Pavilion 4 was the Royal Brisbane Hospital's Drug and Alcohol Unit and it suited me better than anything I'd ever tried before. There was no talk of God, I could get sleeping pills or Valium whenever I felt I needed them, and I saw a therapist there once every week. After an initial assessment, I was prescribed an anti-depressant called Triptinol to help stabilize the mood swings I was experiencing. I was to take them for the next three years. The psychiatrist also recommended that I take Antabuse, a drug that ensured that I would be violently sick the moment I took any alcohol whatsoever into my system. I'd been warned by some of the old diehard drunks who frequented the place not to take it. There were horror stories of people having a few sips of beer and then projectile vomiting instantaneously over everyone in the bar. One of the old reprobates who'd been through the hospital a dozen times or more, told me that Antabuse could kill you if you had a bad heart and drank on top of it. Their advice had just the opposite effect on me. I wasn't frightened of dying; I was frightened of living drunk. I took the Antabuse every day without fail for the next three years. When I was feeling angry, confused, or even more happy than usual, I'd take two pills in the morning instead of one.

Dr. Ruth Cilento was the resident psychologist at Pav 4 and I trusted her from the beginning. I talked to her many times about the *Kathleen R* and she always advised me to follow my dreams.

"Finish the boat and get out on the high seas. If that's your dream, then follow it." When I told her I was an atheist, she just smiled. "Maybe you'll meet your God out on the ocean," she'd laugh, "maybe God's a sailor, too."

*   *   *

For the next three years, Carol and I concentrated on finishing the boat and getting our lives back together. The work progressed steadily and finally, almost seven years from the day we'd begun construction, the *Kathleen R* was ready to launch.

The prospect of leaving Australia and sailing off around the world had brought up other considerations and I found myself wondering about Jean and my children. I'd contacted her on several occasions since she'd returned to Australia, but she'd always refused to talk, so when I phoned her that day, I wasn't expecting too much.

"Hello, Jean speaking."

"Jean, it's me, Brian."

Her voice hardened immediately. "So, it's you again. Where are you calling from this time, some prison somewhere? Are you drunk?"

"No, I stopped drinking some time ago. I've been sober for three years, and I'd like to see the girls."

"How would I know whether you're sober or not? I've heard it all before, remember? Where are you now? Where are you living?"

"I live in Brisbane. I have my own business there."

"Do you really? Well, bully for you."

"Look, I don't expect you to believe me …"

"I don't believe you," she cut in, "I don't believe anything you say. I know you, remember? You're not talking to some stupid little floozy in a bar, Brian."

My stomach was starting to churn. "Look, why don't we meet? It's pointless talking like this."

"I have no desire to meet you, none at all, OK? So don't bother calling here again."

The line went dead. The conversation depressed me but there was nothing I could do. I had no rights whatsoever with Jean and we both knew that.

The following evening the phone rang. Carol answered then passed me the receiver. "It's Jean."

"Hello, Brian?" Her voice came over the line, cold and abrupt. "Do you know Southport?"

"Yes."

"There's a café out on the spit, next to the pub, by the water. Do you know it?"

"Yes, I think so."

"Be there at 12 o'clock tomorrow. If you've been drinking, don't bother coming."

The phone clicked off. Carol was looking across at me.

"I'm meeting her tomorrow at Southport."

"With the children?"

"No, I don't think so."

"What's the point of meeting her then?"

"It's a start, honey, it might open the door."

"To what?"

"Carol, for Christ's sake, I want to see my children. Don't make it any harder than it already is."

She jumped up and left the room but ten minutes later, she was back. "I'm sorry, you should see her. I feel jealous. You've never talked about her. I've never known what happened between you two."

"It's not about her," I said, "it's about the children."

I lay awake in bed that night and wondered if that was the truth. Was it only the children? Images of Jean had haunted me throughout the years and hearing her voice, angry as it was, had brought her back into focus once again.

*   *   *

I arrived at Southport Spit early the following day and wandered along the foreshore, looking at the boats. It was autumn and a cool breeze was running in from the south, stirring the yachts at their moorings and whistling through the rigging.

I saw Jean in the distance, walking through the car park. Tall and slim and graceful as ever, wearing a leopard skin coat that would have looked out of place on just about anybody else. I stood there, motionless, as she approached. Her hair was still dark and curly and two round golden earrings swung as she walked. She stopped in front of me and, without thinking. I reached out to take her hand.

"We won't bother with that," she snapped.

There was an awkward pause.

"Do you feel like a coffee?" I said.

"No, I don't. This won't take long. I just wanted to make sure you're sober, that's all, and I want to make something clear. I don't want you coming down here, I don't want you phoning me, and I don't want you anywhere near the girls. Is that understood? I'm in a relationship now with someone I love, and I don't want you messing my life up again, is that clear?"

"Jean, I want to see the children. I have that right."

"You don't have any rights, none whatsoever and you know it."

Nothing had changed; how could it? We were like total strangers, looking out across the water, separate and lost in our own two worlds.

"How are they?" I asked.

"How are who?" she snapped, flashing an angry look at me.

"How are the girls?"

"You mean Kathleen and Sharon? You haven't forgotten their names, have you?"

"How are they, Jean?"

"They're fine. They're happy, and I want them to stay that way. Just go away, Brian. We don't want you in our lives. Mario is their father now, more of a father than you ever were."

"They'll want to know who I am one day," I said.

"Perhaps." She looked at me. "But not for a long time, I suspect."

I looked away, unable to meet the anger, but then for some reason, she softened.

"Look, it's for the best. They're happy as they are. I may be getting married again. Leave us alone, please, for my sake. Do that much for me."

I couldn't talk, so I just nodded.

We stood there silently for a while, then she turned to me again.

"What are your plans? Do you intend staying in Brisbane?"

"No," I told her, "I'm building a boat. She's almost finished. I plan to sail around the world in her. That's one of the reasons I wanted to meet the girls."

"What, in case you disappear at sea, you mean? How romantic. That could be a nice touch actually, especially if you're insured."

She hadn't changed a bit. We walked back together to the parking area. My car was close to the entrance. I needed to get away.

"I'll write to you," I said.

She was looking at my car.

"You're moving up in the world."

"It's a car," I said.

I watched her as she walked away. She never once faltered in her pace and she never once looked back.

Chapter 34

The River

Three weeks before our planned departure, we slipped the boat for her final painting, cream topsides, a navy-blue hull and the name *Kathleen R* standing out proudly in gold lettering on her bow. It was an exciting time preparing the boat for her maiden voyage, but we were behind schedule and there was no time for standing around talking. Friends that dropped by for a chat were either pressed into service or sent on their way. We toiled from dawn till dusk but the list of things to do seemed to grow longer each day. The marine radio we'd paid a small fortune for refused to work no matter what we tried, emitting only a few faint bleeps at the best of times, and the stainless steel rigging we'd installed turned out to be too long and had to be taken down and shortened.

Finally, one Tuesday evening, she was ready to launch. There were still plenty of things to be done but nothing that couldn't be completed whilst afloat. We finished work around nine that evening and, after a quick meal at the boatshed, I decided to check out our mooring in the Brisbane River. It was a dark, moonless night and when we arrived at the jetty, Carol and I stood at the end of the ancient wooden structure, peering out across the inky black water.

"I can't see the buoy," I told her. "I'll have to row out."

She was tired. "Isn't that it out there, past the big cruiser?"

"I've got to make sure, honey. I don't want any stuff-ups in the morning. If somebody's using it, we'll have all sorts of problems. Look," I told her, "you stay here and I'll row out. I won't be long."

As I climbed down the ladder, the river was running out strongly, the black waters straining against the dinghy's mooring line. I slipped the rope and then, sculling gently, allowed the ebbing waters to carry me out in a wide arc towards where our buoy should have been. I pulled on the oars this way and that, flashing my torch around the anchored yachts, trying to get my bearings until I found the buoy, bobbing and dancing in the torch's beam, it's tell-tale little flag assuring me that all was well. I was turning the dinghy back towards shore when I heard the first scream.

"Carol?" I called out. "Are you OK?"

Her voice came back faintly across the darkness. "Yes, I'm here. Have you found it?"

The scream came again, this time muffled and muted. It was coming from the direction of a thirty-five-foot sloop that swung on a mooring close to mine. I knew the boat, the *Darius Star*. I'd been on board her once, talking to her owner.

A dim light shone softly from one of her portholes and as I rowed towards her, the scream came again, a terrible, piercing, screeching plea, shut off and smothered in mid-stream.

"Help! Heeeeeeeelp! Hel…"

I pulled the dinghy up to the stern of the *Darius Star* and thumped hard on her wooden hull, struggling as I did to maintain my position against the flow of the ebbing waters. For a moment, there was silence but then the top hatch shot back and a head and shoulders appeared.

"Brian! What's up mate? What's all the banging about?"

"What's going on, Mick? What's all that screaming?"

"Screaming?" He sounded puzzled. "What screaming? I was asleep, probably a party on shore."

"It sounded like it was coming from your boat." I was baffled.

"No way, mate. Like I said, I was asleep. You woke me up."

Only his head and shoulders were visible above the hatchway. His face was covered in shadow, giving me no clue to his mood. The dinghy was slipping down river constantly as we talked and every so often I had to take took a few strokes on the oars to stay close to the *Darius Star*. The last time I pulled on the oars, the dinghy ranged up alongside the sloop, level with her aft porthole, and as I glanced unthinkingly into the dimly lit cabin, my blood ran cold. Mick was standing sideways on the short wooden steps that led up the companionway, his arms wrapped tightly around a woman's face and neck. They were both naked. She was struggling feebly, clutching at his forearms, choking in a vicious stranglehold.

"Let her go!" I pulled the dinghy closer. "Let her go, you bastard. I'm coming on board."

"So you want to be a hero, do you?"

He disappeared for a split second but then, as the woman began screaming again, he came bursting up out of the hatchway completely naked and launched himself off the back of the boat and down on top of me. I had a fleeting impression of what looked like a club in his hands as he hurled himself at me, bringing the weapon smashing down onto my head. He landed square on top of me, the force of his body driving me backward into the forward thwart of the dinghy.

The next conscious memory I have is of twisting and turning in the depths of the Brisbane River, half-stunned and breathing in water. I was clawing at the blackness, having no idea at all which way was up, turning over and over helplessly, trying to make sense of what was happening. My eyes were wide open, but I could see nothing, not even my hands in front of my face. Images of Carol swam before me and I wondered vaguely if she was going to be alright. I tried to breathe in again but then, as the water choked me, I realised in a dreamy, far-off kind of way that I was drowning. There were flashes then, in behind my eyes, bright red and yellow streams of light, going off like fireworks in my brain. I had a sensation of bubbles rising upwards and, in one last feeble attempt, I pulled at the blackness with leaden hands. Suddenly, my face was free of water and I was choking and gasping in air. Everything was pitch black. I'd come up underneath the capsized dinghy. As I struggled out from beneath the hull, gagging and clawing at her sides, the dinghy righted herself and I dragged myself into the flooded boat.

As I lay there, half-stunned, vomiting up water, I realized that I couldn't move my left arm. I tried to roll over but I had difficulty turning my head. I peered over the gunwale. The waterlogged boat, kept afloat by its buoyancy tanks, was drifting down river, carried seawards by the ebbing waters. I tried to roll over onto my back again but, as I did, the little boat shuddered to a halt. We'd drifted down onto the anchor chain of a large yacht and as we scraped past, I reached out and managed to grasp the chain in one hand.

As I hung there more dead than alive, one hand holding the chain, the other gripping the gunwale of the dinghy, I heard Carol's voice in the distance, calling out my name. I couldn't answer; it was all I could do to hold on. And then I saw him again, kneeling in the front of a small rubber boat, the bow pushed low in the water, the river carrying him down to where I lay. There was a woman with him, her arms coming around his back; she was grabbing at a short, stubby oar he was holding in both hands.

"Don't, Mick, don't! He's fucked! Don't, please!" She was hysterical, screaming at him and clutching frantically at the oar. "Leave him alone! He's fucked! Can't you see that? Leave him alone!"

I lay there, half paralyzed and helpless. Mick made a few quick thrusts with the oar and then he was down on top of me, the rubber boat pushing into my half-sunken craft. I tried to fend him off, but my left arm was useless. The woman was pleading with him, grabbing at his arms.

"No! You'll kill him! No, don't, please don't!"

The dinghy dislodged as they struggled, and they began drifting downstream again.

"Fuck him!" he was screaming. "Fuck him!"

He pushed her free and then, with a few quick, furious strokes of the paddle, he was back down on top of me, grabbing at the side of the dinghy as he swung at me with the oar. But the woman was pulling at him again and he missed, the oar smashing into the chain, sending shudders along my arm.

I was helpless. All I could do was lie there, hanging on.

"Brian, are you there?" Carol's voice was closer now. "What's happening, are you OK?'

Mick called back to her calmly.

"He's OK, Carol! We'll be there in a minute. Everything's fine."

I realized then that he'd kill her too and I tried to calm him.

"It's over, Mick, forget about it. I should have kept out of it."

"Too fucking right, you should have kept out of it!" His rage was starting to fade.

"It's over," I said again, "let's just forget about it. We're leaving Brisbane tomorrow."

"Do you know who I am?"

"No," I was hoping it was the right answer, "no, I don't know who you are."

He stared at me for what seemed like an age and then finally, he said, "If you go anywhere near the cops, you'll be dead within a week, understand?"

"Yes," was all I could say.

"If they arrest me, you'll be dead within a week, understand?"

"Yes," I said again.

"Leave him alone," the girl was pleading with him again, "he's fucked, leave him alone."

He let go of the boat then and as his dinghy began drifting away, he pointed a finger at me.

"Do not fuck up," he said and then we stared at each other silently across the widening gap until they disappeared into the blackness down river.

A few moments later, I lost my grip on the chain and the waterlogged boat slid along the side of the yacht and began moving off down river, me paddling with one hand, pulling feebly towards the shore. A few minutes later, an abandoned jetty loomed up out of the darkness and as the dinghy drifted closer, I slipped out into the water and grasped a rusting steel ladder that was hanging down from the rotting timbers. I hung there for a while, recovering, the river dragging at my clothes, until finally I began pulling myself upwards, one rung at a time. I climbed slowly, each movement sending a sickening pain shooting down through my entire my back. When I got to the top, I crawled out onto the heavy wooden deck and lay there, vomiting, the blood from a head wound mixing with the bile in a dark pool beneath my eyes.

After resting for a while, I crawled across to a steel railing and pulled myself upright. I stood there in the dark for a few minutes, getting myself together, then I began limping back upriver. Carol came running when she heard me calling.

"Oh! God almighty!" She was shocked. "What happened? What happened to you?"

"Get the ute," I told her. "Get it now, quick."

"What happened? What's wrong with you?"

"I'll tell you later, get the ute!"

When she came back with the ute, I had to crawl into the passenger side headfirst because I couldn't bend my neck. As we drove up towards the police station, we overtook the girl from the boat. She was running half-naked along the street, her hands crossed over her breasts. We stopped the car and she jumped in.

"Drive me home. I live up the road."

"We're taking you to the police station."

"What!" she screamed. "Are you fucking crazy? Don't you know who that is? Do you think he's joking?" Then to Carol, "Take me home, you're fucking insane, both of you. He can have you killed like that!" She snapped her fingers at me and then pointed. "Turn left at the next street, that's it, now straight down to the end."

"You've got to report this ..." I began.

"Fuck you, mister," she snarled, "it's none of your business! Stay out of it! Stop there, by that white car, that's it." As she got out, she turned back. "Go home and forget about it. If you've got any fucking brains, you'll forget it ever happened!"

I watched her as she disappeared through the front door of a dilapidated old wooden house, then we continued to police station. The place was in darkness, so we headed for the late-night chemist up on the main road. By the time we got there, the left side of my body had stiffened up and my face and neck were covered in blood. The chemist cleaned me up as his assistant called the police. When they arrived, I gave them a brief outline of what had happened and after calling for reinforcements, they drove us back to the girl's house. I stood with four uniformed police as the sergeant rang the bell. A heavy, coarse-looking woman opened the door and, after a quick glance at the police, she looked at me.

"You're a fucking idiot, mate," she said, "you were warned." And then to the police, "What do you'se lot want?"

"Is this her?" The sergeant wasn't impressed.

"No." I caught sight of the woman from the river in the hallway. "That's her there."

"You," he pointed, "yes you, come out here."

The woman from the river came out reluctantly. The sergeant was frowning. "What happened in the river tonight?"

"Nothing happened. I've been home all night."

"Tell them what happened," I said. "They'll protect you."

"Who are you?" the girl snapped and then, turning back to the sergeant, "I've got no idea what he's talking about."

The sergeant was getting impatient. "Are you going to tell us what happened or not?"

"Not!" The girl was glaring at him now. "Definitely not! OK?"

She stepped back suddenly and slammed the door shut. I went to bang on it but the sergeant stopped me.

"Forget it." He was shaking his head. "She's a slut, we know them both. They're both sluts."

"But he was raping her on that boat!" I was stunned. "He could have killed her! You've got to do something."

"Don't worry about it mate, they're both sluts, the two of them." He turned away abruptly and began walking back towards the cars. "We'll drive you home. Just forget about it, it's their own business."

*　　*　　*

The following morning, I was woken by the clatter of boots and a loud banging on the front door. From where I lay in bed, I could see the tops of several police cars clustered together on the road outside.

"Open up, police!" The banging went on. "Open the door!"

I rolled over to the edge of the bed. The pain was intense. I'd spent an agonizing night lying flat on my back. I could hear Carol's voice in the hallway, talking to the police. I slid over the side of the mattress and went down onto my knees, curled over the bed as if in prayer. Before I could get any further, the door opened and two plainclothes cops were standing there. The shorter of the two studied me for a moment then gestured to his partner.

"Give him a hand."

I nearly screamed as he pulled me to my feet.

"You need to get to a doctor," the smaller one said, "or a chiropractor." His eyes were roaming around the room. "What do you know about the guy from last night?"

"Not much, we've spoken a few times. He has a mooring next to mine."

"What else do you know about him?"

"Nothing."

He studied me for a while. His offsider hadn't said a word.

"He's a tow truck driver. There's a warrant out for his arrest; we've been chasing him for months."

It felt better standing up, I could move reasonably well as long as I stood very straight. We went into the lounge room and Carol made us coffee as they continued questioning me about my relationship with Mick.

"Do you know his full name?"

"No, we only know him as Mick. He's been onboard our boat a few times. He called here once to ask us to keep an eye on the *Darius Star*. He's got her up for sale."

"He's been here? He knows where you live?"

"Yes, he was here a few weeks ago."

He thought for a while. "Do you own a gun?"

"No."

"You need to get one."

"Why?"

He stood up and moved towards the door. "We'll talk outside."

I followed him out to the front veranda. Two uniformed police were standing there, one of them tossed a cigarette away as we approached. The detective nodded.

"Take a walk."

As they disappeared into the garden, he turned back to me.

"Your mate's a tow truck driver. You know what that means?"

"Yes."

"He's a bad bastard, OK? Six weeks ago, he was causing trouble in a bar in the city. The barmaid refused to serve him and he pulled her over the bar and stuck a glass in her face. Two uniformed cops went up there and he put both of them in hospital with a chair. He's a flip-top. He's got a record as long as your arm and he's dangerous. Get yourself a gun, OK? A shotgun. If he comes here again, shoot the cunt, understand? Just shoot the cunt. It'll be self-defense. There'll be no charges. That's what we'll be doing when we catch up with him. Don't repeat any of this inside, understand?"

We went back inside and talked for a little while longer and then, just before they left, he shook hands with me and said, "Remember what I told you. Get it today and be prepared to use it."

As soon as they had gone, I phoned a chiropractor. He saw me at nine that morning.

"One of your vertebrae is displaced." He was squinting up at the X-rays. "He came close to breaking your back."

"How long will it take to fix?"

"I don't know if it can be fixed. You're lucky to be walking. We won't know the full extent of the damage for a while."

"I'm sailing for Sydney in three weeks."

"Not in that condition, you're not. This is serious. You're lucky you're not paralyzed."

'Lucky,' I thought, 'why do they always tell you you're lucky?'

The treatment was painful but I could move a little better when it was over.

"Come back tomorrow morning, we'll see how you're doing then."

"How bad is it? I need to know. I've spent seven years building that boat and we're about to set off around the world."

"You'll have to postpone the trip. If you can't walk properly, how do you expect to sail a boat?"

.

I sat outside in the ute, Carol next to me, reluctant to speak.

"He's talking rubbish," I told her, "it's not that bad. If I can walk, I can sail. What does he know about boats?"

"Brian, you have to do what he tells you."

A rage was building up inside, seven years of my life building the *Kathleen R,* and now some fucking lunatic could take it all away in a few minutes.

"He's talking shite," I told her. "We're sailing as planned in three weeks. I'll get a different chiropractor."

I was furious, and deep down in my guts, I could feel the old rage starting up again. Nobody on the face of the earth could do that to me and get away with it. I dropped Carol off at home then drove back into the city. When I returned that evening, I brought with me a brand new, twelve-gauge, pump-action shotgun and two boxes of shells.

Chapter 35

Vengeance

The next few weeks were extremely difficult. I could only work for an hour or so at a time. The constant pain in my back draining my energy, compelling me to lie down exhausted several times each day. I worked on the boat as much as I could, fixing the rigging, installing instruments and loading the boat up with provisions for the cruise. Each day, I crossed completed tasks off the list but no matter how hard I worked, there was always more to do.

My friends all advised me against leaving but that only made me more determined. Carol was worried but she knew better than to argue with me. I was leaving Brisbane as planned, ready or not.

One morning, I awoke before dawn, pulled up from sleep by the throbbing ache of my damaged spine and lay there in the darkness, feeling the despair and hatred once again. I thought about John Barrett, one of Carol's friends. He'd suggested reciting a prayer at the launch but I'd refused. I didn't want any weak-kneed, pseudo-Christian crap at the launching of my boat. Willpower and determination had built the *Kathleen R* and she would sail the seas the same way. I lay there, silently wondering about the trip ahead, doubts pushing their way into my unprotected mind. What if something happens out there? How will you cope? I pushed the negativity away, struggled over onto my side and began the daily ritual of getting out of my bunk. Fifteen minutes later, I was standing upright in the galley, hanging on to the chart table, nauseated from the pain.

It was still dark. I lit one of the gimbaled oil lamps and watched as a soft light infused the cabin. Carol was still asleep in the other bunk and I sat there by the chart table, drinking my coffee and thinking about the voyage that lay ahead. We weren't ready to sail. I knew that but I wasn't prepared to delay our departure any further. I was tired of living with a loaded shotgun by my side.

I went up on deck and sat in the cockpit. The first early lights of dawn were beginning to ease their way through a band of dark clouds that had merged with the distant horizon. The air was still and warm with the promise of another hot day. I heard a creaking sound and looked behind me. A solitary figure in a small rowing boat was moving towards us slowly through the moored yachts.

I reached down the companionway quietly, slid the shotgun out of its sheepskin case, clicked off the safety pin, then rested it on the side of the cockpit, pointing directly at the approaching figure. As the boat drew closer, I realized it was an old man, rowing ashore from a night's fishing. I sat there silently as he passed by, completely unaware of my presence.

When Carol came up on deck an hour later I was securing the last of the bolts to the safety rail in the bow.

"Did I wake you?" I asked.

"No, but I could feel you moving around." She hesitated. "How's the back?"

"It's improving. Another week or so and it'll be fine."

She wasn't convinced. "Why don't we stay on here for a while? We could finish all the jobs in a week or two."

"I'm sailing tomorrow. If you don't feel good about it, you could fly down to Sydney. Meet me down there. It might be better that way."

She disappeared back down the hatch and I continued on working. I was exhausted. Since the incident in the river, I'd seen the chiropractor half a dozen times but I was still in a lot of pain. My neck movement was badly restricted and every time I saw him, he advised me to postpone the trip. He meant well but he had no idea what was going on in my mind. Every morning, I awoke to an increasing sense of rage, obsessed with thoughts of revenge. I came up from sleep each day already feeling a fury within, the mad voices from days gone by urging revenge, carried over from dreams and nightmares into my waking consciousness.

'Kill the bastard!' the voices screamed. 'Wait by his boat and kill him! He's got to go back there sometime. Kill him and leave him to rot in the river. You'll be a coward for the rest of your life, if you don't!'

The voices raged at me mercilessly, awake and asleep, pulling me up from the darkness each day, ranting ceaselessly. 'Kill the bastard! They won't even investigate it! The cops have given you the go ahead! Just kill the bastard!'

Some nights, I'd lie awake for hours, reliving the incident and obsessing about revenge. In dreams, I would catch him unprepared in his dinghy, the way he'd caught me. He'd row out to his boat only to find me waiting there, shotgun in hand. I dreamt of the look on his face when he realized that he was gone. I would shoot him in the chest, blowing him back into the dinghy. But no, that was too fast! I wanted him to suffer. I would shoot him in the guts and leave him there to drown, shoving him under with an oar!

Each night, I lay in my bunk with my heart pounding. Replaying thoughts of murder over and over, until a passing boat or a barking dog on shore would jerk me out of my reverie and I'd come back to reality, heart pounding and blood racing. One evening as I came out of one of these fantasies, I realized that I was going mad again. I'd become obsessed with thoughts of revenge and thought of little else all day. I was living exactly the same way as I had when I drank, my thoughts running completely out of control, spending hours each day in fantasies of violence that I knew I would live out if I allowed myself to dwell on them too long.

'He deserves to die!' they ranted. 'Fuck him! Kill him before he kills you! Kill the bastard, then revive him and kill him again, and again, and again!'

Whilst I was in these fantasies, I felt empowered. But then the spell would break and something would turn in me and I would come out of it feeling exhausted and depressed. On one of those nights, unable to sleep for the pain and tormented by feelings of rage, I made my decision. I climbed into the dinghy and rowed ashore, the shotgun wrapped in a blanket at my feet. I left the ute a few blocks from the moorings and went the rest of the way on foot. It was a rainy night and when I drew close to the river, I waited in the cover of some bushes, watching the yachts. Close to the end of the jetty stood a ramshackle old hut, its wooden door sagging permanently open on rusted hinges.

From where I crouched, I could just make out the *Darius Star*, swinging to her mooring. The river was quiet, deserted apart from the usual anchored yachts. I looked at my watch: it was almost midnight. I walked along the jetty, slipped into the hut, unwrapped the shotgun, then stood in the semi-darkness, waiting.

'Are you really going to kill him?' I pushed the thought away. 'Well, are you, in cold blood?' The question angered me. 'Don't start wavering now,' I thought, 'don't fuck this up. Don't think about anything else! Just shoot the bastard and dump his body in the river, fuck him!'

A trickle of water ran down the back of my neck. The tin roof was full of holes. I moved to one side but that made it worse. I moved sideways and as I did, there was an incredible crashing noise. I'd knocked over a stack of empty paint tins. The shock almost sent me through the roof and as the din subsided, I stood, startled, the gun levelled at the doorway, my heart pounding so hard I could hear it.

'Had anybody else heard the din? If Mick was on his boat, could he have heard?' I stayed there for an age, arguing with myself, backwards and forwards.

'Go home, you fucking idiot. Get out now while you can!' But then the other voice immediately, 'Stay, you weak bastard, be a man! Stand where you are until he comes, then kill him. Shoot the bastard and be done with it!'

Water was running down my face. I looked down. The shotgun glistened black from the rain. Do shotguns work when they're wet? I felt a surge of anger. Of course they do! But the thought persisted, what if it didn't, what then?

I looked out of the shed again. The *Darius Star* had swung out of sight behind a big cruiser.

Maybe he knows you're here. Maybe he slipped her mooring and let her drift down river. You've made enough noise, maybe he'll kill you instead. I looked down at my watch. I'd been there for over an hour. I was soaked through and my back felt like hell.

'Are you sure you can kill him, just like that?' The voices were at me again, and I knew they wouldn't let up. I looked down at the gun and suddenly, I didn't want to be there. I stepped out of the shed, threw the blanket in the river and walked back to the ute, carrying the shotgun in my hand.

*   *   *

I awoke the next morning feeling sick and depressed. Carol was sitting on the edge of my bunk staring at me.

"Where were you last night?"

"I was at the boatshed, picking up the rest of the gear."

"You got back late."

"Yes, you know what it's like, we were talking."

"You took that gun with you."

"Yes."

"Why?"

"Why not?"

"I'm frightened. I'm frightened you're going to do something stupid."

She went up on deck then and I knew she was crying. I lay there thinking of the previous night and after a little while, I drifted off again. I woke up an hour or so later, the pain in my lower back dragging me up from sleep. I called out to Carol but there was no reply. I tried to roll over onto my side but I was stuck. Once I lay down for more than a few hours, it was almost impossible for me to get out of the bunk without help. I struggled for ten minutes to turn over, and by the time I made it, I was completely wrung out. I rested there for a few minutes, then began edging my shoulders and torso closer to the side of the bunk. It was agonizing. Every few minutes, I had to pause to recover.

Finally, I was in position. Now I had to roll over onto my face; this was the worst part. Once I got to a certain point, perched on my side ready to roll, the pain was intense and I knew that, once I committed myself to the final movement, I would be hit by a sickening jolt that would make me scream out in agony. Carol would cry sometimes as she watched me, struggling around like a cat with a broken back.

I rolled over, trying to suppress the pain, and then lay there then like a wet rag as the throbbing gradually subsided. The next stage was the easy part. After a few minutes, I slid both feet off the bunk, down onto the cabin floor, and from there, down again onto my knees. Once I had both knees on the cabin sole, it was relatively easy.

I knelt there quietly, waiting for the pain to subside, and for some reason as I did, I remembered the Alexandra Hotel. I used to pray like that sometimes when I was a kid. Kneeling down beside my bed, my face buried in my hands, my hands resting on the blankets.

'Why don't you say a prayer now, ask God for help?' The thought came uninvited, followed immediately by anger.

'Pray!' I thought bitterly, 'Pray to fucking what? Pray to some heap of shite that I believed in when I was a child? Black fucking magic! What a fucking idiot! Pray to what? To the same fucking illusion that you prayed to back then, you weak bastard!' I was cursing myself now. 'You've twisted your back and now you're going to start praying to some fucking Disneyland concept of God again? You weak bastard! Get up! Get on your feet!'

The rage stiffened my resolve and I pulled myself to my feet and limped out into the galley. My face was pale and drawn in the mirror. 'You're doing OK,' I told myself. 'You're doing fine. Don't weaken now, you're doing OK.'

But I wasn't OK, I was totally confused. There were still endless jobs to do before we could safely leave port and I knew I didn't have the time to do them. I had to leave Brisbane; I knew that. I was obsessed with thoughts of revenge but in my saner moments, I knew that if I shot Mick, I could easily end up locked away in some prison for years.

My mind was out of control, one side of me demanding revenge, the other side pleading with me to let it go, sail away and never look back. It was like my drinking days all over again. One side of me was demanding revenge, the other side urging forgiveness. I was being torn down the middle, not knowing which way to turn, and I had no idea which way I would eventually go.

*   *   *

The solution came to me later that same day. I was down below, working on installing the depth sounder, when I remembered Chris Slater. Chris was a well-known Sydney criminal and Chris owed me a favor ... a big favor. I'd hidden him out one time when he was on the run. It was years before, in my drinking days. There'd been a robbery, and someone had been killed. Two other men had already been caught and were serving long stretches. The police had been chasing Chris for more than a year when we met by chance in a club one night.

We'd gotten drunk together and he'd told me of his problem. He came back to my place that night and ended up living with me for the next two months.

By the time the police caught up with him, he had good legal representation and a sound alibi. We became firm friends and, after he'd beaten the charges, he'd been grateful for the time I'd sheltered him.

As long as Chris was in no way connected to Mick, Mick would be dealt with … permanently. That was the way to go. I could stay completely out of it. It was perfect. Justice would be done.

Chapter 36

Sailing

We slipped the mooring lines a few days later, a southerly breeze filling the sails as the *Kathleen R* heeled over gracefully and headed for the harbor mouth. We were on our way.

Our first destination was Moreton Island where we would anchor for the night before heading out to the open sea. It was a clear, bright, sunny morning as we left the harbor, seagulls swinging about overhead, squawking and wheeling above the mast. It wasn't the departure I'd dreamt of but I felt an incredible relief to be leaving Brisbane; we were outward bound at last.

Once out in deeper water, I increased sail and soon we were running along nicely, a fresh southerly pushing us steadily towards our destination. I was still in a lot of pain as I moved about the boat but I could raise and lower the sails without help and I was convinced my back was improving each day. As we reached across the bay, Carol took the tiller and I worked on the dozens of little jobs that were still left undone: storing food away in the various lockers, arranging the galley so that we could cook in rough weather, organizing the charts for the next leg of our journey and making sure everything was stowed safe and secure.

The last few weeks had been a nightmare but now, at last, we were crossing our first stretch of water, the initial leg of a trip that would have us sailing around the world. The *Kathleen R* cut confidently through the blue waters, shouldering her way through the heavier swells, flirting with the wind and the sea as she showed us her grace and speed. The wind increased steadily and by the time we were halfway across, we were reaching along at speed. She moved effortlessly, taking an occasional wave over her bow, shuddering for a second as if to draw breath and then ploughing back refreshed into the next patch of blue ocean, sails filled and taut, eager and confident, the tiller quivering like a spirit under my hand. It was the first time she'd had blue water under her keel and she loved it, coursing down the backs of the rising swells, cutting through the mounting seas confidently, reaching forward, eager and impatient to gain the open ocean.

We came up to the anchorage late that afternoon. We could have arrived earlier but we'd spent time trying out our new gear and becoming accustomed to the boat. We motored in behind the sunken wrecks at Moreton Island and, as Carol stowed the sails, I let go of the anchor and watched as the chain rattled its way down over the bow fitting.

Later that evening, Carol presented me with a gift to celebrate our first day at sea.

"It's too heavy for a book." I was weighing it in my hand.

"It's not an it," she smiled.

"There's more than one?"

"You'll never guess," she said. "Open it."

When I pulled open the wrapping, two inscribed brass plates lay in a small wooden box. We'd discussed getting a plaque on numerous occasions but the idea had fallen by the wayside, pushed aside by a thousand more pressing requirements in the lead-up to the launch. The first inscription I knew well; it was an extract from a poem, "The Nancy Brig".

> *For he was the cook,*
> *And the Captain bold,*
> *And the mate*

On The Nancy Brig.

It was beautiful, exactly what I wanted. I looked at the second.

Lord have mercy,
Thy sea is so large
And my ship is so small.

I stared at it for a long moment not knowing what to say.

"What's wrong," she said, "don't you like it?"

"Why would you give me a thing like that?" I was trying not to be angry.

"What's wrong with it?" She was puzzled. "I had to send off to Sydney for them."

"Send it back." I stood up. "I can't believe you'd think I would put a thing like that up on my boat. You know I don't believe in any of that shite!"

"It's the prayer of the Breton fishermen. I thought you'd like it."

"Carol, I'm an atheist, I find that shite offensive. You should know that. I don't want any pseudo-religious shite cluttering up my boat. It's offensive and it's degrading."

I went out to the cockpit and sat there in the gathering dark. I couldn't believe she'd have bought me a thing like that. Sometimes I wondered if Carol knew me at all. I hated anything to do with religion, from my earliest childhood when my father would beat me if I missed mass, to the never-ending hypocrisies of the Christian Brothers raving on about a loving God whilst they beat you stupid, the whole topic incensed me. I wasn't just against religion, I hated it with a passion and always had. I agreed with Karl Marx. God was a corruption, a disgusting fable, something to be used to terrify and control weak people. As he'd said, it was the opium of the masses.

A small group of people were gathered around a barbecue on the beach, drinking and talking. Their laughter carried out across the water clearly and for the first time in a long time, I wondered what it would be like to have a few drinks. Carol came up and joined me in the cockpit.

"I'm sorry, I thought it would look good on the bulkhead."

I felt bad about the way I'd spoken to her but she should have known better. "That stuff makes me angry; you know that."

"OK, I just thought it was more of a poem than anything to do with Christianity."

"It's nothing to do with Christianity!" I told her. "I'm an atheist. I don't believe in any of that old shite. I don't care if it's Christian, Muslim or Jewish, you know that. It's a con and it weakens people who believe in it. It's fucked up the planet from day one."

She didn't speak again for a long time and we just sat there, watching the people onshore. Finally, she ventured, "But you like the *Nancy Brig* one though, don't you?"

"Yes, of course I do, honey." I felt bad; I'd gone over the top again as usual. "Look, I'm sorry I got angry, OK? I appreciate what you did. Why don't we put up the *Nancy Brig* one now?"

We did, screwing it to the bulkhead just inside the companionway so that anybody coming on board would see it straightaway.

"What does it mean?" she asked.

"Well, like it says, he was the cook and the Captain bold and the mate on the *Nancy Brig,* see? He was on the boat by himself. He was sailing single-handed. He was his own master. He was in charge of his own destiny. That's what I like about it."

"I can return the other one when we get to Sydney."

"No," I said. "Give it here."

She handed me the second plaque.

"Now close your eyes."

When she heard the splash, she opened her eyes.

"What did you do that for? I could have sent it back."

"I don't want it on board, OK? I'm serious. I don't want anything like that on my boat."

I lay in my bunk that night, thinking over what had happened. I was surprised how much it had angered me, but I didn't want any superstitious rubbish cluttering up the boat. I'd built her and I would sail her. I had no fear of the sea, or of God.

*   *   *

We set sail for Sydney two days later. The weather forecast was good and the skies blue as I raised the anchor from the sandy bottom. A few hours later, we cleared the lighthouse at Cape Moreton and headed offshore. We were clear of the land at last and sailing eastwards, reveling in the freedom of the high seas. I had absolute faith in the *Kathleen R*. I'd built every part of her myself and I knew every nut and nail that had gone into her. She was a sturdy, strong little sea-boat and I knew she was capable of taking us anywhere in the world.

We headed seaward all day and most of that evening, the swell moderate, the wind southerly and fresh. We took turns steering, three hours on and three hours off, until I estimated we were approximately eighty miles offshore. Then we turned south for Sydney.

Once we were set on our new course, I navigated by the stars, holding the Southern Cross in the rigging to guide me, only checking the compass occasionally to confirm we were still on track. It was a beautiful night, the stresses and strains of what we'd left behind disappearing into our wake as the *Kathleen R* pushed her way steadily southward under a starry sky. Later that night, the moon arose from a perfect, glistening black ocean, huge, yellow and omnipotent, blessing our entrance to this magical world and assuring us that all was well on the night-dark sea. The yacht sailed along effortlessly, cutting a swathe through the gently heaving waters. It was hypnotic, the boat heeled over on one tack, the sails filled and silent, drawing us onwards through the night, the hull slicing cleanly through the smooth waters, following her course, fulfilling her destiny.

From where I sat steering, I could just make out Carol's sleeping form below in the cabin, her black curly hair spilling out over the sheets. The gimballed brass oil lamps burned soft and low, swinging gently as the boat heeled and danced to the movement of wind and water. My watch came and went and still I sat there, mesmerized by the beauty of it all; the tiller trembling softly under my hand, the boat moving with meaning and purpose, the wind constant and fair, bestowing its grace upon us, devoid of desire, moving with us on the ocean, unquestioning and benevolent, breathing along silently and softly, accepting us as one more part of all that is.

The phosphorescence in the wake fascinated me and I stared over the stern, entranced. Streams of pale light trailed out behind the *Kathleen R* as she sailed steadily through the dark ocean, and sparkles of bubbles, infused with an ethereal light, gleamed out in our wake as if some celestial hand was urging us forward. As I stared transfixed, I fell into a trance. It was as if I was hypnotized. I was conscious of steering the boat but I was caught up in a dream. I stayed that way for ages, peaceful and happy, content to let the hours slip by without interruption and when I came to much later, feeling rested and refreshed, the first faint traces of dawn were just beginning to appear on the distant horizon, sleeves of light bringing into focus the balance between sea and sky, separating the mystery of the night from the promise of the encroaching day.

We'd experienced our first night at sea; the *Kathleen R* had carried gracefully through the darkness of the night and the depths of the ocean. Neptune himself had accepted us into his bosom. We were sailing at last.

Chapter 37

High Seas

There are more sons lost at sea
Than mothers of a broken heart

Anon

The weather began to deteriorate on the second day at sea, the first signs of change appearing as ominous black clouds on the far-off horizon. By mid-afternoon, the breeze had freshened to such an extent that I'd taken two reefs in the main. The southerly swells that had welcomed us with their gentle slopes, slowly turning into waves, their curling tops sending shudders throughout the *Kathleen R* as she beat her way steadily towards Sydney. By the time nightfall came, we had strong winds and white-capped waves. I'd reefed the main down to a bare minimum and our tiny storm jib, thick, white fabric with heavy black stitching, was now pulling us southwards into the night. The *Kathleen R* ploughed steadfastly into the rising seas, cutting through the heavier swells before plunging on downwards across their backs.

Carol was frightened. She'd never seen anything like it before.

"This is what she's built for, honey." I smiled, trying to be positive. "You know that. She can take a lot worse than this."

"Are you OK, can you handle it?" She was worried about my back.

"I'm fine, there's nothing I can't do on the boat. I think I've proved that already."

But I was worried. My back was causing me constant pain, made worse by the movement of the boat. The only relief I got was when I was sitting bolt upright in the cockpit, holding the tiller in one hand and the safety rail in the other.

As the night progressed, conditions became worse. We were slamming into ever-increasing waves and not long after midnight, it became clear that we could not maintain our course. I made a decision to run offshore; this would take us well off course but it would make conditions a lot easier on the boat and us. We had plenty of provisions on board, the boat was fundamentally sound, so the only real danger was the land. The further offshore we were, the safer we'd be.

I stayed on watch all night, strapped into a safety harness, peering ahead into an ever-worsening seascape. As long as I kept her headed seaward, the boat handled the waves well, but every time I attempted to bring her closer to our original course, we'd begin to take a battering again.

Carol had become seasick early in the day and now lay on her bunk, a canvas leeboard preventing her falling out as the boat rolled wildly in the rising seas. I sat in the cockpit, drenched through, the driving rain finding a hundred different ways to penetrate my oilskins.

The *Kathleen R* was magnificent. This was her first storm and she rose to the occasion, shouldering her way through the ever-increasing swells, riding up and over each foaming crest, cutting through the mounting seas, reaching offshore towards safety. Carol was too sick to take her watch so I steered the yacht all through that night.

I don't know when it was that I first became aware of the sound of the wind, a moaning, keening, sighing sound that crept up on me throughout the night, ever increasing in tempo as the weather deteriorated into a full gale. Inching upwards gradually until suddenly I heard it and wondered for a moment what it was. A howling, shrieking, wailing sound, racing unimpeded across the wave tops, screaming through the rigging, tearing at the sails and forcing the

Kathleen R over on her beams end in the heavier gusts. It tore at my eyes, snatching away the tears that formed between my squinting lids, screamed insanities into my ears before rampaging off again into the night in search of other victims.

When dawn finally broke, bleak and grey, I was taken aback. I had never before in my life seen anything like it. I'd read a hundred accounts over the years from all the great sailors. I'd devoured the writings of Frances Chichester, Chay Bly, Robin Knox-Johnston and Eric Tabarly, and I'd spent hundreds of hours poring over stories of small boats and big seas, but nothing had prepared me for this moment; the ocean was enraged.

As the *Kathleen R* climbed up to the top of each swell, I had, for a short time, a broad and commanding view out over our world. As far as the eye could see, there was white water and breaking waves. There was nowhere one could see where the ocean finished and the sky began. Thunderous great, grey, masses of cloud writhed and struggled overhead, merging at some unknown point into a sea boiling like a witch's cauldron.

Then came the decline as the boat was swept back down into the canyon-like troughs between the waves, sliding down the watery walls, greys and blacks and night-dark ocean greens melding together irrevocably with slate dark thunderclouds, ominous and alive. Sea and sky curling up into each other to form one huge homogenous mass, as if the *Kathleen R* was surrounded on all sides, above and below by water. Then up again at the whim of the ocean, climbing and climbing and climbing, and all around waves, endless successions of waves, marching and rolling along majestically and forever. Pushing down on us relentlessly from the south, sweeping, white-topped, breaking seas, pressing us ever northward, the winds, howling and droning through the rigging like demented banshees, ripping at the sails, tearing at the rigging, forcing us ever away, ever offshore, and as I stared out over this tumultuous world in awe, a hundred miles from land and endless watery depths beneath our keel, I wondered for the first time if we were going to make it

I looked down the companionway. Carol lay curled and silent on the bunk below, rolling this way and that, an empty plastic bucket clattering about on the cabin floor. She had vomited all night but now she just lay there quietly with her eyes closed. There was nothing I could do; we were at the mercy of the ocean. As I sat there looking out over this primeval scene, I was struck by the ferocious majesty of it all. The sea wasn't attacking us; it was merely living out one of its many moods. Our survival or otherwise was of no interest at all to the might of this raging ocean.

On the second day of the gale, I decided to change course again and run before the wind. Carol was too ill to do anything and I was exhausted. I'd read many accounts of small boats caught out in gales at sea and I knew that the weakest factor was the crew. So I turned the *Kathleen R* around, stowed the mainsail and began running downwind under our tiny storm jib, dragging mooring lines over the transom to slow our progress and keep her stern on to the seas. I ran north for two days, snatching a few hours' sleep now and again whenever I could, tacking on and offshore to reduce the distance lost and by the time the gale had blown itself out, we were abeam of Brisbane. The weather was still bad and the seas high but at dawn that day, we came about and began to make headway towards Sydney once again.

*   *   *

Seven days from our original departure date, we put into the small town of Toncurry on the Clarence River. Carol had lost a lot of weight and we were both exhausted and dispirited. We needed rest and recuperation.

We spent a week tied up at the fishermen's wharf and we put the time to good use, fixing up navigation lights and checking over all our gear. There was a good chiropractor in town and I saw him several times during our stay. We met other people who were cruising the coast and shared our adventures with them. Most were experienced sailors and we sat around in their boats at night, watching the weather reports on television and talking about sailing. We studied the weather pattern for days and finally, when all augured well, we said our goodbyes, slipped anchor and set sail once again. Our next destination was Newcastle.

When we left Tuncurry, I knew we were better prepared for the sea. Much of the work onboard had been completed, we now had a few sea miles under our belt and we'd survived a major gale intact. The forecast was ideal as we sailed out: a moderate westerly wind coming off the land saw us heeled over on the one tack all day, cutting effortlessly through clear blue waters, the wind continuing on steady into the night and all of the next day. These were absolutely perfect sailing conditions.

During the afternoon of the third day, the barometer began to fall. We were twenty miles offshore and well into our journey, so there was nothing to be done but press on. By nightfall, we were battering along again under reduced sail, the wind shrieking through the rigging. I knew Newcastle had a deep-water entrance and I had decided to make a run for it. By 10 pm, we were sailing towards a group of cargo ships that lay anchored close by each other, just offshore from the river mouth.

Our masthead light had failed again so I was keeping a close watch on the ships as we approached. We had too much sail up, I knew that, but I didn't want to start changing sails at the very last minute. The wind was gusting up to thirty-five knots and the sea was choppy but I felt confident that our present course would have us safe in the river before too long. As I sailed towards the moored vessels, I grew more uneasy. One of the tankers was behaving differently to the others; it was getting bigger much too fast. At first I thought that it was some sort of optical illusion caused by fatigue. She was the same as all the others, a long black hulk against a stormy night sky, her green riding light telling me I was approaching her from the port side. I stared at her fixedly as we drew close. There was something different about her; she appeared steadier in the water somehow.

Suddenly, I could see both her navigation lights, green and red, and with a jolt, I realized that she was underway and steaming straight down on top of us! I shouted to Carol to shine a torch on our mainsail in a desperate bid to be seen. At that precise moment, we were struck by a vicious squall and as the *Kathleen R* went over on her beams end, almost dipping her mast into the waves, the tanker's captain let go with a deafening blast on the foghorn.

As soon as the *Kathleen R* staggered upright, she was knocked flat again by another gust. I tried to free the mainsail, but it was jammed and I screamed out to Carol for a knife. As I grabbed it, a bright red light flared suddenly close by our port side and I caught a glimpse through the rain and spray of another small yacht, obviously in distress. As I slashed through the mainsheet, the sail broke free, thrashing about wildly and cracking like a whip as the *Kathleen R* righted herself and took off again under her jib, heading back out to sea and away from danger. The tanker gave another long, resentful blast on its siren as we slipped down its side and disappeared into the night.

I sailed offshore for hours, chastened by the experience, feeling ashamed at my lack of experience and wondering what could go wrong next. Carol was still seasick but she took the tiller for short periods as I snatched a few minutes sleep here and there.

The following morning the wind had abated but the seas were still ugly. We sailed back towards Newcastle all that day, finally putting in to port around 3.00 pm.

Chapter 38

Catharsis

We stayed at Newcastle for two weeks. I was determined to make the final leg of the journey to Sydney a pleasant one. Every night after dinner, we would go up to the local sailing club and study the weather forecast on television. I wanted to be sure. I knew in my heart that one more gale would finish Carol with the boat forever.

Finally one evening, everything seemed perfect. The forecast was for moderate northerly winds for several days ahead: ideal conditions. We prepared the boat that night and the following morning, just after dawn, we slipped the mooring and set sail once again. As we cleared the river mouth, seagulls swooped and wheeled overhead. The sky was clear blue and there was only a moderate swell as we turned south. By noon that day, we were well underway, a steady northerly breeze driving us swiftly over a smooth, untroubled sea.

Despite the conditions, I was feeling uptight. This wasn't the way it was supposed to be, hanging around in ports, worrying about the weather. I was becoming neurotic, constantly on edge, wondering what would go wrong next. Carol took the tiller several times that day and I could see her confidence returning as she steered the *Kathleen R* through the calm blue seas. We had lunch in the cockpit, throwing scraps of food to a wandering albatross that had been hovering over our stern for hours. At around 3.00 pm, I went below for a nap. I'd be steering for most of the night and I wanted to be rested. I fell asleep immediately, the boat rolling gently downwind, the sound of the sea swishing past the hull close to my head.

When I awoke two hours later, I knew immediately that something was wrong. I rolled over slowly and looked up at the hatchway. Grey-white clouds scudding along, low and angry, had replaced the clear blue skies.

I dragged myself off the bunk, stiff and sore, and pulled myself up the ladder. Carol was sitting in the cockpit, steering. She looked frightened. The boat was heeled over on a reach, travelling way too fast, the skies overhead, grey and ominous.

"Why didn't you wake me?" I said.

"It only just happened the last hour or so. I was hoping it would die down again. You were fast asleep."

I struggled along the deck to the mast. I had lain down too long and my back was aching badly. I managed to get two reefs in the main, gathering the sail together in folds and lashing it tightly to the boom. The weather was deteriorating rapidly and an hour later, it was blowing hard, the wind whipping white spray from the bow and driving it back in sheets across the boat.

"I'll have to change the headsail," I told Carol. "It's going to get worse."

As I spoke, the *Kathleen R* was struck by a heavy squall, knocking her over and rounding the boat up. I pulled on my safety harness and began to crawl forward, moving slowly, clipping and unclipping my harness to the safety points along the deck. When I reached the bow, I secured the harness, wrapped one of my arms through the pulpit and began dragging the headsail down. Every few minutes, the *Kathleen R* would plunge her bow deep into a crest and I would be completely immersed in foaming water as a wave swept over the bow and along the deck. At first, I clung on for grim life but after a while, I became numbed to it all and just went on slowly unclipping the sail hanks, one at a time. There was no option.

Occasionally, I'd hear a shouted warning from Carol and I'd grab onto the guard rail with both hands and hang on tight until the wave had washed over me, then back to the shackles, one after another. I had to get that sail down. I was up there for twenty minutes, shivering and shaking, fingers numb with the cold, until finally, the last hank came off. I stuffed the sail down the forward hatch and then Carol pushed up the storm jib, a tiny sail with only a handful of fastenings.

Once the job was done, the motion of the boat eased and I took the tiller as Carol went below to make a hot drink. I sat there in the cockpit once again, looking out at a stormy sea. I was soaked through from head to foot, my hands were numb and my fingers were aching from the stainless steel fittings. Carol had turned on the radio and the weather forecaster was now giving out a gale warning for the Sydney area. I was starting to feel really angry.

I went down below and did a few quick calculations. We were less than twenty miles north of Sydney Harbour. Another few hours should see us close to the entrance. We could still make it in reasonable time if the weather didn't get too much worse.

Carol offered to steer but I wouldn't let her. I didn't trust anything anymore. I sailed on, hour after hour, staring ahead through the driving rain and spray, squinting towards the shoreline, looking out for landmarks, determined to sail into Sydney that night. The further south we went, the worse the weather became and soon the visibility was down to a few hundred yards. This was the worst possible scenario. We were sailing towards the entrance to Sydney Harbour, our destination obscured by rain and mist. If I miscalculated, we could easily end up on the rocks.

Occasionally, we'd hit a clear patch and I'd grab the binoculars and search for any sign of land. It was during one of those spells, as I was peering towards where I thought the Heads should be, that I suddenly saw white water stretching across our bow. With a sickening jolt, I knew immediately where we were … Long Reef, a notorious area of half-submerged rocks that stretch westward out from the headland at Collaroy. It had been the graveyard of many small boats. I came about immediately, hoping against hope it wasn't too late, throwing the tiller over so hard that the boom came smashing across, reaching down at the same time to turn on the depth sounder. We had less than ten fathoms beneath our keel and there was white water everywhere.

The *Kathleen R* answered the challenge and slowly, ever so slowly, we clawed away from the reef and back out to sea. I watched the depth sounder, all the way counting. Fifteen fathoms, twenty fathoms, twenty-five, thirty. We were safe. Carol took the tiller and I went below. At least I knew where we were now. I examined the chart. If we sailed southwest for an hour, we should be able to come about and, with a little luck, make Sydney Harbour before midnight. I went back on deck and took over the tiller. Carol was looking worried.

"We're not going to sail offshore again, are we?"

"No," I told her, "we'll tack out for a while but then we'll set a course for the Heads. Don't worry, we'll be there soon."

But the weather was deteriorating. It was close to gale force now and I was having difficulty holding our course. The waves, sweeping in from the south, had taken on the same relentless pattern that I'd seen so many times before. Rising up in endless rows, grey-streaked with dirty white tops, marching down on us, remorseless and indifferent. We reached southwest for over an hour, beating into the rising seas and trying to keep track of our progress by dead reckoning. It was hard going. I could only guess at how much leeway we were making but I knew the boat was being pushed sideways as she clawed her way offshore. Finally, I was satisfied and we came about. This was it; if we could make the entrance on this single tack, we'd be safe at anchor within a few hours. We tacked southeast then, back in towards the land, staying as close to the wind as possible without losing boat speed. After half an hour, I began searching through the binoculars for any sign of land. We pushed on for another thirty minutes. We had to be close.

Then suddenly, I saw it again, looming up out of the mist, white water, closer this time, seething and foaming in the rising gale.

"Oh Christ," I screamed out a warning to Carol. "Hang on! We're coming about!"

I slammed the tiller across so hard the boat spun around violently, the boom whipping over my head again as the *Kathleen R* took off on a port tack.

Carol was shouting up from the companionway. "What's wrong? What's happening?"

"Nothing, nothing, it's OK! I'm going to tack offshore for a while. We're doing OK!"

The *Kathleen R* struggled offshore again but the seas were getting lumpier and I spent the whole time getting her up as close to the wind as possible. Carol offered to steer but I didn't want her in the cockpit. She was frightened and I knew the mounting seas would destroy her remaining confidence. I tacked offshore again for more than an hour, staying as close to the wind as I possibly could. The boat was sailing well despite the weather and when I came about the second time, I felt more confident our problems should soon be over.

We sailed back towards the land again, edging ever southwards. Whenever the wind swung a little, I'd grab the chance and pinch her up a little more. We had to make it this time. I stood in the cockpit, peering through the binoculars, willing my boat to the south.

When I saw the first flash of white water, I didn't believe it. At first, it was just a patch way over in the distance but then there was another on the starboard bow and then another. We were sailing directly back down onto Long Reef. I stared at the broken water unbelievingly. It just wasn't possible. I stood there, numb and defeated, and I knew then and there that even if I sailed all day and all night, I would never make it into Sydney Harbour. I looked at the depth sounder; we were back in shallow water again. Suddenly, I had a flash of hope: the engine. We had a brand new outboard engine. It was only eight horsepower and I knew it would not be all that effective in rough water but it might be just enough to make a difference.

I turned the petrol on and primed the engine. I'd let go of the tiller and the yacht had swung beam onto the seas. The sails were flapping and banging about and the masthead was cutting a wide arc in the night sky, high above our heads, as the boat rolled wildly in the troughs. I climbed up on the cockpit seat, slung one leg over the safety rail, braced myself, and then pulled hard on the rope starter. Nothing. I tried again, jerking on the rope frantically with all my strength. The engine spluttered and died, a small puff of smoke belching out reluctantly from the exhaust. I looked up, Long Reef was drawing closer and I could hear the roaring, crashing sound of the waves as they smashed into the rocks. I ripped at the starter again and again and then finally, putting all my remaining strength into it, I gave it one last desperate pull. As I did, I felt my spine go, a searing, tearing pain shooting throughout my entire back as I collapsed off the seat, my head smashing into one of the stainless steel winches on the way down. As I lay there, half-stunned on the cockpit sole, blood mixing with the seawater swilling around my head, I knew that I was finished; my left arm was paralyzed, my strength was gone, and I was completely exhausted. We were never going to get into Sydney Harbour. Never.

Suddenly, something inside me snapped and I forced myself to my feet, overwhelmed by rage. It came up from somewhere way down below, pushing aside reason, smashing its way to the surface to be resolved, no matter what, as I turned my face towards the sky and began screaming obscenities at the top of my lungs. "Fuck you, you bastard! You want to kill me? Well, fucking kill me then! Fuck you!

Fuck you, you fucking bastard! You want to drown me? Well, fucking drown me then, you bastard! I'm not frightened of you! Fuck you!"

I was standing in the cockpit, both hands grasping on to the coach roof, the boat wallowing sideways in the troughs, screaming up at the skies. I could hear my own voice as if from a distance, as if it belonged to somebody else.

"Fuck you! Fuck you! Fuck you! I'm not frightened of you! Fuck you! Do you hear me? Fuck you! Fuck you! Fuck you!"

I have no idea how long I stood there ranting, but finally, there was another voice screaming at me, shrieking at me, forcing its way into my consciousness. "Stop it, stop it! Stop it or you'll kill us both! Stop it, Brian! For god's sake stop it!"

The voice dragged me back to my senses. Carol was standing in the open companionway, tears streaming down her face, screaming at me, over and over and over again. I stared at her for a moment, uncomprehendingly, before collapsing down onto the cockpit seat. The *Kathleen R* had caught the wind in her headsail and she was now heading offshore again, sailing herself. It didn't matter anymore and I sat there like a beaten dog, hunched over and defeated, exhausted and devoid of any strength or spirit. I wondered vaguely if we were both going to drown and realized that that might be the way out. Carol's voice came in again.

"I'm going to radio the Sea Rescue."

I ignored her and sat there, staring back at Long Reef like a zombie. I could hear her voice down below in the galley.

"Mayday! Mayday!"

Looking back towards land, I caught a glimpse of what looked like a headland and I wondered for a moment if I could run the yacht ashore there, wreck her on the beach, get the insurance. At least that would be a way out. The idea died in me. Carol was back.

"They want to know our position."

I just stared at her.

"Brian, they want to know our position!"

"Long Reef, we're off Long Reef."

She wanted me to talk to them but I refused. The boat sailed steadily offshore for an hour or more unattended, beating into the seas, handling the conditions easily, happy to be free of her master.

Every so often, the radio would come to life and I would hear Carol's voice again, responding to questions.

"They want us to put up a flare. They can't find us," she was crying.

I shook my head. "It doesn't matter."

I sat there, defeated and lifeless, my dreams in shreds around me, and when she let off the first flare next to me in the cockpit, I watched without interest. She lit a second one a little later and then shortly after that, I saw them: a navy-blue cruiser around forty feet or so, standing off our starboard bow. Carol was talking on the radio.

"They're going to take us off the boat."

I shook my head.

"I'm not leaving the boat."

"We have to."

"I'm not leaving the boat."

I could hear her talking into the radio again.

"They're going to try to fire a line across to us. If that doesn't work, we have to leave the boat."

I heard the crack of a gun and a rocket streaked across our bow. I crawled forward as if in a dream and began pulling in the line. My left arm was almost completely useless and I had to stop every few minutes to rest. When the heavier rope appeared, I couldn't handle it and finally Carol came up and we pulled it in together and looped it over the Samson post. It took them six hours to tow us into Sydney Harbour.

I sat in the cockpit, entirely defeated. It was the first time since I'd stopped drinking that I'd completely fallen apart and it was the first time since my childhood that I'd acknowledged the existence of God.

Chapter 39

Sydney

The following morning, I came to consciousness reluctantly and lay in the bunk, motionless, willing the events of the previous days not to have happened. The vision that had sustained me for almost seven years lay in tatters around me and I felt sick to my stomach.

The *Kathleen R* sat motionless in the water, the morning still and silent and I lay there like a dead man, unwilling to move. Once I got up and spoke to somebody, I knew that it would make it all true. I tried to drift off to sleep again but my mind would not allow that. I could hear Carol's breathing on the other side of the cabin, peaceful, steady and calm.

After a while, I began the process of getting out of bed, but my back was even worse, and I couldn't even roll over. I was trapped and as I lay there waiting for Carol to wake up, I unwillingly relived the events of the previous day, cursing myself as I did. I should have known that a boat that small had no chance of beating into a rising gale. I should have known that from all the reading I'd done. I should have accepted that and ran offshore. I thought about the sea rescue boat and I felt a deep sense of shame. Now I was one of those despicable sailors who endangered other people's lives. I tried to push the thoughts out of my mind but I couldn't. It was done and there was no undoing it.

'Even if you go on, you'll always know what a fool you've made of yourself.' The voices were back. 'Not so tough now, are you? You couldn't handle Mick, and you couldn't even sail the boat into

Sydney Harbour, you useless bastard! Telling everyone you were sailing off around the world! They'll all have a fucking good laugh now.' It was my back, I thought, but for that, I'd have been fine. But the voices weren't having any of it.

'Bullshit! It's you, for fuck's sake! It's you! You're a fucking dreamer! You're a fucking wanker! You live in a fantasy world!'

I tried to struggle over onto my side. I had to get up.

'We'll see who's a fucking wanker.' I was enraged. 'Chris Slater will sort this out. Mick will pay for what's happened.'

"Brian ..." Carol had risen up on one elbow. "... are you awake?"

"Yes, give me a hand, will you? I'm stuck."

"Were you asleep?"

"I don't know. Help me roll over."

It took us hours to tidy up the boat and by the time we got ashore, I was in agony, bent over to one side and scarcely able to walk. We booked into a local hotel for a few days until Carol found a small apartment nearby.

The weeks that followed were a nightmare. Hospitals, X-rays, back specialists, chiropractors and endless depressions. The prognoses for my back varied depending on who I spoke to. One doctor assured me I would be back to normal in a matter of months. Another told me that, if it continued to deteriorate, I'd almost certainly be in a wheelchair within three years.

I was obsessed with thoughts of revenge and, as soon as I could walk reasonably well, I began the rounds of my old haunts: The Imperial Hotel at Paddington, the Greenwood Tree further down the road, the Rex Hotel at Kings Cross and the Astor at Bondi Beach, all places where Chris Slater had hung out. I talked to barmen and waiters but the answer was always the same. "Never heard of him, we don't know anybody by that name." I'd been gone for a long time.

I was standing at the bar of the Imperial one night, drinking a mineral water, when a man I'd never seen before approached me.

"You've been asking about Chris Slater?"

"Yes."

"What do you want with him, mate?"

"I'm a friend of his."

"What's it about?"

"It's a private thing."

"Is it?" He was looking around the bar. "Look mate, you've been hanging around here for weeks asking some pretty weird questions. You could get yourself in a lot of trouble if you're not careful."

"I'm a friend of Chris," I told him. "If you know him, tell him Brian O'Raleigh's looking for him, OK? Brian O'Raleigh. I've been away for ten years."

"You've been away for ten years? You mean … away, away?"

"No, I was in Queensland. Chris will want to talk to me. We were good mates."

"So what's your problem?"

I hesitated. This wasn't good.

"There was some trouble with a guy in Brisbane." I paused. "My spine's damaged. I'm very pissed off about it."

He was squinting at me.

"Who's the guy in Brisbane, do we know him?"

"You might do, he's a tow truck driver."

"And you want him hit?"

"I didn't say that."

He studied me for a moment longer.

"Does he have a name?"

"I'll talk to Chris about that."

"Give me a phone number," he said.

"I don't have one. We just got back to Sydney."

"You're a worry, mate, you're a real fucking worry." He was shaking his head. "Look, keep coming back in here. If anybody wants to talk to you, there'll be a message behind the bar, OK? Talk to Laurie over there." He indicated one of the barmen who'd been watching us. "If you don't hear anything in the next month or so, give it a miss. Don't come back in here after that mate, OK? And forget about Chris."

Chapter 40

Jim Maclaine

A few weeks later, as I was walking through the city, I heard a voice calling my name. "O'Raleigh, you old bastard! Brian, over here!"

It was John Cox, a Dublin man I'd been in all sorts of scrapes with when we drank together years before. John was the very last person I wanted to meet and my heart sank as he ran across the road towards me.

"Brian O'Raleigh! Holy Jaysus, sure I thought you'd be dead and gone by now! How are ye' doin, for Christ's sake?"

"I'm fine, John, fine. I've been off the drink for three years now and I'm doing fine."

"Sure Jaysus, I don't believe it! Aren't I off the drink myself? Come on, we'll grab a coffee."

We sat in a coffee shop for hours and finally, I told him everything that was going on.

"And you're going to have the poor gobshite done in, is that what you're saying?"

"Yes, fuck him! He tried to kill me, for fuck's sake!"

"Whoa, hold on there, boy! Sure, Jaysus I was only asking! I couldn't give a fuck whether you have him shot or not! I'm concerned for you, that's all, you and Carol. Does she know about this?"

"Of course not, it's nothing to do with her."

We talked for ages. He was a changed man. It was hard to believe it was the same person I'd known before. He told me he'd been seeing a therapist and before we parted, he gave me a phone number and advised me to ring him. I told him I'd think about it.

I was confused. The boat dream had shattered. I hadn't been on board the *Kathleen R* since the night we'd arrived in Sydney. I went to look at her sometimes, standing in the shade of the trees looking down from the hill overlooking the submarine base, spying on her from the shadows as she swung and fretted on her moorings. She looked quite innocent down there amongst the other boats, but I knew that a secret lay between us. I would sit on the grass some days, staring down at her and wondering why it had all gone so wrong. Could it be Carol? I wondered. She was the only one left from my past. Finally, in desperation one day, I picked up a phone and made an appointment to see John's therapist.

*   *   *

Jim Maclaine was a man about my own age, slim, dark hair, glasses and a habit of turning his head from side to side as he looked at you, as if attempting to bring you into focus. I saw him several times over the next few weeks and although we discussed a range of things, I never mentioned what had happened in Brisbane. He was obviously very bright, but progress was slow, so as I walked into his office for my fourth appointment, I made a decision to be frank with him. Jim listened carefully, and after going over the events of the previous few months, I asked him what he thought I should do.

"How would I know?" He was smiling. "My job is to help you sort out what *you* want to do. Do you still intend sailing around the world?"

"Yes, we only stopped off here for a month or two. You know, to tidy a few things up. Fix up the boat and so on."

He sat back in his chair. "And then you're off again, off around the world?"

I was surprised he kept coming back to this; we'd discussed it several times already.

"Yes."

He was smiling again; he seemed to find it amusing.

"So, where's your next port of call, New Zealand?"

"I'm not sure. I guess we could go that way."

"And Carol's keen on the idea?"

"Well that's one of the things I wanted to talk to you about. I'm not sure that Carol and I will be staying together much longer."

"Hmmm ... so that's one of the things you want to clear up?"

"Yes."

"And then there's Mick, isn't there? You were thinking of having him murdered, weren't you? Isn't that what you said?"

"I didn't say that. John Cox told you that and he had no right to. I told him that in absolute confidence! That has nothing to do with anything. It's bullshit."

"So you've given up on the idea?"

"Yes, I have, OK?"

"And that criminal you were trying to contact, what was his name again?"

"I didn't mention his name, it doesn't matter anyhow. Look, this is confidential, isn't it? You're not allowed to talk to the police, are you?"

"No, I'm not and yes, it is confidential, but I do have responsibilities. Are you still planning on having that guy murdered?"

"No, definitely not, that's finished with. Let's just forget about that, OK?"

He was studying me now, his eyes bright and alert.

"So you've forgiven him?" He seemed to be obsessed with Mick.

"Look, that's over with, finished, OK. Now, can we move on? I don't want to waste any more time talking about Mick."

He went off on a different tack. "So how are you feeling in yourself?"

"How do you mean, how am I feeling?"

He was smiling. "How are you feeling? You know, are you happy, are you sad? How are you feeling?"

"I feel OK. I just want to get moving again. You know, do something. I'm not sure I want to be with Carol anymore. She doesn't like sailing."

"So you're thinking of dumping her?"

"I wouldn't call it dumping her. I think maybe we're just not suited, that's all."

"How long have you been together?"

"Twelve years."

"Ummm ... she must have helped you a lot, through your alcoholism, I mean."

"Yes, she did." I was feeling uncomfortable.

"So, do you have anyone else lined up?"

"I knew you were going to ask that. No, I don't. I'm not looking for anyone else. I just want to sail my boat, OK?"

"But if you did meet another woman, that would be nice, wouldn't it? After Carol's gone, I mean."

"I'm not interested. I'm just not interested, mate, honest."

"But if you did meet another woman, say in a month or two, that would be nice, wouldn't it? You know, a new beginning, a fresh start. Leave all the old problems behind. I mean, you're not planning on becoming a monk, are you?"

He wasn't going to let up.

"OK, so I may meet another woman one day. What's wrong with that, for Christ's sake? That's normal, isn't it?"

.

"Of course it is," he smiled, "so what sort of girl would she be?"

"Oh Christ, Jim, where're we going with this?"

"I'm simply asking you what sort of woman would interest you; you must have some idea. What would she look like? Would she look like Carol, for example?"

I decided to go along with it.

"No, she wouldn't. I prefer redheads actually, I always have, or blondes."

"Go on then, describe your perfect woman. The woman you'd like to share your life with," he gestured. "Please."

"Well, she could be a blonde or a redhead. She'd be tall; I like tall women. Attractive ..."

He cut in. "Attractive or beautiful? Come on now, be honest."

"OK then, beautiful." We both laughed. "Yes, she'd be beautiful, why not."

"Long legs?"

"Yes, long legs. What do you go for, short stumpy legs? OK Jim, listen to this. She'll be blonde, tall, absolutely beautiful, long legs, big tits and a great arse. Is that what you want?"

He was still smiling. "Is that what *you* want would be more to the point."

I thought for a minute. "Well, yes, it is actually. What's wrong with that?"

"Anything else? Would she be intelligent, happy, witty?"

"Yes, of course. She'd be intelligent, amusing, loving, understanding, you know, what the Italians call *simpatico*, that special understanding."

There was a pause for a moment.

"That's quite a woman you've described there, Brian." He was looking a little concerned. "There's only one possible problem that I could see."

"And what's that?" I said, eager to solve it.

"I was wondering what on earth a woman like that would see in a man like you?"

I sat there, dumbfounded. Why would he say a thing like that? But he was still talking.

"You're living in a world of fantasy and delusion. You think you can have a man murdered and then run away in a boat with some bimbo who will help you avoid the realities of life? Carol is the only person you've ever met who's supported you unconditionally. Now, you're trying to blame her and your friend, Mick, from Brisbane, for your current situation. Your dream of sailing around the world has come apart at the seams. You're running again, Brian and you're right on the edge of picking up a drink."

The room had gone silent. I hadn't come here for this. I'd come looking for hope, for a new direction. His voice came back again, quieter this time.

"You've told me on three separate occasions that you're an atheist."

I nodded. I didn't trust myself to speak.

"So who were you shouting at off Long Reef?" He was speaking very quietly now. "Was it Mick, was it your father, or was it God?"

Suddenly, my throat choked up. I couldn't speak. Finally I just got up and walked out.

One week later, as I was walking through Bondi Junction, I caught sight of a billboard outside a news agency: *Chris Slater Shot Dead.* It hit me hard, an icy fist clutching at my insides as I went inside to buy the paper.

Chris had been driving his car on the highway outside of Sydney. Somebody had driven up alongside him with a shotgun and blown his head off. My mind went into a spin. Who was the guy I'd spoken to at the Imperial Hotel? Was he a friend of Chris's or not? If he was, would they think I was connected to Chris's death? Could

Mick have heard I was connected to Chris and acted? Could the guy at the hotel have been connected to Mick?

I went in to see Jim the following day and I admitted that I had been planning to have Mick shot. He listened to me without comment and then told me that it was pointless talking unless I was prepared to be honest. I agreed. One of the conditions he laid down was that I'd attend regular meetings of a recovery program for alcoholics that I'd avoided for years. I was desperate, so I agreed to attend at least two meetings a week.

Chapter 41

Recovery

It took me a little while to settle into the twelve-step group, but as I did, I realized it was entirely different to what I'd imagined. There were all sorts of people in there, bricklayers, bankers, movie stars and mechanics. It was like Noah's Ark, there seemed to be at least two of every kind.

At my third meeting, I was introduced to Paul. He'd been one of the speakers that evening and I'd been struck by his simplicity and honesty and later over a coffee, I'd asked him to be my sponsor. He was around forty years of age, tall, greying hair, with such a calm, centered manner, I found it hard to believe that he was an alcoholic. I warned him in our first conversation that I had reservations about the God part of the program but that didn't seem to faze him.

"A lot of us have the same problem when we first arrive." He was smiling. "You'll find your own concept of God, one that makes sense to you."

"But you're a Christian, aren't you?" I was suspicious.

"Yes, I am, but that doesn't mean that you have to be," he said, refusing to be drawn. "You'll work out something that you're comfortable with over time."

"What about the life force?" I said, "I believe the ancient Celts worshiped the life force itself."

"Why not?" he said. "If it makes sense to you, go for it."

Paul helped me a lot in his open, non-judgmental way and gradually, over the months, I became more and more at ease with a concept of a *life force*, a positive, benevolent power that I could turn to in times of need.

*   *   *

Working my way through the twelve-step program was not easy. Some days the principles seemed to contradict every natural impulse in me but, as time progressed and I began to let go of many of my old ingrained beliefs, I came to see just how out-of-balance my life had been.

I also came to realize how I'd lived in my own little dream world since early childhood. From the *Kathleen R* onwards, I'd been a loner, living in a world of fantasy and illusion, fueled for all my adult years by alcohol. Even in my relationship with Carol, I'd been separate and apart. I'd always made all the decisions. Whether we were travelling in Afghanistan or Ireland, building a boat, or moving to another country, all ideas and decisions had been driven by me.

Part of the program suggested that I take a thorough inventory of my behavior throughout my entire life, writing down on paper all of the negative and destructive things that I had done and listing all the people that I'd harmed. When I first talked this over with Paul, I was skeptical.

"Paul, you don't understand! I've been crazy all my life! I was crazy *before* I drank! Once I started drinking, it just made things ten times worse. The list would be endless; it's impossible."

"It's one day at a time," he'd assure me, "and one step at a time."

I was a reluctant starter, but as the months passed, and I worked my way through the program, real changes began to happen, both in my life and in my relationship with Carol.

We began going out together more often, meeting friends for dinner, going to the movies or just walking along the beach in the evenings. Finally, after I'd been in the program for over a year, we were married in a civil ceremony at our place in Sydney; John Cox was my Best Man.

Paul was one of the wedding guests, and when I spotted him having a quiet smoke in the back garden, I slipped out the kitchen door.

"Time out?" I asked.

"Yes," he smiled, "I've never been good with crowds."

"You sponsored half of the people in there."

"That's what we do, Brian, we pass it on. We live one day at a time, and we pass it on."

He lit another cigarette and we stood there not talking for a few minutes. I'd come out for a reason, but I wasn't sure how to start. Paul was a bit of a loner and intensely shy. The only time you ever heard him talk was when he was called to speak at meetings; then everyone listened. He had quiet, laconic way of telling his story, but anytime he spoke the room sat hushed and silent.

"I came out to thank you, Paul. You saved my life. Without you I'd probably still be out there drinking. Now I'm married, we're expecting a baby, we're living in a nice house, and I've got a good job. I just wanted to thank you, mate."

He tossed the cigarette on the gravel path, stubbed it out with his shoe, and turned to leave.

"Pass it on." Was all he said.

We spent our honeymoon cruising Sydney Harbour, sailing by day and anchoring in a different bay each night. The weather stayed perfect throughout; the spell had been broken.

Chapter 42

Trevor

The first time I saw Trever he was sitting in the back row of our meeting room one evening looking anything but happy. Leather Brando jacket, hard face, cold grey eyes, and an aura that screamed, *don't even look at me.* I went over as soon as the meeting ended but he saw me coming, turned quickly, and left the hall. I watched from the veranda as he climbed on a black Harley and rode off into the night.

"You know him?" Jack, our secretary, was standing behind me.

"No," I said, "never seen him before."

"Probably won't see him again either," he shook his head, "he looked pretty crazy"

"You didn't look too good yourself the night you arrived," I told him.

He was there again the following week but left just as quickly. The next time I saw him was a month later, at a coffee shop up at King's Cross. I was reading a newspaper when he approached, helmet in one hand, a mug of coffee in the other.

"You got a minute?"

"Sure," I nodded, "grab a chair."

The first thing you notice about Trever is his eyes; cold, grey and emotionless.

"I listened to your story the other night," his eyes were roaming around the crowded café like a hunted animal. "You been in a fair bit of shit yourself, mate, eh?"

"Yes," I nodded, "I was pretty crazy when I drank."

"You done time?"

"No," I said, "oh, a little when I was a kid, you know, boys home stuff."

"Yeh," he nodded, "me too, but no jail. Long rap sheet, but no jail."

There was hardness about him that was beyond tough.

"How long you been sober?"

"A few years." I told him.

"How do you last that long?" he shot me a quick look and then away again. "I'm off it five weeks and I feel like fucking necking myself."

We talked for two hours. Trevor was Sergeant at Arms for one of Australia's most notorious bikie gangs. He'd been hooked on whisky and speed for years, but his habit was out of control now, and his comrades were beginning to wonder if he was getting a little too crazy.

"If they knew I was talking to anyone about this stuff I'd be in deep shit," his eyes met mine abruptly, hard and questioning.

"Anything you tell me is confidential, mate" I told him, "but no names, okay? If you get back on the piss, I don't want you worrying about anything you might have told me. I don't want to hear any details, okay? No names, no places, no dates, no dead bodies."

"Suits me," he snapped and strode away.

Trever joined our group six weeks later, angry, suspicious, but desperate to stay sober. We talked a couple of times after the meetings but there was a belligerence about him that cut short any meaningful exchanges.

.

He became a regular, turning up late most nights and leaving early. People tended to avoid him, uncomfortable with his appearance and manner. He always took a seat at the back of the hall, his helmet on the chair next to him to deter any unnecessary encounters. He wore his leather jacket, jeans and biker boots like an amour, his body stiff and taught, as if ready to jump up and leave at a moment's notice. It went on like that for months and, although I tried not to judge him, I doubted he was going to make it. Then one night around midnight I woke from a deep sleep, Carol pulling at my shoulder.

"There's someone knocking on the back door."

"Back door?" I struggled up, grabbed a pair of jeans, went out to the kitchen, and peered through the window. Trevor was standing in the garden, helmet in hand. I opened the door.

"It's past midnight, Trevor."

"Yeh, I know. I was at a meeting, some would-be tough guy rabbiting on. I got home, couldn't sleep."

"You sober, mate?"

"Course I'm fucking sober! Sobers the fucking problem."

"Keep it down, mate," I told him, 'look, you better come in."

He entered cautiously, his eyes roaming around the room.

"Your misses asleep?"

"Yes, hang on, I'll close the bedroom door."

When I came back, I put the kettle on.

'What's going on, Trevor?"

"She okay?"

"Yes, she's fine, she's asleep. I'm going to make some tea. Want a cup?"

"Yes, thanks."

"You want to talk about something, mate?"

"Yeh, I'm going crazy. All this fucking sober stuff. I'm worse now than I was before!"

"Not true," I told him, "you might feel worse, but that's only because you've stopped drinking. What you're feeling now is stuff you been suppressing for years."

"So, what are you now, a fucking shrink or something?"

He was bristling.

"Look, Trevor, we all know you're a tough guy, but if you're going to come knocking on my door in the middle of the night, you need to leave the Rambo stuff outside, okay? You're in deep shit mate, that's obvious. You're an argument away from a drink, and I'm not going to be that argument. If you want me to help you I can, and I will, but only if you're prepared to listen. If you're not, then you're wasting my time and yours too."

He'd fixed his eyes on mine for the first time since we'd met. It was like staring through a grey prism into a very angry madhouse. There was a silence for a while, and I figured he was wondering whether to leave.

"You've come this far, mate" I told him. "You're going to have to talk to somebody if you want to stay sober."

He stood up and walked over to the kitchen sink, staring out the window into a pitch-black garden.

"You ever killed anyone?" His voice was so low I barely caught it.

"No." I told him. "Nearly. I nearly killed a guy in the West one time."

"Pissed?"

"Yep, drunk as a monkey. I almost beat him to death. He was in a coma for three days and in hospital for months; head injuries." I went over to where he stood, "Look mate, there's a guy in our group who did time for murder, maybe..."

"No," he stopped me, "You're the only one I trust, but you said you didn't want to hear anything."

.

"I didn't say that, mate. I said I didn't want to hear any details. No names, no places, no dates. That's how I did it when I joined up. I told my story to a guy I trusted. Names don't matter, it's what we did that matters." He was on the very edge. "Look, I'm going to go and tell Carol not to come out here. Just in case. There are two doors between here and the bedroom. If you want security, you've got it, okay?"

When I got back, he was in the chair again, staring at his knuckles.

"She okay?"

"Yes, she's fast asleep. She won't be interrupting us."

"Okay to smoke?" He was holding up a pack of Marlborough.

"Sure."

We sat there for a while longer, Trevor staring down at the cigarette pack, moving it around the table, shaking his head occasionally. I knew where he was, and I knew what was going through his mind. When I'd finally got up enough courage to talk to another member about my past, I'd been terrified. When you've spent much of your life hiding things you've done, refusing to take responsibility, not admitting that you've harmed friends, family and strangers alike, it's sometimes almost impossible to face up to your own rotten deeds.

So, I did what my sponsor had done with me; I told him about my own past. I told him how I'd abandoned my first wife and children. I told him about the friends and families I'd hurt, the people I'd betrayed, the degraded life I had lived, the people I'd conned, and the crimes. And I realised once again as I talked, that this was the only possible way that the wretched, drunken life I had lived for so many years could possibly be of any use or value in the world.

After a while he began talking, cautiously at first, telling me that he'd done similar things, identifying with the degradation, and adding parts of his own story. Once he began, he talked for hours, pausing at times, battling internal demons. He broke down twice.

Once about the stabbing death of a close friend, the other when he talked about a broken marriage and the loss of his children.

He spoke of things that I'd seen reported on the news or in the newspapers, and as he talked, the guilt and self-loathing that were threatening his sobriety became more and more apparent.

It's difficult to understand what happens when two people get together to confess their darkest secrets and sins, but as the night went on, the shocking things we shared created a sense of openness and honesty, and with that came the possibility of hope and redemption.

I listened in silence most of the time, touching him on the shoulder occasionally when he broke down. What struck me more than anything else that night was the terrible, self-destructive nature of alcoholism and drug addiction.

Towards dawn he began adding details of how he felt about each incident. Musing over how many people's lives he'd damaged, both friends and enemies, and finally, as the first glimpses of light began to silhouette the taller trees at the far end of the garden, he looked up.

"I'm fucked mate," he whispered, "how do you come back from all that?"

"You come back the same way you went in," I told him, "one day at a time. One decent act at a time. One kept promise at a time."

He shook his head, but there was a glimmer of hope in his eyes.

"That's how you come good?"

"Yes. That's the only way mate, one day at a time. The same way we got sick. You've already started, Trev. All you've got to do now is keep going. You can make it, brother. I made it, you can too."

He shook his head again.

"You really believe this shit, don't you?"

"So do you, mate, otherwise you wouldn't be here. Like I said, you leave Rambo by the side of the road and you take a different path.

You can't undo what you've done, but you can make amends. And from this day on, you can choose to live a totally different life."

"You know what troubles me more than anything?" I knew what was coming, I'd been there myself, "My kids. I haven't seen them for years. Restraining orders, all that shit. She took off to Melbourne. I never blamed her. She's a good woman."

"That's where the one day at a time comes in, Trevor. You've got no idea how all that will work out. Right now, you work on your recovery. No booze, no drugs, no crime, and you work the program one day at a time. That's what gets us right."

He stood up and walked back to the window, staring out at nothing. I went over.

"What you just did took a lot of guts." I told him, "You've joined us at last, mate. You might not realize it just yet, but this changes everything. This is the beginning. I did it with a guy called Peter, it saved my life."

I put my arm around his shoulder. He stiffened momentarily, then turned and gave me a hug, slapping me hard on the back to let me know he was still macho.

"I've never trusted a man in my life, not even my mates on the road."

"Tell me about it." I said.

It was 6am. I made coffee and took a cup into Carol. When I returned, he was out in the garden helmet in hand, checking out the flowers.

"Carol does all this?"

"No," I smiled, "I do."

"You're a good bloke."

"We're all good blokes when we get sober, mate."

"One day at a time, eh? You reckon that's the way to go?"

"There is no other way, Trevor. It's one day at a time."

I watched as he walked away.

I've seen a lot of remarkable recoveries, but Trevor's almost certainly tops the list. From a drug crazed, sociopathic, alcoholic biker, to a guy who returned to school at the age of 38 and now spends most of his professional and his private life helping others with similar problems, is quite a leap for any human being. He still rides his Harley, probably always will. That's Trevor.

A year later he moved to Melbourne to be close to his children. I'd get a postcard occasionally, over the years. Trevor on his bike somewhere, one of his kids on the back, half concealed in an oversize helmet. So I was surprised a few years later when the invitation arrived.

The presence of Brian O'Raleigh
is requested at the wedding of
Trevor and Giselle Clarke

The wedding ceremony was something else. It was held in the grounds of the Re-hab Clinic where Trevor was employed as a program manager. The guests were an eclectic mix of professionals, patients, priests and politicians. Psychiatrists, psychologists and counsellors rubbed shoulders with groups of recovering alcoholics, whilst several leather clad bikers chatted with a local member of parliament.

"You're a friend of Trevor's?"

He was standing just behind me, looking awkward and shy. The white collar slightly soiled, his nose and cheeks bearing the tell-tale stains of chronic alcoholism.

"Yes, Father," I held out a hand, "Brian O'Raleigh. I've known Trevor for years."

"Please, don't call me Father." we shook hands, "It's Tom. I'm a client here. They think I'm an alcoholic. If I get stay sober, I'll be forced to retire."

"Your first time here?"

"Yes," he shook his head, "I met Trevor at a wedding last year. I was drunk. I mucked the whole thing up. He followed me out to the car, and we talked. He told me he was an alcoholic." There was a sudden roar of laughter and we both turned to look over to where Trev was standing with his wife and a group of friends. "They call him Oda," the priest was smiling, "Short for ODAAT; you know, one day at a time. That's his mantra. You stay sober one day at a time."

"That's how we do it," I told him, "one day at a time."

Father Tom was still staring across at Trev.

"He's more like a priest than any priest I know. It's hard to imagine him being really crazy, isn't it?"

I looked back at Trevor. No, I thought, it's not hard to imagine. Not if you'd have met him the night he arrived. It's a thing I'd noticed, the ones who come in totally broken, often clean up pretty good.

Chapter 43

Fatherhood

I continued to see Jim MacLaine on a regular basis, and he became an important part of my recovery, helping me with all sorts of problems on the road back to normality. Although we'd just married, Carol and I had been together for twelve years by then and a lot of unresolved problems lay between us. On one visit, she came too, and I sat there, listening as she explained some of the difficulties we were having.

"He's always been like that." She was really getting into it. "It's always the same. He wants everything his way. He wants to build a boat, so we build a boat! He wants to travel to Afghanistan, so off we go to Afghanistan! He wants to sail around the world, so off we go around the world ..."

We'd been arguing for some time about whether we'd continue on sailing.

"Hang on," I butted in, "we talked this over and you agreed ..."

"Talked it over," she demanded, "with you? How can anyone talk anything over with you? You're right all the time!"

I was surprised at how angry she was.

"And he's always been like that," Jim interrupted, "ever since you first met him?"

"Yes." She flashed a look at me. "Always! When Brian talks, it's as if everyone's supposed to agree with him. He has that sort of personality."

.

"You mean that you find it hard to disagree with him?" Jim asked.

"Yes, it would be hard for anyone to disagree with him."

"And you think that may be a part of the problem?"

"Yes, of course it is." She was warming to the topic. "He's been crazy all his life, he'll tell you that himself. He's always done crazy things."

"So he's always been crazy?" Jim was looking thoughtful. "Ever since you first met?"

"Yes, he was drunk the first time I met him on a boat on the way to England. He was abusing the waiter at the table!"

Jim nodded. "So how come you stayed with him for so long?"

Carol paused. "How do you mean?"

"Well," he smiled, "I was just wondering why anybody would want to stay with a person like Brian for twelve years?"

"What do you mean?" She was becoming confused. "What are you getting at?"

"I'm not getting at anything really." He leant forward. "I'm just wondering why anyone would choose to stay with a violent, antisocial, unpredictable alcoholic for over twelve years."

She paused for a moment.

"Because I loved him?" she offered hopefully.

"Is that what you'd call it?" Jim queried, "Love? How could you love a person like that? Are you sure it was love, or could it have been something else? Could it be that you *needed* to stay with him for some reason?" He smiled. "You don't have to answer that now; think it over for a while. Why would any woman choose to stay with a person like Brian for such a long time?"

Sitting there listening, I wasn't sure whether I was being insulted or not, but when we left there that day, we were both in a more thoughtful mood.

*   *   *

Our son, Christopher, was born a year later. He came to us at three o'clock one Sunday morning. I'd rushed Carol to the hospital the previous day as soon as the pains had started, all of the advice we'd been given flying out the window as I panicked and drove like a lunatic to the hospital.

I sat by Carol's bedside all that day, holding her hand and talking to her. We'd both done the pre-natal classes, practicing breathing techniques and all the various exercises but it was still a difficult delivery. Finally, there he was: tinges of blue and pink, crying and struggling but alive and well, the last remnants of my atheism dissolving entirely as I witnessed the miracle of birth. After he was cleaned and wrapped and Carol had settled down to sleep, I crept out of the room and, standing in the garden of the hospital, I knew with absolute clarity that I'd been blessed once again. I was forty years old as I looked up at the same stars that had shone down on Kathleen's birth, but I knew this time it would be different, this time I was sober.

Chris was a happy, contented child and he settled into our home like the blessing he was. We took him with us everywhere and when he was only a few weeks old, he went out for his first sail in the *Kathleen R*. Cruising Sydney Harbour, keeled over to a breeze, Carol steering and Chris snoozing in his wicker bassinet below, I wondered once again why I had been chosen to be saved. Grace, as a friend had told me, was indeed an unearned gift from God.

In the months that followed, Carol and I talked less and less about sailing and when she fell pregnant again a year or so later, I knew that the dream was over, and I advertised the *Kathleen R* for sale. It was a difficult decision, but we needed a home of our own. I refused so many offers for our boat that Carol began to wonder if I was serious about selling her, but I was determined that she would go to the right person. Finally, Peter Corrigan came along and when he told me he was looking for a small boat that was capable of sailing around the world, I knew that I'd run out of excuses.

A few weeks later, I stood alone on the cliffs at North Head, watching the *Kathleen R* sailing outward bound from Sydney Harbour, a small green pennant bearing the Irish harp, flying from her masthead as Peter had promised.

Chapter 44

Liz

After the *Kathleen R* was sold, we returned to Brisbane and bought a house in the bayside suburb of Wynnum. I began a small construction company and when our baby girl came along a few months later, we settled down to raise a family.

Elizabeth was a delight from the beginning, a cheeky, smiling little girl who charmed everyone who met her. As soon as she was able to crawl, she was everywhere, emptying cupboards out onto the floor, fishing down the toilet bowl with coat hangers, or chasing the cat around the house until it was forced to disappear next door in search of peace. She had a natural, spontaneous sense of humor and nothing seemed to worry her. By the age of three, she enjoyed doing exactly the opposite to anything I told her, laughing hysterically when she realized that she'd upset me. She was the original tomboy and she hated dolls and teddy bears with a passion. I bought her stuffed toys of all types: lions, tigers, fairies and beautiful china dolls with long, black hair and blinking eyelashes. Nothing worked. She refused point blank to touch any of them.

One day whilst I was in the city, I spotted the most incredible looking teddy bear in a store window. I went in and spoke to the assistant who told me it was one of a kind and had been especially made for the shop. The bear was wonderful. It was big and round and fully dressed in a white cotton blouse, long flowing colored skirt, a bonnet that tied under its chin and an expensive looking pair of leather shoes. It cost a small fortune but I had to get it. I was convinced that this was the bear that would convert her.

They wrapped it up carefully and that evening when I arrived home, I told Liz that I had a very special surprise for her.

"Is it a doll?" She was looking at me steadily.

"No," I told her, "it's not a doll, but you're warm. It's something really special and I want you to think about it when I give it to you."

"What does that mean?" she said, staring up at me, wide-eyed,

"Well, you know how sometimes we think we might not like something but then, when we actually give it a try, it turns out that we do like it after all. Do you understand that honey?"

She shook her head. "No."

"Well, what I'm saying is that I want you to have a good look at your present before you make up your mind whether you like it or not, OK?"

"What's wrong with it?" she said.

"There's nothing's wrong with it," I said. "It cost me a small fortune. I'm just asking you to think about it before you decide whether you like it or not."

Carol joined in. "Why don't you just give it to her?"

As soon as Liz saw the parcel, she guessed. "It's a bear." She was smiling.

"There you go, honey." I handed it to her. "Open it up and you'll see."

We stood there watching as she began tearing off the paper. As soon as she saw a furry leg, she knew for sure.

"It's a bear," she said loudly, "it's a teddy bear!"

She pulled off the last few bits of paper and held the bear out at arm's length.

"Isn't it beautiful, honey?"

She was hugging the bear and I gave the thumbs up sign to Carol.

"It's the only one in the world and it's all yours."

Liz was talking to the bear and kissing it. "Nice teddy. Good teddy. You're a good boy, aren't you?"

"I think it's a girl, Liz," I said. "It's got a skirt on."

"No, it's a boy," she replied.

"Well, it's dressed like a girl," I said.

As I turned away to say something to Carol, there was a shriek that made me jump and I looked back to see Liz running towards the open French doors, gripping the teddy bear by one arm. As soon as she reached the veranda, she hurled the bear over the railings and watched as it went flying off into the bushes. Then she ran off, shrieking and laughing hysterically. She'd fooled her father once again.

*   *   *

Occasionally, Carol would go out for the evening and I'd look after the kids by myself. They always loved those times because we did things then that Carol would never do. During the tropical downpours of the Queensland summer, we'd grab umbrellas and run off down to the park, screaming and laughing, tearing around in the pouring rain until we were all saturated, laughing and slithering around on the flooded grass.

Once we got home again, they'd want some more fun. One of their favorite games was the mosquito hunt. This enthralled them more than anything. At their pleading, I would get out the vacuum cleaner and after putting on my official safari hat, a baseball hat on back to front, the game would begin. Chris and Liz would go off hunting in different parts of the house. Liz upstairs, Chris downstairs. Sometimes it took a while, but sooner or later, there'd be a scream.

"Mozzies!" You'd hear the squeal from one of the rooms. "Mozzies, I've found one, dad! Quick, come on, quick, quick!"

I'd grab the vacuum and head for the stairs, crouched over as if hunting big game. "Shhh," I'd whisper, "they'll hear you! Never call them mozzies! They know what that means!"

"There, over there!" Chris and Liz would be jumping out of their skin.

I'd pretend I couldn't see anything. "Where, where?"

"There, on the ceiling! Quick, it'll get away!"

"Shh!" Chris would try to calm Liz down. "Shhh, you'll frighten it."

Then we'd plan the assault. "You hold the tube, Liz, make sure it doesn't get stuck on anything. Get ready, Chris! When I say 'power on', you flick the switch, OK?"

"We know what to do." They'd be frustrated with all the orders. "Come on dad, do it!"

I'd climb up on a chair, creeping up slowly on the poor unsuspecting mozzie, snoozing on the ceiling.

"Ready, Chris?" I'd whisper.

"Yes, dad," he'd whisper back, all eyes.

"Ready, Liz?"

"Go on dad, get on with it! Do it now! Get the mozzie!"

"Power on!"

Chris would flick the switch and I'd gradually move the nozzle closer and closer to our unsuspecting prey. There would be a long, agonizing pause and then suddenly, pop! And it was gone, sucked down into the bowels of the vacuum cleaner.

The kids would go wild, cheering and jumping up and down as if it was the greatest thing in the world. After I'd caught the first one, it was their turn.

"Me! Me!" Liz would be grabbing at the vacuum tube, struggling with Chris to be next. Some nights, we'd spend hours on the mozzie hunt and it became one of their favorite childhood memories.

Chapter 45

Kathleen and Sharon

It was some time after Elizabeth's birth that I began to think about Kathleen and Sharon again. I hadn't seen Jean for years by then. I'd called her occasionally, but she remained abrupt and unpleasant and she'd always warned me to stay away. But watching Elizabeth grow and change had brought my daughters back to me and I knew that I had to try to reconnect with them someday. I phoned Jean one afternoon after finishing work. When she heard my voice, her tone changed abruptly.

"Oh, so it's you again. Where are you this time?"

"I'm in Brisbane. We moved back here last year."

"Are you still married?"

"Yes, we have two children now, Chris and Elizabeth."

"Well, isn't that nice. Let's hope you look after them a little better than your first two."

"Look, I don't want any unpleasantness. I just want to see the girls."

"Do you really? Well you can't, alright? I don't know what's wrong with you. You pop up every few years from God knows where and say you want to see the girls. Well you can't. The girls are happy the way they are. They're not interested. They don't even ask about you anymore and that's the way I like it."

"I don't believe that. Kathleen's eighteen now and Sharon's sixteen. They have a right to meet their father if they want to."

"Well they *don't* want to, OK?" she butted in. "And that's that!"

There was a long silence; this was exactly what I'd wanted to avoid.

"OK, I'll write them a letter. I'll address it to you ..."

"I'll just tear it up, Brian."

There was another long silence and I sat there, wondering which way to go.

"There's nothing I can do about that, I guess, but someday you'll have to explain that to them."

There was a pause for a moment or two and then the line went dead.

*   *   *

Two weeks later, Jean called me one evening at home; she didn't bother with any small talk.

"We're coming to Brisbane on Friday morning. I want you to be in the car park at Garden City Shopping Centre. Stand near the main entrance on the right-hand side. I'll be arriving at 10.30 am. You can talk to the girls in the car. Don't try to get in the car. If you're drunk, I won't bother stopping."

I waited until she had finished.

"I won't be there, Jean. I'm not going to meet the girls under those circumstances. It would be degrading, for everyone."

"It's that or nothing, take your pick."

"We'll talk about it later," I told her. "I won't be at Garden City."

She called me again the following week.

"You can meet the girls tomorrow at Southport. There's a boatyard out along the spit near Sea World. Do you know the place?"

"Yes, I think so."

"I don't know how long we've got; we have other things to do. We'll play it by ear. If it gets awkward, we'll just leave. And, by the way, I've never said anything bad about you to the girls. They think you're a sailor. And I don't want you telling them you're an alcoholic, OK? We don't want to hear any more of that nonsense."

"Anything else?"

"Just be there at 4.00 pm and don't be late." There was a pause. "Don't let them down."

I stood by the waterfront the following afternoon, feeling nervous. When 4.00 pm came and went, I began to worry. By 5 pm, I'd given up and was heading back towards my car when I saw them in the distance, walking towards me. Jean was waving and, as they drew closer, Kathleen broke away and ran a few steps towards me but then she stopped and waited for her mother to catch up.

Jean looked angry. "I said 4.00 pm at the boatyard!"

"This is the boatyard!"

"Not this one, the one near Sea World!"

"Mum." Kathleen was looking at Jean. "It was a mistake."

We stood there awkwardly.

"Well," Jean said, looking around, "this is your Dad."

The girls were smiling at each other and casting quick little glances at me. There was another pause then and Jean took my arm.

"Come on, we might as well get some exercise while we're here."

We walked off along the foreshore then, the girls trailing along behind, giggling and whispering together. After a while, they caught up with us and walked along next to Jean.

"Where are you living now?" Kathleen asked. Her eyes were like her mother's.

"I live at Wynnum. It's about an hour from here."

Sharon was on the far side, looking around Kathleen's shoulder.

"Mum said you got married again. Have you got any children?"

"Yes, two, Christopher and Elizabeth."

"Do they live with you?"

"Yes."

"Look, I'm starving," Jean butted in. "Why don't we get something to eat?"

We sat in a café by the waterfront; the sky was dark and overcast and the place was deserted.

"Can we go and look at the shops, Mum?"

"Yes, but don't disappear. We won't be here much longer."

They smiled at me as they walked away.

"Well, what do think of your daughters?"

"They're lovely," I told her. "They don't seem too intimidated by all this."

"Why should they be? What did you expect? You didn't think they were going to make a big fuss of you, did you? They have their own lives; you're just something of a novelty, that's all. They think of Mario as their father. They've known him for twelve years."

"I know, you told me. I don't know what I expected."

After we finished the meal, we found the girls and drove back to Jean's place. It had begun to rain and the sky was almost black as we arrived outside her apartment.

"You can come up for a while." She flashed a look at me. "You've hardly spoken to the girls."

Once they were back home, Kathleen and Sharon relaxed and soon they were chattering away, asking me all sorts of questions.

"Mum said you used to be a sailor. Have you sailed around the world?" Kathleen's face was open and inquisitive, all the shyness gone.

"I built a boat once, a few years ago. We wanted to sail around the world, but it didn't work out that way."

"Why not?"

"Well, we had a baby instead."

Jean cut in. "And for some unknown reason, he decided to be responsible for once in his life."

"Mum," Kathleen looked surprised, "we're just talking, don't be like that." Then, turning back to me, she said, "That was Christopher?"

"Yes, that was Chris. He was the first."

"The third, actually," Jean snapped. "You never were much good at math, were you?"

It was like walking in a minefield.

"Do you believe in God?" Sharon was sitting on the other side of the room, studying me.

"I believe there's a higher power. You know, like a supreme intelligence or spirit of nature. That's how I feel about it. I see God in nature."

"So you're not a Christian?"

She was more intense than Kathleen.

"No, I was brought up Irish Catholic but I gave all that away years ago."

"Mum says we're half Irish."

"You are, you're half Irish and half Gypsy."

"No," Sharon said, "we're half Irish, a quarter Gypsy and a quarter English, because of Granddad."

"Yes, I guess that's right."

"Are you a Buddhist?" Kathleen was sitting next to me on the couch.

"No, but I like Buddhism. Or at least, I like what little I know about it."

Sharon cut in. "So you do believe in God then."

"God, the Buddha, Christ … they're all just names, Sharon."

"So you're an authority on God now." Jean was there again. "We have come a long way, haven't we?"

"Stop it, mum," Sharon cut her off, "you're being really silly." She looked back at me. "Go on, so who do you think the Irish God is, then?"

"I don't know. I've been told that the ancient Irish worshipped the life force itself but then Christianity arrived and changed all that. I suspect it's still there, though, underneath all the Catholic stuff. They're a wild bunch."

"What he's trying to say is that the Irish are all bloody mad." Jean was smiling now. "And that's pretty close to the truth."

"You've never been to Ireland, Jean." I was getting tired of her pettiness.

"No, I haven't and I have no intention of going there either. I've met enough Paddies to do me for the rest of my life."

"Well, you're sitting in a room with three Paddies now, so I'd be careful about slandering the Irish, if I were you."

The girls broke out laughing and finally Jean joined in too and just for that moment - for that second in time - it felt like a family.

*   *   *

Jean called things to a halt shortly after and on the way out, she whispered that she wanted to talk to me privately. The rain was beating down heavily as we ran across the road to my car. I was feeling good about the evening but, as soon as the door slammed shut, it all changed.

"Well! That was quite an act you put on in there."

"What?" I said. "What's wrong now?"

"Look, you might have fooled the girls in there but you don't fool me, OK?" She was angry. "You haven't changed a bit, have you? Still the same old conman with all your old Irish blather. I wouldn't trust anything you said." The rain was zigzagging down the windscreen, the coursing droplets twinkling in the reflected lights of the passing cars. It was pointless saying anything. "Well," she went on, "you didn't expect me to believe any of that old rubbish, did you? *The Life Force,* for Christ's sake! *The Celtic Gods!* The girls think you're wonderful, the poor sods. They have no idea at all about the likes of you."

I looked across at her, her dark brown eyes glittering. She was still very beautiful.

"You've been angry for a long time, Jean."

"Angry, you bastard, after what you did to me, why wouldn't I be angry? And now you think you can just walk back into our lives and play the wonderful, long-lost daddy!"

The car fell silent and I sat there, wondering where we were headed. Jean was staring fixedly ahead through the misted windscreen, glaring out at nothing. I had no idea what to say. It was as if I'd never stopped drinking and we'd been transported back to one of those terrible rows from years before.

And then, I suddenly realized that that was the way she saw me. She'd never known me any other way. And I remembered how it had been with Carol when I'd first stopped drinking; she hadn't trusted me for ages.

"You're right," I said, "you shouldn't trust me. There's nothing to base it on."

"What does that mean?" she snapped.

"Well, the only way you know me is how I was when we were together. I forget that sometimes."

"And you're trying to tell me you've changed, is that it?" She was glaring at me. "Well, I've heard that one before, remember?"

There was another long silence and finally I said "Look, all I can tell you is, I haven't had a drink for years. I live a different life now."

She'd turned her head away and I knew I was wasting my breath.

"There's no way I can convince you of that. I guess if we keep meeting, you may come to believe me over time."

She looked back at me.

"You won't be seeing us again. I wanted the girls to meet you, that's all. Just once, just so they know that you actually do exist. You won't be seeing them again after tonight, not for a long time, anyhow."

It was painful listening to the hatred in her voice but it was pointless arguing. "I understand; I know you're thinking of them. You've brought them up well, they're lovely girls." She was right. What reason did she have to trust me? "I'll stay away until you say otherwise."

She'd gone quiet as I spoke and I guess she could see that I was upset. There was a pause then that seemed to go on forever and we sat there, alone with our thoughts, the rain beating down on the roof of the car.

"I guess I'd better be on my way," I said after a while.

She didn't answer, but I knew that she was staring at me. I couldn't look at her, unwilling to meet any more of the hatred in her eyes.

"I have no idea who you are." The sentence came from nowhere. "I know you're Brian O'Raleigh and I recognize your face, but I have no idea who you are. You seem to have changed completely."

"I told you ..."

But she cut me off. "No, don't say anything. I have to go. The girls will be wondering where I am." She leant across suddenly and kissed me on the cheek then she pulled back just as quickly and opened the car door.

"I'll call you next week," I said.

"No, don't. I'll contact you. I don't want you calling the house. And I don't want you talking to the girls. Not yet anyhow. Promise me that."

"I won't, I promise. I'll wait for your call."

She was bending down, peering into the car, a black umbrella framing her face. "Goodnight, Brian."

"Goodnight, Jean."

The rain was belting down hard as she ran back across the street and as I sat there, watching her go, I couldn't help wondering what our life would have been like together if things had been different.

——

Chapter 46

Chris

For the next few years, Carol and I developed our business and renovated the old Queensland style home we'd purchased. I enjoyed the design and construction side of things, but my favorite part was the garden.

When we'd bought the place, the backyard was a wilderness and the first thing I did was to begin planting trees. Every morning before going to work, I'd sit in the garden and meditate for a while and Chris got into the habit of sitting out there with me. He had no idea what we were doing but he was such a naturally peaceful child that he'd sit there cross-legged in the silence without ever questioning it. One evening when he was around five years of age, I was planting a tree at the far end of the garden when Chris came out and stood watching me as I dug the hole.

"Can I do that, dad?" He was staring up at me.

"Sure," I said, "give it a try." I held the shovel for him and together we poked around until we had a reasonable sized little hole.

"Right, that's enough. Now give me a hand with that tree." It was only a small tree, but he was enjoying the whole thing. "That's it, son, now get some soil around it. There you go, that's it."

I showed him how to put water in when the hole was half-filled with soil and then how to put the rest of the soil back in and tamp it down lightly with his hands.

"That's right. You've done a great job, Chris. That's got a good chance of growing into a big tree now, the way you put it in there, depending on the leprechauns, of course."

He grinned; we'd talked about leprechauns before.

"What's funny about that?" I said.

"There's no such thing as leprechauns, you know that."

"Keep your voice down," I said, looking around, "we've only just put that tree in. We don't want to upset the little people. If you upset them, they won't bless the tree and it might never be able to grow then."

"That's not true, dad." He was shaking his head. "There's no such thing as leprechauns. I asked mum and she said you were only joking."

"Chris, please, keep your voice down! They might hear you. Look son, your mother's not Irish; she's never even met a leprechaun! Leprechauns are Irish, you should know that."

I was on my knees as we spoke, Chris standing next to me.

"That's not true, you're telling fibs again." He said it very firmly, but I could see the hope in his eyes.

"Look," I said, "you'll never ever see them if you don't believe in them … that's a fact. But if we were to sit out here quietly all night, you'd see them for sure. I mean, they've obviously heard us banging about here so they're bound to want to know what we've been up to and you can't miss them, of course, they're about that high." I held my hand up to about his shoulder height.

He was shaking his head again. "I don't believe you, dad. You're telling fibs again."

"They'll be dressed up in green, son. It's the only color they wear."

"It's not true." He was becoming more adamant. "There's no such thing as leprechauns, mum told me."

"And you don't have to worry about mistaking them for just another small human being because they always carry a shillelagh with them, in case they're attacked by a cat or a big mouse or something."

"That's not true, dad." He looked amazed. "That's just not true."

"And of course, you can't mistake their ears. They have long pointed ears that come up like this at the tip." I pulled both my ears up as much as I could and the expression on his face changed immediately.

"Do they, dad?" he whispered, eyes wide. "Do they really?"

"Oh yes, son, never deny the leprechauns, it's bad luck if you do."

We went back inside then and spent the rest of that evening drawing little green men with shillelaghs and the places they lived in. From his earliest years, Chris loved all things Irish.

*   *   *

Occasionally throughout those years, I'd dream of the *Kathleen R* and wonder where she was. Was she still sailing the oceans of the world, her graceful form cutting through tropical seas? Did she miss us or was she happy with her new owner? Sometimes, late at night when these things troubled me, I would creep into my children's bedroom. Chris's red hair poking out from beneath the sheets or Elizabeth's serene face as she lay flat on her back, sleeping, her arms spread out wide either side, would let me know that we'd made the right decision. The oceans of the world would be there forever. My children needed me now.

The End

Brian O'Raleigh

Brian O'Raleigh was born of Irish parents and raised in the English seaside town of Blackpool. After a troubled childhood, including a violent, alcoholic father, recounted in his memoir – *The Boy in the Boat* - Brian travelled alone to Australia at the age of seventeen, running from his demons and a growing dependence on alcohol. In 1967, he volunteered for the Six Day War in Israel, but later, disillusioned with that cause, spent the next ten years travelling Europe and Asia. On returning to Australia, he worked for several years at mining camps and construction sites in the outback. Finally, after coming to terms with his own alcoholism, he married, started a construction company and settled down to raise a family. He then began writing and to date has completed three books:

- *The Boy in the Boat.* A Memoir
- *Waking Walter.* The memoir continued.

The following books will be available July 2022

- *Passage to Inis Mor- Could a legend save his life?* A modern-day mystery set on one of Ireland's most beautiful islands.
- *Endor's Way* - a dramatic and compelling murder mystery set between Australia and Ireland. Available January 2021

Other Books by Brian O'Raleigh

Endor's Way

Available July 2022

Brian O'Raleigh

Chapter 1

Bondi Beach

The body washed up on Bondi Beach around 3 am, the time of arrival established by its presence amongst the flotsam and jetsam that marked the furthest extent of the incoming tide. Empty beer bottles, old tennis balls and multi-colored plastic thongs lay scattered recklessly along the high-water mark, intertwined with seaweed, bits of rope and the odd piece of driftwood. Rejected, along with Jameson, hurled back from whence they came by an angry, disillusioned ocean.

He'd been a handsome man, but as he lay there face up waiting for a savior now long overdue, you could never have guessed that. The crabs and little fish that had escorted him on his long, slow, drift from the foot of the cliffs at North Head to his final resting place on the beach at Bondi, had been pulling at the edges of the gaping chest wound that had terminated his life.

I arrived at the beach around 8 am; it was a miserable day, grey clouds hurrying furtively across a darkening sky and the wind, coming in from the south east, was keening over the ocean swells like a requiem for lost souls.

The early morning jogger who'd stumbled across the body just before dawn was being questioned by the local police just out of the weather near the entrance to the surf club. I glanced at her as I got out of the car. She was around forty-five or so, tall, blond and skinny, her arms folded tightly across a Spandex plated, anorexic chest, still pale and visibly shaken from her grisly find.

I nodded to the sergeant and moved past them towards the beach. Another half a dozen uniforms were on the windswept sands, close by the wading pool. Two of them were moving about securing the flapping yellow tape that determined where the public stopped and started; beyond that a small crowd of vultures in anoraks and track-suit pants hovered uselessly, drawn in by the scent of death, straining to catch a glimpse of the unfolding drama.

As I approached the main group, the uniforms parted to reveal the kneeling figure of Carl Seagan, doctor, coroner and, if the critics were correct, one-time abortionist to the Sydney social set. As he recognized me, his face took on a slight frown.

"Glad you managed to make it before the tide came back in, Harrigan," he said, turning back to the body.

Before I could respond, his assistant, a worried-looking young man just out of medical school fumbled: "I'm sorry, sir, it's your partner; Detective Jameson..."

Passage to Inis Mór

Available July 2022

Brian O'Raleigh

When 38-year-old Conner O'Rourke returns to Ireland after an absence of some thirty years, he is on the verge of suicide and running from his demons. His advertising agency in Australia is bankrupt, his marriage is falling apart and he's hearing poetic voices in his mind, telling him to return to Inis Mór. His Irish grandmother, whom he hasn't spoken to in years, has contacted him saying she's critically ill and must speak with him before she dies. When he arrives on Inis Mór- a wild, windswept, rocky little outcrop some thirty miles off the West Coast of Ireland - she has already died, leaving him a cottage and a dilapidated old sailing boat built by his grandfather.

A mysterious old seaman appears, offering to help him rebuild the boat and, as they work together, the old man tells Conner stories and legends of Ireland: stories of adventure, courage, and passion. Conner is inspired by the old man's stories … but will he find the courage to follow his own heart?

Brian O'Raleigh's books are available at Amazon & Kindle.com

Made in United States
North Haven, CT
03 July 2022

20930507R00228